HOW CHAMPIONS
THINK
TO
WIN

The Power and Possibility of Creative Mind

A. A. JAMES

HOW CHAMPIONS THINK TO WIN
Copyright © 2016 by
A. A. JAMES.
e-mail: kingdommotivationministries@gmail.com
+2348075080572, +2348066194123,

All rights reserved.
No part of this publication may be reproduced, stored in a retrieval system or transmitted in any way by any means, electronic, mechanical, photocopy, recording or otherwise, without the prior permission of the author except as provided by USA copyright law.

All characters appearing in the illustrations of this work are fictitious. Any resemblance to real persons, living or dead is purely coincidental.

The opinions expressed by the author are not necessarily those of Revival Waves of Glory Books & Publishing.

Published by Revival Waves of Glory Books & Publishing
P.O. Box 596| Litchfield, Illinois 62056 USA
www.revivalwavesofgloryministries.com

Revival Waves of Glory Books & Publishing is committed to excellence in the publishing industry.

Book design Copyright © 2016 by Revival Waves of Glory Books & Publishing. All rights reserved.

Published in the United States of America

Paperback: 978-1-68411-051-3

Table of Contents

Dedication 5
Acknowledgements 6
Introduction 7
Chapter One: GROW YOUR COURAGE AGAIN 9
Chapter Two: DEVELOP UNLIMITED MIND 42
Chapter Three: THINK YOU CAN AND YOU WILL 68
Chapter Four: BELIEVE IN YOUR TALENT 106
Chapter Five: HAVE THE FAITH OF GIANTS 149
Chapter Six: LEVERAGE WITH YOUR RELATIONSHIP ... 174
Chapter Seven: THE LANDMARK OF STARTING 208
Chapter Eight: TAKE STEPS IN POSSIBILITY 237
Chapter Nine: TAP THE POWER OF NEW IDEAS 253
Chapter Ten: THE NEED TO BE CHANGE CREATIVE 287

Dedication

This book is dedicated to the source of all inspiration and creativity—God.

Acknowledgements

Things are made to happen by deliberate hands and minds, the same with this work. Rolling out big thank you to my heart blend and queen, who has been an awesome part of my life, for your patience and understanding of what it means to dwell with someone like me—Debby, what a gift you are to me and our children. Our two inquisitive and ever happy daughters—Prisca and Lydia, I bless God for giving us you. My parents in the Lord and in-laws, Pst. & Pst.(Mrs) Mike Oyedele, words can never quantify your mentorship impact in my faith walk, what a blessing you have been. Never will I forget you, my awesome mother—Eunice, for your care and cuddling in bringing up such a number boys and a girl with your late darling in such an exemplary way, from my heart I say I love you. And to all the gifted hands, who contributed their potentials to the climaxing of this project, grateful thanks to you all.

Introduction

Two young children were once asked by their anatomist father in a family garden, "How come those trees can't move about as do other living things—the animals?" trying to test their knowledge. "Because trees are stuck to the ground." The two kids chorused. "Why are they stuck to the ground?" he asked innocently. "Because they grow in two directions—their stems grow upward while their roots grow downward, both in opposite directions at the same time unlike animals that grow upward only—above the ground." They replied with assurance.

How childish their answer could be, but how illustrative it is to us. The same thing with human beings, many people are not moving like the rest because they are stuck to the soil of time and they are stuck because they too also try to live in two directions. They tend to flow into their past and at same time try to grow into their future, hence stuck to a spot which is every day. The greatest machine ever invented is the mind; the Creator has designed it to run the course of our lives depending on the program we develop in it, to run forward, backward or stand still, depending on the side to which we gear it. We are all born equal but won't die equal; because we never use our minds equally.

No matter the race you are from, we are all in the same race, so all equally equipped though differently challenged. Man was a product of creation, but partly of invention as well—being made from existing resources. The same way the Creator expects him to dominate his world through discovering unknown things from known or existing things. Mind architectural framework poses the highest form of disadvantages or advantages to all races and dreams. What stop some people are what get some people started. The dream you let go today someone else will pick up tomorrow, either in your generation or the next. Anyone can fail successfully if the mind is well programmed. When you cut trees, thinking you have silenced them, you will be surprised that when they come back they hardly show up with one bud but with multiple stems.

There is more hope for a tree in greater form. Just like when a stone is dropped in the path of gentle stream, though it seems like an obstacle to its flow, but the stream will naturally split into channels rather than being stuck and skillfully flow by—when you can't push through split through. When your dreams face truncating failure, what do you do? When life challenges stand in your path, do you remain dogmatically static or become diversified in your thinking to overcome? Every life obstacle could be handled, just with an attitude; all you need is that stream wisdom and a courageous hope. Dream harvesters are always goals desperate—they spend time to cultivate their ideas and find a way to bypass or level up with the necessary obstacles through mind dexterity and faith power. This journey will surely change your perception and system of thoughts; you will without fail unveil and discover the mighty champion in you.

Chapter One

GROW YOUR COURAGE AGAIN

~Courage will add life to your
days and days to your life~

A father of two, who works with waste disposing company, once drove the garbage truck home. On the truck was clearly written "Goods Only". The sound of the strange horn jacked the family up as his kindergarten boy rushed out in curiosity only to see his father parking a waste truck. Deeply engrossed, beholding the truck, he tried to read what was written on it "Goods Only". He turned to the newly employed dad and said with excitement, "I like your truck dad, it is permitted to do good things, I mean to carry good things only." His father replied, "Yes! It is for 'Goods Only'." The other day the man drove home with the truck while on duty, as his route includes his house street. Just as he slowed down to a park and was about to off load the garbage bin in front of his house, his son sprang out to greet him on sighting the truck through the window.

He embraced the lad and asked him to go back to his mum as he was on duty. Without wasting time, he reached out for their garbage bin, lifted it up into the truck, and emptied it. The little boy, who was about turning to go inside shouted, "Dad that is wrong, are you ok? Stop doing that; do you not realize that this is the bin where mum always drop the bad food, broken toys and the rest of the rubbish? Nothing in that bin is good anymore." The father stood amazed at the strange reaction of the boy. In a shock he asked, "What's wrong." The young lad curiously said further, "Dad, look and read—"pointing to the write up on the truck, "Goods Only." "You are going against the rules and that's wrong." "I am not going against the rules," the man calmly replied, "The garbage are also goods, the truck is specially designed for them."

Afterward, his elder brother, pumping out of the front door, who had been watching the scenario came closer, standing in between father and his younger brother said, "Dad, I think you are right after all, my science teacher once taught us how the garbage is being recycled to create a new product." The relieved father added, "That is true, everything you see in that truck is rubbish now, useless and appears to be of no value, but there are potential goods hidden in them."

~There is a potential in your past, a purpose
for your now and a plan for your future~

Your life may seem full of mess in the past, rubbished and abused, but there are still hidden good messages. Your dreams might have been sagged with the passage of time. People could have taken your cloth of many colors; situations might have pushed you to hell boundary; you are messed up and betrayed; but what life streams of rejection, abuse, desertion and failure must have left behind is your future and your desire to feature—these two are a permanent gifts to every soul. Messed up past does not make your life not worth living. Your failure may turn out to portray rubbish but your life is still invaluable. Your life is for "goods only" ultimately, by God's pre-planned program though seems stormed now, at the end it will be "Goods Only". He promises to land you in expected end not eventual end. However, you will be a wise partner in this project by rising with faith and not resigning in fate.

When a building contractor was through with fixing two bank security doors, he asked his two trainees, what is the difference between a security man who closes the bank's door, removes the key, but forgets to lock it and the one who closes the bank's door, locks it and forgets to remove the key? The two smart trainees replied, there is no difference really, they have things in common—they both closed the door and they both had missed something. He asked again, if you are a customer who arrives so early, seeing the two doors; one with the key in the hole and the other with no key, what will be your comment? "I will conclude that the one who left the key in the hole has failed in his duty," replied, the senior. "But when a bank worker comes, moves closer to the two doors and makes attempt to enter through, he will discover after all, both of them have failed in a way only that one is pronounced to every passer-by and waiting customers while the other will be revealed to those who move and study closely." The junior trainee interrupted.

So is all who ever succeeded and all who ever failed in the past, they all have one thing in common—they all made attempts and they all made mistakes. The former's door may appear to be secure from afar and so are successful people they all have secret lapses when you move close to their lives and living, though they are tagged hero you will discover that the door was unlocked. Likewise, those who fail have appeared to make blunder, when people see the key on the door from afar, but they have achieved something—they conquered the fear to start and are armed now with how it will not work.

~Everybody has courage in a way; some
use it to dream alone; some to start it, some
to quit it and some to rerun and finish.
It takes courage to do all~

MAXIMIZE YOUR PAST

Three Arabian travelers doing business in camels and gold at one season decided to travel around neighboring countries within the space of ten years. As they reached an island in the suburb of their focused city, they saw three shrubs growing by the riverbank. They settled there for a while and in the meantime, the shrub began to bear peculiar fruits, some sweet, and some bitter on the same tree. In order not to induce clashes, they chose to take the tree one per person. When the fruits were ripe, they began to pluck the fruits, all looked ripe but some would be sweet and some very bitter like a gull. After few days, they realized they needed to move because of their animals. Each of them thought of what to do with his plant: the first said, "I will pluck all the fruits available and load them on my camels so I can live on all." The second said, "I will uproot the plant, tie it on my donkey, and take it along to replant for continuity of pleasure as soon as we settle. The third said, "This is what I will do, I will gather all the seeds of the sweet types I had taken and go away with them. The other two laughed at his foolishness.

When they got to the next land each of them off-loaded his goods to settle down. When the first opened his sacks of fruits, he discovered they all were rotten, not only that, the camels were about giving up the ghost due to the stress and suppression of the load they carried. The second waited for his last two donkeys, which were at the rear carrying his uprooted tree to arrive. When he checked the tree it was almost dry and the animals too almost dead from the burden of the load. Quickly, he replanted it while the third of them brought out the sweet fruit dry seed and planted them. As the nature of the plant is, with a fruit bearing short duration; after the next two months of settling the one planted by the third began to bear fruits while the second's planted tree finally dropped the last leaf, leaving behind a dead stem.

Humbly, they begged their third man for fruits to eat; plant and survive. When the time came for them to depart, they had learnt their lessons,—they all went for the sweet seed alone and intentionally left behind the trees as they journeyed ahead. This is the picture of our pilgrimage, the tree is our past, and the sweet and bitter fruits are the experiences, experiments, and lessons. The wise among men will only go for the sweet fruit's seed, which are the lessons from the past's rising and falling, go ahead and plant it in the future, with an unburdened heart and life speed. When you try to carry with you the whole load of the past the sweet and the bitter moments you live a depressed and oppressed life ahead. Two rivals contest for your present: the past and the future but you are the referee.

You are like a boy standing on a tight rope, with his father standing on the right while the shadow of his father reflecting on the left. He has the choice of where to jump to when the wind begins to blow: either into the arms of his father on the right side or on the left side into his shadow and you know what will happen. But that is what you do anytime you shift your thought to the past—you are jumping over into the hands of the passing shadow, the end of the day is always depression and emotional injuries. No matter how good or bad the past is, see it as a rehearsal to act your today and perfect your performance tomorrow.

~Everybody has past, but not
everybody passes it behind~

When Michelangelo was to paint the vaulted ceiling of a chapel between 1508 and 1512, Michelangelo covered the ceiling in Rome majestic frescoes, or paintings created with wet plaster with main scenes showing biblical stories and the Hebrew prophets. Perhaps the best-known fresco shows God creating Adam. Michelangelo worked perched on a platform about 18 meters (60 feet) above the floor. His paintings covered 930 square meters (10,000 square feet) of ceiling area. Most of the times, he did the painting lying on his back. Each day fresh plaster was laid over a part of the ceiling. Michelangelo then had to complete that portion while the plaster was still wet. He could not undo mistakes.

This is the picture of life sometimes, your job is not to undo mistakes, but to learn from it and lean on the experience. Today we talk about the great artwork with no reference to the mistakes made by this famous artist because he chose to move the brush ahead despite the odds. Each day provides us with a fresh plaster of time to paint out lives on it with our best ability and trusting God to make the best of our shortcomings. However, sometimes we lie on our back thoughts until the day's fresh plaster hardens to a rock of yesterday on which no one could write again. All your mistakes can be recycled with great new lessons turning out of the assembly line of time. God is working out everything out for your good. The basic thing to establish is that your life is worth living, and your future is worth having. Your today's garbage will be processed and managed by God, to garnish the lives of your contacts tomorrow.

Life may rid you of your past success, bully you out of your comfort zone; you might have lost everything visible to time, but you are not empty, your future is still in the enclosure of time. What more could your life still contain after all the flood of storms, nothing but the space of the future, it has not succeeded to encroach into that. Men may take from you your treasure, but your future is a blessed space, it is a blank check, on which you can choose to write anything; you can dream anything and can reap anything. In a junior high school, there used to be a bully who happened to be the most intelligent of his peers at the same time. So, combining his intellect with his muscles he contributes a threat to the rest.

At the beginning of one new session, a young boy was admitted newly, and was not happy with the behavior of this tallest boy in their class. One day, the newly admitted was asked by the class bully to remove his baggage from the airtight locker, which was reserved for special items but could temporarily be used by new intakes until space is being created for them. The young boy replied, "But I have every right to keep my goods here." The bully insisted, "Get them out now." Before they knew it they were creating a scene, other pupils were already gathering around the show. The boy replied, though you may force me to remove my goods, you could not remove everything there.

The bully was furious; as a well-respected great IQ student, he replied "What do you mean; that I can't remove everything from the enclosure? I have all it takes physically and mentally." With his patience running out, he drew closer to the locker, grabbed the goods of the new intake and flung them out. Everybody was quite while his gang hailed him as usual. Afterward, the new pupil replied, "Is that all you could remove?" He answered, what else is there? The young boy replied, "Light." Before all he reached out to the black cotton nearby and covered the glass door of the locker. "What else? With challenging tone he screeched, "You small for nothing!" shouting. The calm ruddy scholar replied in low tone, "There is still air inside."

Now, everybody was enjoying the show. He hurried, went to get a vacuum cleaner, disengaged the hose, and fixed it into the locker, within seconds he had suctioned out every air inside. Confidently and arrogantly, he exclaimed to the curious and cheers filled mixed crowd, "I have proved my superiority again physically and mentally." As his gang was about to hail him, the young lad said, "Friend, one more thing to remove," everybody was silent, eager to hear the final straw. They were confused, what more could be inside? After the short tensed silence, he uttered; "Space." It is obvious how helpless the bully became. Your future is the space that the storm has not succeeded in encroaching.

~Your emptiness is but the preparation
for your being filled, and your casting
down is but the making ready for
your lifting up~ Charles H. Spurgeon

I was once exposed to the power of God's recycling mercy when I was reading the lineage of the Lord as compiled by the tax master disciple. Matthew listed that forty-two generations were involved from the patriarch Abraham before the baby king. In other word, forty-two women were the matriarchs involved. But of all only four names were specifically mentioned: Tamar, Rehab, Ruth and Bathsheba. Out of the four, three played harlotry and one a widow—a non-Israelite. Why would God select such people of the rotten past to be the pipeline to convey the world's River of life and joy? In addition, why is it that it was their names that were specifically mentioned? This is the good news, that you can join the queue as you bring your past before the same Maker.

Just as the weather is the costume of the sky, it puts it on and changes it as often, likewise circumstances are like dress to our lives we should learn to undress them to fix in tomorrow's outfit. God expects us to always pass through situation and not situation passing through us turning us to a passive tool in His hands—we are not destined to *fail through* but *pass through* indeed. The spirit of adaptability when it comes to challenge driven change is the greatest and best attitude; it is the king of discipline when we want to develop our strength to work with inevitable weather. It is a symbol of a living mind and thriving hope. It separates the weak from the strong, boys from men, dreamers from sleepers, wishes-driven souls from will-driven souls. Challenges should be seen as a forerunner of change, a link to your best life ahead. Do not try to edit your past nor make your future a revise edition of world's script; today is a new page, write a fresh script for your tomorrow using the pen of courage and ink of goals.

Your hope is in the future and your future is in your hope. Have you noticed that when a tree is cut it comes back to thrive starting with more than one stem at ago compare to when it was initially planted. When you miss it you should bounce back, more resourcefully and equipped yielding much more accomplishment. Human beings use their brain, the animals use their instincts to survive, and the trees use their endurance to survive. But we can imbibe this attitude of the trees. Whatever befalls you in the race of life keep focus on what is before you. The future belongs to those who disown the past and become renowned with their today.

The story of a duck, ducklings, a fox, and a crocodile could be useful to drive in the power of dwelling on today to put your future to flight. At the bank of a river was duck with its duckling playing with one another. Just at a stone throw was a crocodile sleeping on the bank of the water as well. Suddenly a fox emerged from the bush and tried to attack the ducklings, they quickly out of fear dashed into the water to join their mother. The fox attempted to catch the last one, which hurriedly joined the rest. Because of fear, they continued to swim farther in the water. However, unknown to them, they have used the sudden water wave to disturb the sleeping crocodile.

The mother duck assumed all was over when it unexpectedly observed the approaching reptile. They all fled while the animal pursued. Within few seconds it had closed up the distance between them, the whole duckling team said to one another no need of swimming anymore; we are already its food. The end of the river's breadth was just few meters away and they had already given up, that if it can come close as this in a few seconds then in the next seconds it would catch up with us especially on the ground. As they were thinking, they heard the mother shouted, "Swim the more, faster to the ground." They thought, "Will that not amount to foolishness? Can we outrun a reptile on the ground?" Finally, they obeyed. As they reached the dry ground, the crocodile emerged as well. After taking few steps, the mother shouted at them all, "Now use your wings."

Suddenly, it dawned on them that they could fly; like a stunting aircrafts, they all leaped up into the air living on the ground the hungry and disappointed reptile. When in the air the ducklings asked the mother what gave you the strategy and assurance that we could still escape? "Because I knew the animal can't fly, but we too can't take off from the water. If we had continued swimming in the water trying to solve the problem, it would have caught up with us. And the reptile knew as well that was why it gave all its energy to the start-up." The mother duck explained.

The water represents your past, the dry land your today and the air your future. The fox represents the challenges you met when you were born while the crocodile represents the ones that surfaced because you were born. If you want to conquer those past chasers and barriers, you need to leave the water. You are like a duck that can walk, swim and fly, but can only take off to the air on the ground. If you want to soar in the future treasures you need to take off from today. Start your life from today, hurry out of the water of the past, you cannot defeat the reptile of depression and regrets in such terrain. The future provides you with unlimited space to fly and fly but your launching pad is today.

You should be a pupil of your past to learn from it and not to lean on anymore; a teacher of your today not a preacher of past; and a classroom for your future and not with a mushroom thinking. Your hope is in your future and your future is in your decision. Your past depends on your future for the final changes but you can watchfully choose to allow your past to finish the future. Life is like a stone of rock, or a log of wood, you are the sculptor with the tool of mind to carve out whatever you can see hidden in it. Some things that happen to you simply happen for you if you see them as life teachings. The beauty of a flower comes out in the heat of the sun. You cannot erase your past, but you can overlay paint on it, drawing the picture of the future you see like a famous artist once disclosed, "I paint my dream."

When you try to remove all the blocks of failure in your building of success, you will discover many holes in the building. Sometimes, some people have only the roof and the part of the foundation remaining, which never stand, or last. These are those, who live so carefully, in shallowness that they never make mistakes but also live and leave with the greatest mistake of living by default.

~Use what is left, for it is the only
possible right thing to use~

I once read of an aged woman who just did something that thousands of high school students do every single year—she got her diploma. You might not think it is that big of a deal, but she isn't your average high scholar. She is 103 years old. She waited 90 years to see her dream fulfilled. Marie has lived in Spring Green, Wisconsin, for her entire life. She told NBC that she was part of a large family that struggled (as most did back then), and finding a way to get to and from the River Valley High School was an impossibility for her. So she sadly dropped out of school after eighth grade and became a caretaker to her younger brothers and sisters. "I was born in 1911, and there was no way that country kids six miles away could go to high school." Marie said. Decades later Marie, now living in an assisted living community, told a staff nurse, she deeply regretted the decision to leave school. The nurse reached out to school officials and put a plan in motion to help Marie finally get the degree she wanted for her entire life.

So, on one good Friday, Marie finally got her dream fulfilled. River Valley High School presented her with an honorary high school diploma, some 87 years after she would have originally graduated. She made hay while the moon shines. Gold is never too old to sell, true dream, do not die with time when lived, they rather die of time. Those who spend their morning singing I could, their afternoon saying I would will spend their night sighing I should.

MAXIMISING YOUR STORMS

~Never forget that God tests his
real friends more severely
than the lukewarm ones~
Kathryn Hulme

In a Sunday school, a young boy asked the teacher as they concluded the story of how David killed Goliath; he said ma, "Why was David particular about the smooth stone that he had to leave the battlefront, passed by many stones as he went down to the brook to get them?" "Why can't he use any other stone?"

Secondly, "What makes those stones to be smooth?" The teacher replied him, "David preferred smooth stones because they work best in the sling and to disarm the target. When a smooth stone is slung by the sling, it smoothly slips off the sling with little friction and hasten better accuracy. Moreover, they will not quickly ware out the sling as they glide off it. David had to bypass other stones he met on the way because they were not prepared; God can bypass thousand just to get a man after His own will—a man that he has trained with the tool of life storms and challenges. A man coming from the wilderness where he had fought the lion and bear over small matters. God doesn't use a man with rough character; He will first polish you in order to unleash the potentials in you."

He taught further, "Remember David was the last to be presented to Samuel as potential king and God rejected the first six, by-passed them and went for the last to be presented—David. In addition, what makes the stones smooth is a long tasking process and that is why many stones could not pass through it. Those smooth stones were once rough edged before. One day, the river dragged them along, and for many days, months or years they were being dragged along by the river.

While in the process, they were forced to rob against the rock, at the bottom of the river and against themselves. They met many stony obstacles on the way, which they collided with, and still moved on. All these processes had an impact on the stones; they brought about abrasion and attrition leading to wearing and chipping of the stone edges and at the end they came out smooth. One more thing they do is that they stay in the location—the river brook so they can easily be found and used like David did."

One of the 50 richest Jews in his third term as mayor of New York City, was a former equity trader who used some of his $10 million severance package after being fired in 1981, to develop what became the global financial news and media company. At age 68, he net worth $18 billion. He could have resigned to fate and complaints, but he was fired to re-fire. What happens to you is one thing, how you see it is another thing and what you do with it is the ultimate thing. After a native farmer harvested a yam tuber, a hole was left behind in the ground. At night, a little frog unknowingly jumped into the hole—never knew how deep because it was dark. When it began to dawn, it realized the danger—the hole was a bit deep for its exit.

Nevertheless, it tried to escape, but succeeded only in stamping claws at the mouth of the hole slipping back with some sand granules chipping off the wall of the hole, falling in to the base. He continued the unsuccessful trial many times, each time the sand granules fell into the bottom of the hole. When the farmer got to the farm with his two sons who were working with him, the children discovered the frog in the hole and became excited at the captured live toy. They immediately began to play with the creature, they kicked sand on it in the hole several times, and the frog as well would try to jump out unsuccessfully, pulling down more sand with each sliding. For three days, the scenario repeated itself, the frog trying to jump out and the boys, running to the hole every morning to catch fun there by kicking sand on the frog.

On the third day, the frog was already tired and starving. Meanwhile the sand that fell from the wall with it when sliding down at each escape trial and the one the boys kicked at it to make jest and fun of it had begun to fill up the hole gradually, reducing the depth. The third day episode actually reduced the depth to a bearable height of escape. On the fourth day morning, the exhausted creature woke up from sleep and thought within itself, no need to jump anymore. It had given up after several trials. When the boys came at the early hour they quickly rushed to the hole, found the frog lying down on its belly exhausted. Assuming it was dead, they went to inform their father about what they had been doing behind the scene for four days. Moreover, they were afraid that it would be unhealthy for the dead frog to be where they get food.

When the farmer got there, he said there was no need to remove the frog; it is good manure when finally decompose. Therefore, he took his shovel and began to fill the hole with the purpose of burying the creature as natural fertilizer. Immediately the heavy blow of sand touched the frog, it was unlike the granules of sand the boys have been kicking; this one really hit hard. As the pain dawned on it, unprepared and unplanned, it jumped up and landed outside the hole; the two boys ran away while they watch the creature as it took three more hops to disappear into the bush.

People may kick dust of criticism against you as you struggle to reach your goal; you may fall and roll ahead, but all these factors are materials to convert into a ladder for your rising. Joseph said you meant it for evil by selling me out, betraying me and stabbing my heart, but God meant it for good to save lives including yours. You may want to give it up like the frog when you are closest to the realization of your goals; all you need may just be one more attempt and you are up there. Thank God for the storm He sends to stir us up, like the scoop of sand that landed like an avalanche on the frog which made it to make an unplanned attempt, and that was it. God allows storms not to stop us, but to top our efforts.

Optimize your inevitable

~Often we as strong in life as the resistance
we face in the way not really as the assistance
we receive~

I did a little bit of aerodynamics in my university days; they instructed about the significance of the shape of material when it comes to air lifting. When you visualize the experiment in the wind tunnel, you will have a vivid understanding of the role of shapes in aerodynamics. The wings of airplanes are major factors that contribute to the lifting power. In other words, what determines whether a material will fly in the face of the wind or get overturned is simply the shape and positioning of the material. The shape of your mood has a lot do in determining whether life circumstances will drift you up closer to your dreams or overturn your aspirations. Sometimes, the miracle you need is just an obstacle on your way. An adventurer found himself lost in the desert due to a faulty compass, which he still believed was working well. At a point, he encountered a mountain standing directly across the path indicated by the compass as the right route.

He felt discouraged as that route indicates the nearest distance to inhabited village. Having no choice after much complaint, he decided to make holes in the rock for footing to climb up. On getting to the peak, he took his telescope and looked around. Suddenly, he discovered that following the compass after the rock was a large expanse of dry land afterward an endless sea. He continued looking around and discovered that just to his right, was a footpath, barely two kilometers away leading to a closely laid out village. He said, "Thank God I climbed the mountain, and never turned back for a plain ground, nor sat there complaining." His compass could have led him to a new adventure, which he might never complete, had it been he had a choice to bypass the mountain. However, climbing the mountain gave him a bird view of direction. There are some mountains, you must climb in life to make your journey counts; and your make efforts amount to a monument. Keep your eyes focused on resources in your challenges. When you fall in the path, rise up forward, the road is becoming shorter, at least by six-foot head.

~When failure is inevitable make it enviable~

Some of God's best for us are only visible in the moment of trials when all people are running for their comfort then life rolls out its increase. This is succinctly portrayed by an inspiring artwork of a young man, which was tagged, thus "This Incredible Sidewalk Art Is Only Visible in the Rain"—A sidewalk artist knows that a rainy day can make a person feel pretty blue, which is why he decided to create artwork that can only appear on a rainy day. "Rain works are pieces of street art that only appear when they are wet and their messages or images designed to make people's rainy day a little bit brighter," The young man lives in Seattle, which is, of course, known for its rainy weather, making the entire city the perfect canvas for his craft.

Some of his messages are very witty. However, they are meant to bring a little joy into the life of everyday citizens, so that even on a rainy day, they still find themselves walking on the sunny side of the street. Making use of something called a biodegradable super hydrophobic coating that repels water after setting for 24 hours. He could have been complaining about the incessant rain of the city or just move out in disappointment. Likewise, the beautiful artwork can only be accessed by those who defy the rain and dare the chill weather. You are only being polished not punished. The belt is hanging out in the combat zone not comfort zone.

Red hot advantage

When the iron is hot is when the blacksmith takes the advantage to bend it to his desired shape. Some vital decisions are taken, often, at the points of unpalatable life circumstances. We could see clearly our errors and carelessness of which we can take the atmosphere of the moment to stamp along time lingering positive choice. When the prodigal son was on the verge of suffering, he took a vital decision that changed and retraced the course of his life. When Paul had the Damascus way encounter, he took the greatest decision of his life and purpose. He became blind to see. Sometimes you need to become lame to walk; you may need to become dumb to speak. What you are passing through could be for you to pass a decision for God's will. Some training comes like mocking, some like storm, and some like pains.

A boy unexpectedly came across a nest with a bird brooding over newly hatched young ones. Being in the night, he climbed the tree and gently captured the whole team, took them home as a pet. Then, unexpectedly the mother bird escaped and flew away. The boy became furious and chose to turn the little birds into cheap toys. Every day he will come to the open throw them up together catching fun, the young birds will struggle in the air as they spread their wings, to softly bang on the ground. Sometimes they will sustain injuries, scream as they suffered hatch treatment from the boy. What used to pain more was the fact of seeing their mother flying around, perching on the surrounding trees looking at them in all their ordeals and wondered why it would not just come and rescue them. But the mother bird never bothered to do that because it knew that as long as they persevere and endure, all things would work out for good for them one day.

Day in day out the boy continued to catch fun and trouble these little birds. But a day came, he took the duo out of the cage, threw them up as usual. But something unusual happened, to his surprise they never landed in their back yard as usual, rather, they flew away to join their waiting and watching mother on the tree. All the while the boy had been training these birds indirectly how to fly thinking he was maltreating them and catching fun.

The same thing with us what life sometimes subjects us to is a preparation for our next future flight. We are being strengthened, trained, and polished by the whole process. Often we wonder why God is not stretching forth His mighty hand of deliverance and bear us on His wings; but He has the advantage of seeing the whole picture. He is rather employing life challenges to polish us, but it seems as to punish us. Imagine all Joseph passed through, it was not that God forgot him and His promises to him as revealed in his dreams; but in all, the scripture will say every now and then "...but the Lord was with Joseph: in slavery, in prison, in the pit; why didn't God make him to skip all these?

~Believe things happen
for you not to you~

A curious toddler inwardly wondered how his parent used to get long straps of tissue paper from the same roll all the time. One morning he tried to do the same but did not have the capacity to hold and unfold it much. Playing with it on the table it suddenly fell off and on it rolled on the floor. As it rolled forward, a very impressive length of the tissue paper was unfolded. The toddler was happy of his achievement. Sometimes your hidden potential will only surface when you are tried and tilled. When you drop down from your privileged zone and you choose to intentionally fail forward.

You are only passing through, you are not failing through. Are you passing through fire? God said, "I will be with you and you will come out as refined gold. Are you passing through water? You will not be drowned, you will come out washed and watered. Are you passing through the valley of the shadow of death? David said, "I will fear no evil for thou are with me." Everybody must pass through, how you come out is a factor of your attitude in the tunnel. It is not what you are passing through that matters most, but where you are passing to and who is passing through it with you. Fall on your knees, not back when things go tough.

When Joshua was about to be installed as a new leader of millions journeying in the wilderness; a young man of experience and good records—saw no giants as unconquerable, dared what his colleagues feared; he was equipped with this truth despite is record. God bypassed all these and not for once nor twice admonished this daring young mind with a burning zeal to be strong and of good courage, because He knew there would be falling and rising on the way. Joshua actually faced the reality of life challenges as they lost the second war to the city of Ai. Joshua fell on his face and lamented over their failure, but the LORD said to Joshua: "Get up, why do you lie thus on your face?" Successful people carry the scars—scars of missed stepping but not the coward stopping. God does not prepare a table before us in front of our friends, nor our well-wishers but our adversaries. He did not create us for adversities, but recreate us through adversity.

    Tough time is a language of love we find so hard to learn with God. Failure could be a process to success and success could be a process to failure depending on how you handle it; depending on how we chose to see it in the light of choices. The star and dark sky reveal mutuality of success and failure; the stars lighten the sky, the dark sky reveals the star. Failures will double the fame of your success tomorrow and success will cover the shame of yesterday failures. When a strong mind fails, he stands to become stronger, when a weak mind fails he sits to become weaker. Failure points us to our weakness, and one's weakness is a pointer to a training topic. God is charging you, saying, "Have I not commanded you? Be strong, vigorous, and very courageous. Be not afraid, neither be dismayed, for the Lord your God is with you wherever you go."

> ~When the world pushes you to
> your knees, you are in the best position
> to pray~ Anonymous

    Resolve for strength on your knees do not dissolve the remaining ones by lying on your face in dejection and rejection. Just like the story of a hawk with newly hatched one. They lost their mother—their potential model for flight lessons as they were about leaving the nest. These little ones will rather land on the ground rather than on the branches of trees and playing kids will quickly come to chase them away or throw stones at them. They have always been wondering about other birds' ability to perch on the branches. They were scared about how the branch will first oscillate back and forth, up and down as if it would break or fall off their legs. Therefore, any time they attempted it they would quickly fly away in fear.

One day one of them tried to emulate other birds while others felt pity for it because they were afraid that it might fall off from a broken branch. As they flew in the sky, it dived down and perched on a tender branch. As usual, the branch began to oscillate up and down. The little bird was afraid, but clung its claw tightly the more, after all, if it breaks I had fly away so why the fear. After a good number of oscillations, the branch began to settle down; it finally slowed down to a bearable and comfortable state. When life challenges come, hold on, do not let go, with time and trust it will end up as rocking chair to make your life amusing.

~Your dreams shrinks or expands at the
dimension of your courage~

KEEP GOODS ONLY BEFORE YOU

One gracious thing about God is the picture He tries to paint in our mind. A young adult once asked this question in one of our bible study classes. He asked, "Why can't God show us the process we will pass through as we decide to embark on His will?" I happened to be conducting the teaching that day and this was what I told him. God will only give you the end picture and not the process if He does you will likely withdraw. He only showed Joseph the throne picture but did not show him the persecution at home, the pit, the Potiphar's house slavery and the prison but the palace. He only spoke to the children of Israel about the land flowing with milk and honey, but not about the wilderness and the red sea nor the giants. God chooses to show us the end picture only, so that we can have it kept at our front.

When he showed the process to the Lord by the revelation on the mount of transfiguration through Moses and Elijah it took great grace for Him to go ahead in the garden of Gethsemane. What you need to focus on is the product from following God's will and not the process. I once read a shocking discovery that right from birth our eye lens remains in the same size till the old age. It is one of the few parts of the body that do not increase in size as one grows. A good lesson can be learnt from this that it is like God wants us to keep a constant view about His love and plan for us from birth till death. His plan for us is unchanging and such He wants our view to be unchanging about them no matter what is happening around us. God designed us in a way that our lives cycle around what we think about most. There is a force of attraction that keeps a life around the orbit of the mind's picture and ultimately, what you live around with will determine the amount of drive and energy you will draw for your journey. The solar system depicts this at a glance. The earth is glued to the orbit of the sun, which actually serves as her ultimate source of energy.

~Life is not just about defining your strength,
 life is more of refining your weakness in the
 furnace of storms ~

There is a power of attraction that keeps you heading toward your imagination. In the eleventh chapter of the scriptures, just after the dispensation of the flood, men on the earth had a unified language which matured into a unified mind-set. They told one another let us build a skyscraper notwithstanding the crude state of their technology. When God viewed their joint project, He exclaimed! "Behold, the people are one, and they have all one language; and this they begin to do: and now nothing will be restrained from them, which they have imagined to do." In other word, their lives will one day hit their imagination; their achievement will one day meet up with their mind picture; their dreams will someday become reality. Not on the scale of trial and error or event of chances, but of certainty, nothing can be restrained from them.

All they need are three fundamental tools: unity, one language, and imagination. When as a man your entities: spirit, soul and body are in unity of purpose and keep voicing one language, with your spirit, in your mind and actions, imagination will crown the victory. Hence, a need to keep living dreams in front of you every day.

After many years of fruitless and rigorous labor, the frustrated Jacob decided to quit his contract with his uncle and set out for greener pasture. To reverse this, a new deal was struck to retain him; the selfish, bossy uncle protested, why leaving? Name your salary expectation and I will consider it. They agreed on color separation; you will take the white products of the herd while all the specked, the spotted will be mine. Jacob being a mild and creative God driven man, set out on the process of imagination to achieve cross breeding. He set before the animals a picture of what he wants their life to produce. As they continually come to drink and conceive before the spotted and speckled rods they reproduced the picture set before them.

The figuration they beheld continually became their imagination and nothing could restrain them from giving birth to their imagination based on the new configuration. The same thing is applicable to human being, what you behold continually makes up your imagination, in turn duplicates in your life, and eventually dictates your boundary. Many times, I have seen couples after many years of marriage tending to resemble each other—tending to look like twins facially. I do not have any scientific explanation for this or to prove this; but I can infer that, they look at each other too much, and eventually begin to look like each other. This law of reflection is firmly established in the word of life, and what I am trying to liken it to is the power of imagination. But we all, with open face beholding as in a glass the glory of the Lord, are changed into the same image from glory to glory, [even] as by the Spirit of the Lord. What you are continually exposed to with open face or eye of your mind, is what your life will be tailored toward. Having established the possibility of mind replication, then it is necessary for your life not to be dreamless.

When you choose not to place a dream before you or to quit after falling, you are close to the boundary of hopelessness and depression. Failing is neither a misery nor a mystery but a tool for gaining mastery. It is just common sense. If every man will have it recorded by dear mothers how many times they fell when trying to stand and walk as a toddler I know the number will be appreciable. Yet, as a young kid, you never quitted, something kept on making you to stand and try again. You propped on the wall, on the walker, around the couch sometime clung to your parents' wears, all efforts channeling towards your goal. Let me tell you, there was something pushing you not to be content with crawling on all fours.

I agree that biologically and anatomically you were destined to stand straight, but there was something as well that was propelling such constant falling and rising—the picture of others around you standing and walking. You were surrounded continually by your siblings standing and walking on their legs, your parents, neighbors and visitors. Therefore, you kept on trying to live what you saw incessantly. Like it was earlier said, what you place before you will influence the power of drive and the volume of zeal that will be available to you. Today is the result of your past but resources for your tomorrow. The days behind could be full of guilt, but those ahead are full of gifts from God. Your mind can only focus on one thing per time, when you remember the past, you forget the future meanwhile.

~To put the past behind you, you must
accept that you've moved beyond it ~ Ruth

Pursue a clear picture

The past has already determined who we are; but to predetermine who we shall be should be the job of today and you have the say. You cannot be defined anymore by your past, but you can be confined by it. In life you must always see where you are going to move on and do everything you can to keep the sight. As a driver, you do not press the throttle without firstly having a clear picture of the road. When it begins to rain, you turn on the wiper; when the dusk is approaching you turn on the headlamp; when the windscreen is layered with dust you press the button to release cleaning liquid on the screen; when the sun rays are pointing directly in your eyes you pull down the sun shade device—you do everything to have a clear picture of what lies ahead.

All these efforts are geared towards one reason—to have a clear picture of the road ahead. Likewise, you must do all you can to have a clear picture of what your life wants to dive into. That is why God said write the vision and make it plain that he who reads it may run. One of the reasons you need to dream again is because dreams become clearer with time. The frequently you dream, the more fine-tuned the picture becomes. You need to allow God to give you a fresh dream rather than allowing the foxes of life to choke your mind.

In one of the miracles performed by the Lord, a blind man was involved. He took the blind man by the hand and led him out of the town; "And when he had spit on his eyes, and put his hands upon him, he asked him if he saw anything. And he looked up, and said, "I see men as trees, walking."

"After that he put [his] hands again upon his eyes, and made him look up: and he was restored, and saw every man clearly." In the first vision of the man, he said he saw men walking like trees. It is obvious that his vision was lopsided; again, Jesus touched him and this time asked him to look up and then he was given a clearer vision, and his sight was restored. When you are confused about your vision in life, go for second touch looking *up* for second time like the blind man before looking back at life. God is ready to give you clearer and brighter dreams.

At the age of seventeen; wearing rainbow like raiment, this young mind had dreamt and again dreamt. In his first dream, he narrated to his siblings, "Hear, I pray you, this dream which I have dreamed: For, behold, we [were] binding sheaves in the field, and, lo, my sheaf arose, and also stood upright; and, behold, your sheaves stood round about, and made obeisance to my sheaf." And his brethren said to him, "Shall thou indeed reign over us? Or shall thou indeed have dominion over us?" And they hated him yet the more for his dreams, and for his words. And he dreamed yet another dream, and told it his brethren—"Behold, I have dreamed a dream more; and, behold, the sun and the moon and the eleven stars made obeisance to me."

~Life can only be understood backwards;
but it must be lived forwards~
Søren Kierkegaard

Before talking about the above account, look at these two scriptural phrases: "dreamed a dream more" and "dreamed yet another dream". I challenge you today to dream yet another dream and to dream a dream more. Back to his dreams, the first of the two dreams was a bit illustrative. Joseph had seen the sheaves of his brethren bowing to his, but the second one was more illustrative and dramatic, really carrying the details of his future enormity. Now the sun, the moon, and the eleven stars were bowing to him. In other word, the world was bowing to him. Though Jacob retorted, "Do you mean I, your mother and your brothers will come and bow before you," but this dream can be further translated as meaning something else.

Firstly, Rebekah, his mother had died by then, and eventually it was only his eleven brothers that came to bow to him. Jacob did not bow but rather blessed Joseph. What am I saying, when Joseph dreamt again, it was like the dream became bigger and clearer. The world not just is family came bowing. When you allow God to work in you after falling, He will place in your mind something bigger and clearer. Like to say that, Joseph did not dream twice following the text of this scripture. When he dreamt about the shelves and told his brethren, the text says, "And they hated him yet the more for his *dreams*". Note the word "dreams" this was before the celestial dreams of the sun moon and the stars. So this young mind was dream addict—he dreamt not just once or twice but again and again. When Joseph was dying, he told his brethren that they should carry his bone along since he was sure that God would visit them and take them out of the land. He was still dreaming at the point of death. He was so sure of God's promises to his great grandfathers to the extent that he was making plans towards it in his absence.

God asked Jeremiah, what do you see? He is asking you in addition, "What do you see? Before our Lord Jesus finally went to the cross to vanquish our foe, He had already dreamt of his end. In the third book of the gospel, Luke wrote, "And he said unto them, 'I saw Satan as lightning fall from heaven.'"

When Satan tries to batter your dream, God has a better plan for you. When it seems that the dream of Joshua was hitting the rock after suffering a defeat in the war with the city of Ai, God told him to get up from the floor where he fell to discouraged. He revealed to him where Israel missed it and rekindled his dream, but not only that, He made the process much clearer and better with new strategy of ambushing the enemy. Eventually, he won the war by this new strategy. Do not let your dream slip off, nor sleep off, dream yet another dream and dream again like Joseph. Keep your eyes single at a time; focus your strength on goals.

~It's okay to look back at your past,
just do not stare ~ Benjamin Dover

THE FUTURE IS THE HOPE NOT THE FEAUTURED

A retired soldier was telling his son how he escaped being killed by the opposing force. He had tried to counsel him to retake his training as a student after he failed, but the boy was thinking of going back to be a factory worker—what he did before putting in to further his education. He narrated, when we were sent to the hot zone, we had the cause to cross over a valley with a long rope stretched across the valley, which demarcated us from the camp of the enemy. After the operation, we were to return. As I was in the middle of the tight rope as the last man to cross, the enemy reinforced and came with heavy bombardment. They fired at my colleagues and both parties exchange shots, but there I was in the middle of the rope in the air. It was getting dark. I had to stand still like a statue so I won't be noticed by the advancing sharpshooters. But luck ran out on me as one of them sighted me and fired at me. I was holding the rope with my two hands and fortunately for me, he missed me which was very unusually of such well-trained shooters. The bullet went straight in between my two stretched arms, but I was not completely lucky as the bullet hit the rope I was holding on to right in between my two arms.

Before I could say Jack, the rope lost part of its fabric and rapidly tended to break off. In a twinkling of an eye, I had to make a decision: either to hold one side with my right hand and let go of the left part or the other side with my left hand and let go of the right. "My son, which side do you think I should hold on to?" He asked.

He said my right hand was towards my camp and the left hand was towards where I was coming from—the foes camp. The son almost shouting, replied, |"Dad you dare not be silly, you must have thought so fast and wise and clung to the right rope with your right hand so that as the rope finally breaks you will dive with it and land in your camp though crash landing." "My son you are right, my instinct made the decision before I was able to think it out. I naturally clung to the right side as the rope broke off and away I swung with it to land on the side of my colleagues where I was heading.

When the rope failed, I had two choices or two places to hold on to, forward or backward. And as you said, wisdom demands I hold on to the forward rope where I headed initially. The same with you, your journey had been divided in to two by the impact of challenges; now that you had failed in your path of advancement you have two choices: either to hold on to the rope of hope of your dream side or you cling to the rope of quitting that will swing you back to your odd past—where nothing exists but enemies in the likes of frustration, depression, underutilization of your gifts and loss of time spent to get to your present position.

But you can choose to hold on to the right side of the rope and land in the camp of your future, with a price of crash landing which is better than to be a prisoner of war in the hand of the enemy—a prisoner of hope and fading wishes.

A notable leader once said "The most important thing I do at the beginning of a new year is leaving the old year where it fell. Regret and negativity can kill our drive." Continue to face the sunlight of tomorrow that the shadow of your past might be kept at the back. A wise man once put it thus, "It's good to learn from the year you just lived, but if you stare at it too long, regret over the opportunities you missed or mistakes you made will blossom."

~You are not fully responsible for your
past but you are truly for your future~

In a biology class one brilliant girl wearing a pig tail hair style stood up towards the end of the class. That day they had been taught about primate and other animals. Before then, a history teacher just left the class and had taught them about the beasts of burden—how men in old age made use of the animals for transportation and comfort. How they used to place load on them and sit on them. So as the biology teacher was rounding up the curious girl asked "Ma, why did God make the animals to be walking on all four and human beings stand straight up; was it for us to use them as beast of burden with ease?" The teacher replied, "Possibly God had us in mind." After the class was over the psychology teacher who had been waiting outside and over hearing their last conversation walked in. "How many of you are carrying burden in your heart, mind or on your head about the results of your past failures and fallings?" he asked after exchanging greetings. Many of them, including the girl that asked the question raised up their hands. He said, "You are carrying the burden like the beast of burden because you are mentally living like them. All your fours are on the ground you have not stood up from where you fell. You have been crawling in life and that is why life was able to place on you the burden of dejection, self-condemnation, low self-esteem, anxiety, fear of future failure, mockery of people, and conclusions of critics. Why do not you shake them off by standing up on two legs while using your hand for future pursuits?"

~Your past is late, but if you do not leave
the funeral as soon as it is over, you can be
late for your future~

Your plans may fall apart, but let not your goal fall apart; plans are tool if one doesn't work go back to the tool box and in your inner get the another strategy. It is your plan A that failed which is the alpha, then go for plan B which is *beta*. You cannot renew your past you can only review it. Guard your heart from your failure and your head from your success. Everything is a change both success and failure. No matter how good or bad the past is, see it as a rehearsal to act your today, and perfect your performance tomorrow. Everybody has past, but not everybody bypasses it behind. Run with time and march with the seasons so your age can match your stage at the closing hour. Daily define your goals, redefine your plans and be confined in your dreams. Often it needs to be near to be clear.

Focus rightly on the left

Whatever befalls you in the race of life keep focus on what is before you. The future belongs to those who disown the past and use today to crown the future. Two rivals contest for your present: the past and the future but you are the referee. There is no failure strong enough to make you useless; always know that you are still less used. Live today with responsibility for you cannot live your past in reality anymore. Your future can't walk toward you neither can your past, which ever position you find yourself is your goals of thought. If nobody believes in you, it doesn't mean you are nobody. Your value is unchanging in the eyes of God.

A defaced, roughened, soiled, and messed up 100-dollar bill retains its value anytime any day. Learn from your past but do not live to learn about it. You may have no reason to laugh about your past, but tomorrow is pregnant with reasons to laugh. A wise heart once said something that shows how important this is and how far we need to go to keep negativity at bay—"I find a quiet place to be alone and have a forgiveness session," he said. "I scour my heart clean in preparation for the 365 days by forgiving those I need to forgive. And I always include that person who often seems to disappoint me most. . . myself."

~When a goal fails, set another one;
to be goalless is close to being hopeless~

Let your past be in your head, your future in your heart, and your today is your hand. There can't be a future without past, but there can be a past without a future; so choose to think onward, fight forward and dream toward. At every axis of time coordinates, our life is the sum of three parameters: past, today and tomorrow. Today cannot continue nor tomorrow begins until yesterday mentally ends. When you lavish today on yesterday you spend your time; tomorrow is the only good soil to invest and harvest your time. Do not wait for the future to come meet you run towards it.

Overlook your past and look over your tomorrow. A river cannot flow farther than the sea; your past cannot take you beyond today so empty it into the sea of today and let a new course be structured on the other side of the sea. Do not live with a mirror before you rather place a plain glass so you have no business with scenes behind. The car windshield was made of bigger plane glass size compare to the reflective side mirror of small area. This tells you that you have little to see at the back and a whole lot at the front. However, some people make a side mirror of their windshield, making it reflective to often view past scenes and choose to look through the side mirror occasionally at their assumed imaginary future.

~The more you past is real to you
the more your future is unreal to you~

A businessman who just got bankrupted resolved to go back to his village and narrate his failure in the city to his family. He had spent the past days to cry and lament of the silly mistakes he made about a wrong deal. Going back home, he boarded a canoe with his son who was following him to their riverside home village for the first time. While on the water, the kid who had never ridden in a canoe before watched the canoe man as he skillfully maneuver the oar. He observed that the man used the oar to drag the water backward and in doing so the canoe moved forward. So he asked the father why it is in such way.

The canoe man heard his question and interrupted the father and son—said, "My son; that is the law of progress on the sea. You must use what you have at hand to push what you do not need backward in order to go forward. I have the oar in my hand and use it to drag the water I do not need behind since our goal is to reach the dry land ahead—that the canoe can go forward." The boy curiously demanded, "What if you want the canoe to go backward what would you do?" "I will have to paddle the water forward," said the man. The boy looked at his father and said, "Dad, that means as we are going back to our village because of your failed business, we are like paddling the water we do not need foolishly forward—your failed past." The man suddenly realized his foolishness he had been pushing his past failure forward into tomorrow using the oar of today, hence his life had been going backward to the remote. He inspired himself, "If I want to go forward and be a business tycoon I must use the moment I have at hand to push my past bitter water backward to gain forward momentum in to my dream."

~To the wise the past is too long to
be remembered today; to the fools
the future is too long to be
remembered today~

You are designed to go forward. Dreams are nurtured in the womb of time, but do not mature in the tomb of past. When you have given your best, you are a winner it does not matter if you get an award from men or not, for your reward is in heaven. You cannot do anything when you cry in pain but you can do many things when you try again. Not that God only instructs us to go forward, He as well designed us to go forward—all our senses are directionally forward likewise all our body openings. The only part that opens to the back is the anus, which is meant to throw out the unwanted parts of our system.

The majority of things you have behind you in your past are really unneeded for your future growth. If today is a horse, I think the past is the laden cart, and must I drag it into the future? No! This is what I will do; I will leave the comfort of the cart and sit on the horse, on my way to the future. The cart is just an implement I can ride faster without it. Let go of the past lest the future passes you by. Failure is only the echo of a success ahead. The strength of success is sometimes the length of failure before the access. It is better to have a flat tire in the garage than a broken wing in the sky, for when the flight is on it is too late to gauge the tire. Success without mistake has a fake process.

> ~99.9% of what is holding us down
> in life do not have hands; we lend
> a helping hand~

Turn the experience into insight

Some goat kids often passed under herb whose leaves sometimes fall off when dried. They used to find it so delicious when they feed on the fallen leaves. However, they were never satisfied as they hardly got enough to share. So they often looked up to the nearest branch to feed on the fresh leaves directly, but despite stretching themselves up none of them could have its mouth to pick them. Eventually, they resolved to feeding on the dry ones. There was a day one of them ran into a ditch as they were running home from the approaching rain.

The other left it behind until their owner discovered that one was missing. Right there in the ditch under the tree the young kid witnessed that before the rain started the wind will first blew, the thunder rumbled and at the end, the rain started pouring. Meanwhile, fresh leaves were blown down one after the other on the ground before they were finally blown off by the wind; in the same vein, the branches of the tree were forced to bend lower by the wind in the meantime.

One day they were under the tree resting from the sun; suddenly the wind began to blow as it had been whenever it was about to rain, they all fled to the ranch shed for safety, but unfortunately on getting there the ranch door had been jammed by the wind, so thought within themselves on what to do. Quickly, their instinct told them to return to the tree for cover as a lesser but available alternative. To their surprise, they discovered that one of them which had been looking fresh was there. As they approached from afar, they saw it eating fresh leaves on the ground and occasionally from the tree lowest branch, including the fruits, which naturally, all of them were not able to feed on. They saw how the wind shook the tree for some fresh leaves and fruits and sometimes force the branches to bend lower for the reachable height of the goat.

All the while, this had been the act of the bold kid. He waited behind a bit when the thunder starts rocking and others fled, he waited longer enough for the wind to blow eat and then run off when the rain begins to drizzle ever since it discovered this, on the day it fell into the ditch. Often it had ended not raining only thunder and storm that left behind great drops of fresh leaves. They just discovered that it was getting fresher.

Many have lost great opportunities to fear of economic weather, they have been so careful not to make loss that they make no plus. Dreamers know when to take risks and when to wake up from the risk. The fact that the thunder is rocking doesn't mean it will be raining. Many have developed the pessimist spirit that they see danger in everything in color red. Even when they are in aircraft, they thought of a flat tire.

This reminds me of the story of four lepers in the bible. They were being left at the city gate as lepers, not permitted to enter. A time came when there was a great famine in the city, the enemy had the city besieged which caused the famine. However, God worked out a miracle according to His word through a prophet, that there would be plenty the following day. These lepers thought within themselves: if we remain here in the city outskirt we would starve to death; if we go into the city the famine is there severely—we will still die, but if choose to approach the enemy they might choose between two things to kill us or to spare and serve us food. Therefore, with this common sense they went for the third option.

On getting there they met no one in the camp of the enemy, God had made them flee and they left behind their goods. These lepers got there and became richer overnight than the entire city. They ate and delivered the whole nation from famine to fulfill the word of the Lord. In life, we are always faced with these three choices: to stay where we are in our stagnation; go to the city to join the multitude and experience their fate or to reach out to the dared and feared by faith to save our generations.

See through the tears

John Ray Grisham, Jr. is an American lawyer, politician, and author, best known for his popular legal thrillers. His books have been translated into forty-two languages. John Grisham graduated from Mississippi State University before attending the University of Mississippi School Of Law in 1981. He practiced criminal law for about a decade, and served in the House of Representatives in Mississippi from January 1984 to September 1990. He began writing his first novel, A Time to Kill, in 1984, and it was published in June 1989. As of 2012, his books had sold over 275 million copies worldwide. A Galaxy British Book Awards winner, Grisham is one of only three authors to sell 2 million copies on a first printing, the others being Tom Clancy and J.K. Rowling. Grisham's first bestseller was The Firm. Released in 1991, it sold more than seven million copies.

Grisham said the big case came in 1984, but it was not his case. As he was hanging around the court, he overheard a 12-year-old girl telling the jury what had happened to her. Her story intrigued Grisham and he began watching the trial. He saw how the members of the jury cried as she told them about having been raped and beaten. It was then Grisham later wrote in The New York Times, that a story was born. Musing over "what would have happened if the girl's father had murdered her assailants", Grisham took three years to complete his first book, A Time to Kill. Finding a publisher was not easy. The book was rejected by 28 publishers before Wynwood Press, an unknown publisher, agreed to give it a modest 5,000-copy printing. It was published in June 1989. While other juries were crying, he saw an inspiration through the tears. He saw a brain child the twelve year old girl's case can give birth to. He turned her past failures to a path to success. Sometimes tears are welcome but do not let them tear the future opportunities and possibilities apart.

Failure is like a trash bin you have to close your eyes to dig it out and get the gold coin at the bottom; people will mock you for your foolish art and act; even your senses will knock on your thought asking you to get back to the common. But in the dust lies the gold. Do not cry over spilt milk, try to recover, though in the process you might need to take the sand along, the prices you didn't plan for, but do not look at the old scars, focus on the new start for potential star to emerge, the more you spend time to complain the more difficult it is to explain the way forward. The more we mourn our failure the more it enlarges in strength and the cost to reactivate the passion inflating.

~Today is the evidence that you had
a past and that you have a future~

A sinner fails one to six times and gives up but the righteous man fails seven times and rises up. A renowned leader and author once said, "I block the last week of the year and spend time reviewing my entire year's calendar. I believe that evaluated reflection turns experience into insight. So, I evaluate what I did so that I gain insight for what I should be doing in the New Year." A missed target is a feedback either of your no plan, little plan or average plan; but often we refuse to listen to the report with hidden process for progress. Often our failures want to feed us back, but we feel bad to listen. Many times, we back the feedback from our mistakes by focusing on the pains. Every time we fall and hit the floor there is an echoed from the impact, one of pain another of gain, we choose which we listen to and the one we hasten to embrace. Falling may seem to reduce you to nothing but let it be that it is a lesson to induce you with something. As long as you stare at the sea all you will see is your image merely existing and staring back, if you want to send waves of living impact beyond your shore you must jump into that sea of challenge not to sink in laxity but to diligently swim, generating waves at each stroke of goals.

~Better to fall seven times and then
rise, than to rise seven times and then fall~

POWER TO GATHER THE PIECES

When Jesus finished the miracle of fish and loaves, he told the disciples to gather the fragment and amazingly, it was able to fill twelve baskets. Gather all the lessons in your past and pack them in the basket of the future you will discover the oceans of wisdom collectable. No past is so bad not to have a good lesson to teach. When he was two years old, this adopted child of two college professors suddenly and inexplicably stopped growing, and his health started to fail. A team of doctors gave him six months to live after they diagnosed him as suffering from a rare disease that inhibits digestion and nutrients in food. Intravenous feedings of vitamins and supplements allowed him to regain his strength, but his growth was permanently stunted. Confined to hospitals for long periods of time until the age of nine, he quietly plotted his revenge on the kids who taunted him and called him "peanut." He recalled many years later that subconsciously "the whole experience made me want to succeed at something athletic."

Sometimes his sister, Susan, went ice-skating at the local rink, and he would go along to watch. There he stood, a frail, under grown kid, with a feeding tube inserted through his nose and down into his stomach. When he wasn't using it, one end of the tube was taped behind his ear. One day, as he watched his sister whirl around the ice, he turned to his parents and said, "You know, I think I'd like to try ice skating." Talk about two adults, looking at their life-threatened child, with glances that were unbelievable! Well, he tried it and he loved it, and he went at it with a passion. Here was something funny at which he could excel, where height and weight were not important. During his medical check-up the following year, the doctors were startled to discover that he had actually started growing again. It was too late for him to reach normal size, but neither he nor his family cared. He was recovering and succeeding. He believed in his dream, although he had little else to hang on to.

None of the kids taunts him and teases him today. Instead, they all cheer and rush to get his autograph. He has just completed another dazzling performance on the world professional ice-skating tour, with a long string of triple jumps, complicated maneuvers, and athletic moves, capped off with a racing front flip that brought him to a sudden stop inches from the audience. Although he has retired from professional skating, he remains a coach, mentor, and commentator revered by everyone in winter sports.

At five feet three inches and 115 pounds of pure muscle and electrifying energy, former Olympic gold medal figure skating champion Scott Hamilton stands as tall and as proud as any winner does. Scott's size did not limit his faith and reach. His passion birthed a dream and a dream gathered his disintegrating life. Tree lives to the maximum potential because they are not living under the roof of men; men sometimes fail to achieve all possibilities because they live under the roof of their mind. Common failure is as if water poured on the floor you can cry over the liquid and watch the sun of time dries it off or choose to spread a wool of smartness and suck back needful portion.

~Successful people look lucky, but
they always have the lock key—
persistence~

When a beautiful looking young woman approached a counselor, pouring out how frustration of what she had become and how her life had been shattered beyond coordination. After much lamentation, the man asked her, "What is your dream for life is?" She said to be a mother of outstanding kids and be a world-renowned entrepreneur. He said that is all you need to pick up your life. The elderly man from a well of experience brought out a jig jaw puzzle, which was plane on both sides and the other have an eagle drawn on one side vividly. Then he cast them on the floor separately, the puzzle pieces got mixed up. After, he asked the woman to fix them back one after the other. She started with the one with planesides. For the next thirty minutes, she could not figure out the re-arrangement. Then he asked her to move to the next pieces. In the next three minutes or so she was done. He asked her why she failed to achieve one, but the other despite the fact that they were equally muddled up.

She replied, "I simply traced the picture of the eagle since I saw it together as a whole before you mixed it up. With that, I rearranged the broken pieces. But the other has no picture to trace it out." He told her, "Your dream is all you need to gather your pieces. Once you know what you want you can use what you have now as leverage. Your end picture will provide you with strength of focus which will enable you to maximize your challenges and juxtapose your past experience with today's experiment to rearrange your future expectation." Pass through fire, pass through water, pass through the tunnel, fail thorough none—at the end your life story will become a template for success pilgrimage.

~From the womb of adversities our
diverse abilities are born~

Chapter Two

DEVELOP UNLIMITED MIND

~When you get to the top,
you discover a new sky~

In the house of an old couple was a beautiful aquarium given to them by their son. In the aquarium was a goldfish that had lived there for some months when another feral fish was put there. Directly in front of the aquarium was a big television. The couple was lovers of wild animal life and every day they tuned their TV to wild life channel watching often the deep ocean life. The old gold fish had lived its life watching the television with the couple being placed in its front. Every now and then, it would see other species of fishes in the glass box like itself. It would see them swimming in the screen just like its own aquarium. All the while, it had seen many types of fishes, different species, colors, and sizes. Always wondered why they too stay in the glass—another aquarium like its own as it thought of it? With time, the convinced aquatic creature concluded that God created all fishes to live in the box of glass.

When the feral fish was brought in as a fingerling, the gold fish tutored it as well to believe that all fish were created to live with limitation. Day after day, the feral fish according to its nature grew bigger than the goldfish and got to a point that the aquarium could not contain it again. The old couple thought of how to preserve the fish for they loved it. They concluded that the best thing to do is drop it in the ocean so it could live well. As they took the fish away the gold fish felt sorry for it and wish its soul rest in perfect peace for it knew there is no other place to live, the only habitation of the fish is the limited glass boxes like the two in the living room—the aquarium and the TV. Now that my friend had outgrown its size, it must have been taken to the kitchen as a food. From that time, the gold fish refused to eat so as not to grow big. Meanwhile the couple went to the nearby ocean and dropped the feral fish there.

On diving into the ocean depth, the fish thought the end had come, but gradually it began to explore the ocean. Seeing other fishes swimming everywhere without limitation, gradually it began to change its orientation and swam freely and gladly with them. After a while, the feral fish remembered the school of thought of the goldfish that all fish were destined to live in a confined glass box, it means it was a wrong philosophy and ideology. Back at home, the goldfish had stopped growing and began to turn weak.

At a time, the couple looked at it and thought that they should not lose in two ways. If the fish should die in the aquarium because of its depreciating health, it will pollute the treated water; moreover, it will not be good for food anymore. Therefore, they took a step, dragged out the gold fish and took it to the kitchen for a roasted meal for their pet. The fish thought within itself, as they did to the feral fish it is my turn to be killed and eaten. It thought within, I ought to have been eating all this while and not have lost in two ways. Often our common sights determine our common sense. Our reachable information and exposition inform our mind orientation and limitation. How big your mind is how big your life is. Many times our minds are disciple by our beliefs, while our beliefs are discipled by what we behold often.

Then we consolidate it by the aged minds' words and experiences. Freedom of speech has gained such a worldwide attention and often been fought for by human rights activists, but no one propagates the freedom of dreams. Every older generation wants to impose their periodic discovery and conclusion on the coming one. The beginning of maturity is not the ability to carry out plans, but to stand at the center of ability to plan according to your pattern. You do not carve your life philosophy on great mind's conclusion; there is no final discovery.

MAKE ROOMS

~Give minimum attention to your success
give maximum attention to the process~

One cool morning our two plus old little girl woke up to get prepared for school earlier than usual. After taking her bath, she went to lie down on the bed probably to relax. Some minutes later we heard her muttering disgustedly, the mother and I jointly asked what the matter was. The little girl replied, "The bed is making me to sleep." We both laughed and laughed. We never really knew what could have happened, possibly, she was trying to stay awake and feel our activities, but was dozing off until she could bear it no more and voiced out uncomfortably.

Many a time in life, we discover we want to go beyond our past fits, we kind of being tempted to conclude it just can't work out further or farther. We look around and all we see is what we have achieved and become. However, the problem sometimes, is our achievement. The young girl said the bed was making her to sleep in other word the comfort of the bed was making her to sleep though she could not understand it that way. Our own bed is our achievement that has made us so comfortable that we sleep live and let the big picture dream slip off. The room for improvement has no wall; it has no roof only extendable foundation.

The size of the earth is fixed, but the world is not; the size of your brain is fixed, but your mind is not; the size for your past is fixed, but your future is not; the size of your age is fixed but your stages are not. In a little town in the polar region during the Stone Age, was a surviving old woman. The little town has a unique feature, they had no dusk, half of the year is all the daylong—it will be sunny and the rest of the year is all night long— it will be all dusk, no sunlight at all. In addition, to crown their predicament they had no time technology as at then. A time came that two polar explorers got to the island and met this surviving woman with an oyster shell used to make a long chain hanging around her neck.

After narrating the history of the town to them, they asked her, so how do you know your age in your generation? The woman pulled out her shell chain. These two explorers were confused. They said please explain. She said everyone in our community is given the responsibility to develop our village in a way, so anytime you are able to build ten huts you add one shell to your chain. In other word, you determine your age by your value or achievement. So I want to ask you, how old are you by the measure of your exploits? Time measures our age, goals setting and getting measure our value. The question is how old are you? How long is your shell chain? Mind aging is the actual man aging.

Forget a quiet get together with cake and presents for her milestone birthday, all she wanted was some adventure. And the South African great-grandmother most certainly got what she desired when she went skydiving on a Friday in celebration of her 100th. With 15 members of her family by her side, Harwood successfully landed her tandem jump, which she described to the Associated Press as "wonderful" and "exhilarating." Granted, she already has two big skydiving jumps under her belt, the first of which she took when she was 92. And if that's not enough, Harwood will be continuing her thrill-filled birthday with (of course!) a cage dive amongst sharks. Physical ageing is inevitability, but mental aging is choice of responsibility.

Give room for your potential

Your dream is the limit of your sky, your faith is the limit of your dream, your mind is the limit of your faith, and your library is the limit of your mind. A middle class plumber was about dying and wished to will all he had to his teenage daughter. He knew that his daughter had been used to withdrawing to her shell when playing with her mates. She always thought of taking a small part of their activities. She used to see herself of not being able to accomplish much like her peers. However, his wise and thoughtful father knew that she had within her more than she was delivering.

When he interacts with her and gives her assignment, she always comes up with an idea but she was so myopic in her view of reaching out. When this man was about to die, he thought of how to leave a lifetime lesson for her. He thought repeatedly and resolved on what to do, which he did. When the letter of her father's will was handed to the girl she couldn't find anything legible enough to worth reading in the envelope save a shrunk balloon. However, she kept on thinking about what was written on the back of the envelope, "Always blow your mind" just as he used to charge her while alive.

One day, after many years, the girl, now a mother picked the envelope where she had carefully kept it as a thing of legacy even though seems useless, she brought out the balloon and gave it to her little son who quickly grabbed and blew it up. As the balloon was growing bigger before the mother, the write up began to show up on the skin. When he finished blowing it, on it was clearly seen, legibly written—her father's will and gifts for her. When the father of a little girl was about to die he blew a balloon and on it wrote the will, deflated it to its original shrunk shape, enveloped it and at the back of the letter he wrote, "Always blow your mind, dream wild."

One of the most powerful earthmovers for talent digging is the boundless dream future. Your best will require a testing ground to surface. The bigger your dream the easier it is for your gifting to find expression. Joseph could not know he had the capacity to be a good business manager until he found himself in the house of Potiphar. He could not have known he could successfully keep a whole prison full of dejected and condemned in good mood with little or no supervision from the prison warder. He could not have been in a position to develop the gift to interpret dreams for his inmates. He could not have known that he could build a storage that can feed the whole world for almost seven years. Moses could not have discovered that his stammering tongue could still be so powerful to read out the whole book of Deuteronomy. When you begin to allow God to work through your mind to enlarge your thinking coast, you will gradually begin to see His gifts and wills for your life becoming spelt out, readable, understandable, and reachable.

Joshua dreamt big, he saw the giants as surmountable, the city conquerable at the end he became the leader of thousands in place of Moses. He dreamt so big that God found him a good tool. He dreamt so big that those leadership abilities in him surfaced. You cannot compare the aero skills of a bird reared in the cage to the one that grew outside captivity. The one in the cage can only stretch his wings, but never could say how high and wild it can fly because it is caged. Likewise, when your mind is caged in myopic future, you cannot maximize your potential.

In one of CNN news of Environment and Parks official once reported that dumping of live goldfish into the ecosystem has resulted in freakishly large fish. The invasive species has no natural predator and is thriving in poor water conditions, "The biggest one we've caught is the size of a dinner plate." The dazed environmentalist said further, "That's the crazy thing about domestic aquatic pets, you have them in your aquarium and they are this cute little thing and then you release it into the wild and that constraint of size and food is gone and because of that some of these species can get really big."

There are three environments that determine the growth of your dream: your mind climate, your mentorship climate, and your method climate. There is nothing that can't grow bigger if subject to the natural habit for growth. Some people keep their dream in the aquarium of excuses like the economic meltdown, background held down, educational shortfall, just name it. The truth is that your dream won't grow bigger than you orientation. The officials said, "Further that we are estimating hundreds of thousands are in flowing rivers and water. My biggest concern is people are doing this because they think it's the humanitarian thing to do. We really need to correct misinformation. "It is illegal to dump or transfer live fish from one body of water to another.

Aquarium owners who no longer want their finned friends have a few options: Contact a retailer for a possible return, give the fish away, donate it to a school, or talk to a veterinarian about humane disposal." Look at those four ways to dispose a growth intended goldfish that is exactly how people dispose their dreams in lieu of an occasion for advancement or opportunity to expand it. Some return it to seed idea; they shrink back to where they started, to live 'safe'.

The second option is to give it away. Many have sold their ideas to companies or traditions that later on ended up a big deal. Like the man that actually discovered one of the world most popular beverages, he got the formula, sold it for peanut and the rest is history. The third option is to donate it generously and nonchalantly. There is a time to be generous there is a time to generate. Just like the story of the poor wise man in the second book of Solomon, who delivered his city from war yet was never recognized afterward. The forth option is to give it to veterinarian in other word you can give your dream to people who will help you determine its course, the way they thought it best, possibly in their own interest. No one can fill pregnancy like the woman; no one can help nurse your dream like you. Get the golden idea out of the aquarium of illusive limitation in to the flowing river of dreams

HAVE A LASER VIEWPOINT

~Inspiration is offshoot from imagination accidentals~

When rainbow is still a white light, it poses no beauty but for us to see. But placing a prism in front will bring forth the rainbow in it. The prism is not the one that produces the spectrum, all the while they lie in the white light. That is how many never have smart spectacle to see the opportunity behind the common. Not all opportunities carry a sign post but they all post a sign in a way. Dell also was a man with a laser sight, a unique ability to see beyond the white rays. Recognizing the financial advantage in selling PCs directly from manufacturer to user, cutting out the retail middleman, he started PCs Limited in 1984 and, beating IBM and the rest of the heavyweights at their own game, had driven the renamed Dell into the Fortune 500 within eight years. Everybody looked at those times of America's depression but few saw the opportunity within. Some opportunities are dumb and lame they can come to you neither can they call to you. When opportunity is not honking around, you hawk around for it.

Hear him speaks: when I called he didn't hear, so I came he didn't open, then I knocked he didn't answer, so I opened he didn't see me, then I tapped him and he left the room; he locked the door behind with me inside. Opportunity comes to everyone in a life time but some live and died leaving him behind in the infinite room of time. Just as we have colour blindness, I think sometimes men suffer from opportunity blindness.

> ~He has no right to complain who
> had the opportunity to do it better
> passed him by~

One of the top 10 CNN Heroes of 2013 was a creative woman. This young passionate woman ended creating *an oasis of greens in desert*. Her pressing passion puts up a path. After discovering the inadequacy of fresh food supply by first-hand experience with her own brother, she did something outstanding from low standing tempo. Access to fresh food is an issue for many communities throughout the United States. According to the Department of Agriculture, nearly 10% of the U.S. population lives in low-income areas more than a mile from a supermarket. Discovering this problem sparked something inside Emmons, who had recently left her corporate job to find more meaningful work. "I really thought it was an injustice. ... Healthy food is a basic human right," she said.

More than 72,000 people in Charlotte, North Carolina, lack access to fresh produce. When Robin Emmons discovered this problem, she took action "I decided to rip up my whole backyard and make it all a garden, and it just kind of snowballed from there." Today, Emmons has 200 volunteers helping her tend 9 acres of crops on three sites. Since 2008, she says, her non-profit, Sow Much Good, has grown more than 26,000 pounds of fresh produce for underserved communities in Charlotte. At first, Emmons donated her locally grown, chemical-free fruits and vegetables to churches and food pantries.

But she soon started selling them herself in the neighborhoods that need them the most, for what she estimates is about half the price of organic produce sold in stores. "When I see people coming to the farm stand ... I feel encouraged," she said. "I feel like I am giving them a gift —a healthier, longer, better, more delicious life." How could one have thought that a back yard piece of land will end up feeding a community; she was not the only one with such space behind her house but she has a laser sight. She could see when everyone could have been looking. Every day we bypass hidden forest and plantation in the seeds like the small mustard that we overlook because we can only see as big as the lens of our mind.

~Places do not make people great,
rather great people make great place~

Heroes see success as a little failure

One day I visited a government secretariat for an appointment; as I passed through the lobby, I saw a sign that was interesting, it reads: no waiting, no loitering, keep moving. And conformably, the environ was so serene, everybody appeared to be at duty post. Every success is a seed; it is harvested to be invested. The same I say to you, no waiting, no loitering, and no stopping in the school of success. Your best per time is just a tip of the Ice Berge of what you can do. There is neither perfect idea nor accomplishment for we must have missed a part concealed to us. Therefore, in every phase of success there is a phrase to make to a clause, in order word there is still a missing action.

Discovery is ever a process to the endless that there is no final discovery, the down to heart state of science and innovation of our generation is soon a discovered primitive brain for the approaching humanism race. In the scripture, a prophet having just delivered God's message successfully, was on his way back, when he decided to rest a while. Along the line, a deceiving old prophet caught up with him and truncated his success. Your success now is not a resting point but a starting point for the big picture success. A father was asked by his little boy who was having problem riding a bicycle, "How can I learn the art? The father requested, "What do you do anytime you mount it and you discover you are not balance?" He replied, "I stop to keep me from falling." He said you will never learn it that way, you need to keep moving, and then the bicycle will keep standing. You need to move on to sustain your tempo. Success becomes a temptation when we fail to attempt greater heights.

You can still make hay while the moon shines

The future is not as far as you think that you can be safe postponing and it is not as near that new dreams are too late. Wise men say future begins today not tomorrow, so they live every day as if there is no tomorrow; the little mind says there is always new tomorrow, today is too soon to start with and the future will always wait ahead; the weak mind says the past ends today, so every day they live in past. People who live on wishes will do it twice: in the morning; I wish to be, and in the night; I wish I had. Wishers always have their horse behind the cart, dreamers before the cart. Dreamers have great passion for their great future which makes them to drive in to the time ahead while wishers have great compassion for their great past that keeps them in island of memory. They wish their past could overtake their days and walk into the future. There are many heroes that started very late so to say. Colonel Sanders of KFC, age could be to your advantage not always otherwise.

BREAK YOUR THOUGHT SKIN

A young man went on fishing in the evening of one summer days. He let down his hook in the sea and waited for a catch. Suddenly, something in the sea began to drag the fish line with him. In fear of being pulled in to the sea he quickly cut the fish line and let the sea creature went away with the bait and the hook. He went to the man who sells fish line to procure another one. Again, he went fishing and just as it happened in the first it happened again, a sea creature got hooked with the bait and began to pull the line. The boy began to fear again as he struggled with his line and the boat not to be dragged in to the middle of the sea. He finally let go of the line—he cut it off. The third time he went to the man to buy fish line, the man became worried and asked him, "Young man what is happening? You have come to buy fish line these three times; it is unusual of fisher men." After the boy narrated his ordeal the man just laughed and laughed. Young man you have been losing big opportunity because you cannot handle it immediately. He asked him do you have an anchor in your boat he said yes. He said, "Next time you catch a big fish let down your anchor and let time and patience work it out."

The boy did not really understand but left with the counsel. When it got to the river, he began fishing. Not quite long, after catching four small fish the hook picked a giant fish again. So the boy just pulled out his anchor and let down to the bed of the sea. As usual, the big fish tried to drag the boy with the boat as it struggled to make away with the bait the fishing equipment fixed to the boat. The fish tried to drag the boat but the anchor held it back. It was a tug of war. At the end, after about an hour the fish began to become weak. The boy invested time as the old man had advised; at a point the fish stopped pulling as it had expended all its energy.

As he discovered this, he began to pull the fish toward the boat. When he was sure the fish was captured finally, he removed the anchor and paddled both the fish and the boat to the bank. Sometimes in life, when great opportunity comes that we do not have the capacity to handle, we immediately cut off our focus from thinking about it or pursuing it; I am not able to handle this, I do not have the capacity or the resources. When we conceive such a big dream, we become scared of our own aspiration and immediately began to see why it will not work out and opt to let it go. However, like this young fisher boy, we can let down the anchor of hope and determination that one day it will be possible. We should learn to hold on to a dream no matter how big it may be. The vision is not for today but tomorrow.

No matter how stormy the goal is if you can hold on you will see the storm enveloped and the possibility dawning. Just like the pouring of rain, wind may come first with sound of thunder and lightning in abundance, anyone who wants rain will not run away because of the prelude.

Andrew Johnson's, the 39th president of the United States who served as the nation's chief executive during a time of serious problems at home and abroad dreamt of ruling the world power as an illiterate. But

Johnson's lack of formal schooling and his homespun quality were distinct assets in building a political base of poor people seeking a fuller voice in government. His tailor shop became a kind of center for political discussion with Johnson as the leader; he had become a skillful orator in an era when public speaking and debate was a powerful political tool. His lack of formal education became stack of opportunity to have a like mind and ready-made audience to leverage a platform for his political carrier.

Life is full of opportunities that are married to adversities; they are masked with excuses. There is always a solution to obstruction on the path of a dream for those who incorporate change in their philosophy. The advent of space tourism occurred at the end of the 1990s with a deal between the Russian company MirCorp and the American company Space Adventures Ltd. MirCorp was a private venture in charge of the space station Mir. They suddenly discovered that the cost of execution and maintenance of space machines could not be taken care of by the fame and praise they got in return. So they had three options to go bankrupt, quit or seek a financial light.

To address the financial challenge of generating income for maintenance of the aging space station, MirCorp decided to sell a trip to Mir, and Tito became its first paying passenger. It has never been heard that ordinary man can board space craft as they do air craft trains and cars. But a man who was pushed to the wall made a window out of it to design the closest route of escape. Tito, who paid $20 million for his flight on the Russian spacecraft Soyuz TM-32, spent seven days on board of the ISS and is considered the world's first space tourist.

However, given the arduous training required for his mission, Tito objected to the use of the word tourist, and since his flight the term spaceflight participant has been more often used to distinguish commercial space travelers from career astronauts. Orbital space tourism continued to grow following Tito's mission, with flights to the ISS by South African computer millionaire Mark Shuttleworth in 2002 and American businessman Gregory Olsen in 2005. These travelers were followed by Iranian-born American entrepreneur Anousheh Ansari, who became the fourth spaceflight participant and the first female fee-paying space traveler when she visited the ISS in September 2006. The following year American billionaire Charles Simonyi joined the ranks of spaceflight participants when he shared a ride with two cosmonauts on board Soyuz TMA-10 for a 10-day stay on the ISS.

The sixth spaceflight participant, American video game developer Richard Garriott, was launched in October 2008. Since 2007 Space Adventures has offered a spaceflight around the Moon on a Soyuz spacecraft for a fee of $100 million. They became diversified at the point of adversity, and were able to solve the financial challenge.

When we are talking about focus, we should not confuse it with flexibility. I think CEOs have learnt from the legend Ford, not to be plan addicted like he was color addicted. God gave us a skin free mind so we might expand our thought nucleus. Be flexible in your plan construction and execution. That space company could have closed up or run under distress if they had limited their program to only scientific exploration but a digression in to tourism change the look of their financial bottleneck. There could be up to 10,000 ways to do whatever you are doing, but there is one that will work out best; think it out like Mr. Thomas Edison.

Make goal arrows of your dreams

To dream without goals to pursue is as a fish put in a cage and placed in the ocean, it feels the water, feels at home but not free at home; experiences the water but can't explore the ocean. A young boy was trying to pass a pictorial message to his friend. He had spent hours drawing a page long comic story in a plane sheet of paper, colored it and perfected it. It was like a dream of his heart to share with Jerry his neighborhood friend. When he was done, he remembered the last warning his mom gave him never to leave the house until she is back, so not wanting be naughty he thought of how to pass his pictorial story to his friend whose apartment is directly facing theirs.

After much thinking, he resolved on what to do. In the next couple of minutes, he shaped the paper using his art skill into paper aircraft. With such a pointing aero friendly object, he called out his friend and threw the paper work aircraft across into to their apartment. What the boy did is what it meant to turn your dream in to a goal for a launch. Goals are the carts to your dreams. Start now; start somehow. No matter the speed of the wind, it can't lift when the wings are clipped. He who finally starts is bold. If you can hear the ladder speaks, it had tell you, you can rise with me to any height as long as you can use my first rung first. To start is the art of winners and craft of finishers but not all dreamers.

~Dream without goals is lame;
goals without dream is blind~

A son of a meteorologist followed his father to the field and saw him placing two measuring container in the open as it was about raining. One was very big and the other very small with their mouth sealed. The man asked his son to make hole in the cover using the nail in his hand since the cover had stock due to rusting. After the rain they went back to pick them up. Both were not filled up. The man asked his son which of the two containers do you think will contain more water? He said, "The big one." When they got home he asked him to empty the two containers in the measuring cup, to his surprise they contain the same volume of water. He asked his father why.

The man replied, when I asked you to make hole in the lid the other time, how many holes were made? He said just one on each. He asked what their sizes were. He said the same. Then he told him it is not how big the space is but the openness of the space to receive that determines the final content. He said further, "Many are full of great dream with big future but they have small goal per time not because of resources but fear and lack of diligence." It is not how fast you think but much more, how vast you think of technical knowhow to scale the heights. Just like in the game of football to be a winner you must have outstanding goals not just dribbling performances.

Your dark night is for a purpose

Considering the story of a newly wedded couple wrote by a marriage counselor; it reminds me of the fact that the darker the sky the brighter the star. The duo chose to spend their honeymoon in a hotel to avoid distraction and enjoy the best of themselves. However, horribly, it turned out to be a battle moon as they hit the ship at the deadlock rock over an argument. In a rage, the husband removed the wedding ring and threw it out of the hotel window. A while after, their storming emotion was calmed and they got things resolved; the problem now was how to get the diamond ring back. Once again, in harmony, they jointly went for the ring hunt amidst green grass of the hotel landscape. After tireless search in the scorching sun, they gave up, but the husband being a melancholy person, brought up a suggestion. Honey, "Why do not you let us wait until dusk?"

The sweet heart in amazement wondered, how can that be sensible or yield positive result, if we had failed to see it in the sunshine how much difficult will it be in the dark night? The husband having a good knowledge of diamond was soon proven right. When it was dusk, they left their room for the night search. As they got to the grass landscape, they were greeted with a shining and sparking stone of diamond attached to a gold ring.

The new groom was harmed with the fact that diamond alone shines in the dark and with such atmosphere; they could locate their lost wedding ring quickly. So is your gifting and talents, they are best discovered in the dark moment of challenges and trials. They shine out into visibility. The thickest darkness is an opportunity for the faintest light to shine and be seen as a star not to complain of its weakness or the darkest night.

A team of college basketball players just returned from a lost match. They felt they had disappointed their coach because of some stupid mistakes they made on the court. When the basketball team got to the training hall, they mistakenly took the extra ball down stairs from the locker room, which was meant for the coach's use. The big march they lost was still-hunting them and everybody was discouraged while some thought of quitting the tournament. Their coach, well aware of their morale, used their mistake to teach them a lesson. He shouted; "Guys, you have taken extra ball with you; can I have mine back?" "Oh! Sorry, can I throw it up to you?" said the captain of the team. He told them not to throw it. "It's alright, let me come up with it," the young captain answered. But their coach replied, "No, stay there." They were confused and thought maybe he had changed his mind and not demanding for it again.

They continued to lament over their loss. The coach shouted, "I said I want my ball up here!" The confused captain almost shouted back, "But you said I should not throw it nor bring it up, what can I do?" The coach replied, "I said I want my ball rising to the top." Then he brought out another ball from the room stretched it out in the veranda and slammed it very hard on the court floor the ball hit the floor where the team were seated and up it bounced to the top while the coach quickly got it back.

After the short exercise, he shouted again, "I want my ball up, do not throw it and do not bring it." The captain quickly understood the game, took the ball slammed it on the floor but the force could not lift it up as desired. He picked it up again; this time hit it very hard on the floor and up the ball rose to the veranda while the coach quickly grabbed it. With the ball in his hand, he came down to meet them. Gazing at all of them one after the other, he sighed; afterward said to them "When you fall to the ground you are naturally equipped to bounce back and the harder you hit the floor the higher you have the potential to bounce back. Mistakes are like bow string that seems pulled backward, if you position yourself again they will shoot your plans to your targeted goal. You can't tell a kite how to fly but you can determine where to fly by just holding the string. It may seem drifted by the wind here and there but at the end it will follow you home. Life is like a kite in the wind, though it seems to blow where we do not wish, but if we hold on the end of the string as we go on, we will finally have it following us." The old coach told them. Dream to succeed and proceed to dare the rare; from the rear proceed and dare your fear.

~Dream to win and win only to dream again~

Learn to sieve opportunity from adversity

A great inventor once said opportunities come around dressed in workshop overall so many never recognize it. Many times we wait for the door of opportunity to open that we may walk in why we overlook the open window and complain all through for the key. Life is 20% of what it looks like and 80% of how we look at it. Challenges of life should be like a pair of glasses, it ought to, at most succeed in changing our length of view and not the strength. We will see outside what we look for but we should look for what we see inside of us. Foresight literally, can be inferred, to mean four eyes: two in the socket and two on the target; two here and two there; two for today and two for tomorrow. Your eyesight can deceive you but your foresight cannot.

~I can't will always be employed by I can~

Success defined is 90% of a refined failure and 10% of furnishing. Either failure or success everything is just a process, a means to the end and never means an end. Every success is a fruit of yesterday and a seed for tomorrow. Every success is like a stair case one step should be a stepping stone to the other not a monument. When you get to the top you discover there is another horizon. Those who take time to reflect on today will shine brighter tomorrow. Today is the building that yesterday foundation can withstand, and future structure will stand on today's re-construction. Success is but a very little infinitesimal failure, for every success today of a man is like a shadow of failure compare to major breakthrough success in later life. That is why we sometime laugh at our past pride-childish achievements so to say.

Dream dreams that will scare you to pursue alone—dreams that will interest God to invest His bigness. Dream dreams that will brace up your weakness and embrace your strength. Limit sometimes implies what your weakness cannot overcome but which your strength can turnover to a platform for a new summit if you awake the hero in you; if you feed your strength and stop feeding on your weakness. Those who want to go fast do not grow fat; likewise, those who want to go far do not grow fear. Stretch your limit; give room for your potential by sometimes closing the door to the available.

~Be content with what you have
but do not be contained by it~

RULE YOUR INNER WORLD

In the 25th chapter of proverbial book of king Solomon, he said a man that has no rule over his own spirit is like a city that is broken down, and without walls. An elderly woman having an empty lead tin covered and a plastic bottle filled with sand both dropped to the bottom of the drum. She tried to pick them but her hand would not just reach. So she decided to play smart by pouring water in the drum at least to recover the plastic bottle as she expected it to get floated on the water at the brim. As she began to pour the water, she was surprised to see the lead tin began to rise up while the plastic bottle remained at the bottom of the drum. At the end she got back the lead tin but the plastic bottle remained at the bottom, she was surprised and disappointed.

What determines what floats is the law of floatation and not the nature of the material. It tailors down to what the material harbors; empty space or crowded space. It is not the nature of your problem that finally determines where you end your journey but the nature of your mind. When you allow your mind to be crowded up with fears, worries, anxiety and depression you discover you cannot rise above the water of life. Give no room for fear and anxiety. Fill a bottle with water and leave just little space at the top. Take it up and give it a shake, you will discover that the water will be troubled with bubbles springing up and the water will become unclear to see through until you stop shaking for it to settle down.

If you have a piece of broken glass corked inside it you will observe that it becomes strenuous to sight it. Now add more water to the one in the bottle and fill it to overflowing, afterward cork and try to shake it. You will discover that the water will stay still and clear—no bubbles, and whatever you cork within will still be clearly sighted. When you allow a mushroom size of anyone of enemy's weapons— fears, worries, anxiety and depression, to inhabit your heart, you will be surprised that it can trouble your entire heart that it becomes practically impossible to see what you once believed God for. Jesus thought us that a little leaven leavens up the whole lump. Life's storm may shake you but can get you troubled as long as you provide no space for fear and its relatives.

Step out on fear

Billy Graham often paddled a canoe to a small island in the river, where he would preach to the birds, alligators, and cypress stumps. What was the young preacher trying to do? I envisage he was trying to build self-confidence and skill. He ended being acknowledged as a worldwide state man whose ministry reached out to millions of souls through his crusades and broadcasts. A retired astronaut was travelling in the train with his son. On their way, the son asked, "Dad what inspired you to join such a sensitive team and record such a success?" He replied, "John, it was not so from the beginning, in fact I was afraid to ride in a plane for years. I always went by the land or at worst by sea—I was afraid of the heights and sky."

His son asked, "How then you finally came about flying not even in the sky but now above the sky?" He said, "John I never knew I could do it until I stepped out." Taking the first step is a great way to open up the door to your potential. He said dad do you mean you actually had the ability all the while you dared not ride in the air? He said, yes, my son you can't know your potential until you step out in faith. "Dad I need more explanation," he said. His father said inside you is a great potential but it will not materialize until you take the initial step. Inside every seed is a tree and in the tree is a forest but until the seed is thrown out and buried in the soil, it cannot reproduce, not even a fruit.

Then the astronaut asked his son to bring the ball in his hand; he asked, "John what is the speed of this ball?" He said, dad what do you mean? It is stationed—its speed is zero. Dad you should know as a once professor of physics. His dad said, "No John, you are wrong the speed of this ball is 120 miles per hour." He protested it is not possible. He said won't you mind losing the ball? The boy replied, you can always buy me another one just explain the mystery of 120m/hr. Then he opened the window of the moving train, outside they saw a hare running in the desert; his father said, what is the average speed of that animal from your knowledge? His son said roughly it could run like 50ml/hour. Nodding his head the man dropped the ball. To the boy's surprise the ball ran faster than the rabbit for a while. The little boy exclaimed dad, see! The ball is running on the second rail track at unprecedented speed faster than the rabbit!

Then both the ball and the rabbit were left behind as their train rode on. The boy was surprised and convinced. His father seeing his successful illustration smiled and said, "John Martin, the same with you, your life will look ordinary or stagnant until you step out on an adventure then your potential will surface." The young chap was so pleased with the train lecture; afterward he said dad, one more thing, "Why did the ball later stop as I could see when I gazed out backward?" His experienced physicist dad said, the ball should not have stopped but for the air resistance and friction. The law of motion says an object will remain on a spot or continue in uniform motion unless an external force acts on it. So remember in life as well, there will be friction and resistance of challenges that will want to reduce or stop your potential but never give up to them, as you can see our train is unstoppable by the same wind resistance because the engineers keep the fire burning.

KICK START YOUR STYLE

~Men are only privileged to include
in your life not to conclude it~

People based their opinion on their ability and past experiences and try to make everybody take their conclusion as a status quo. A teacher in a high school wanted to teach his students what temperature is all about. He brought out three bowls of water one at room temperature; he poured some iced cubes in the water of the second bowl and the third one he placed on burner for a while. When he was done he placed the three bowls of water on the table all looking the same at sight. He faced the class and called out six of the students in the class to step out for the experiment. He told the first set of three to deep their hands in the bowl of water containing dissolved iced cubes while the other set of three was asked to place their hands in the bowl of water retrieved from burner.

After few seconds, as they were appearing to be unable to cope with the temperature, he told them to withdraw and to immediately deep their hands in the third bowl at room temperature. When they had done that he asked them for comments. He asked what the present water feels like.

The first three who were withdrawing from the cold zone shouted, "Sir this is hot," the remaining three boys exclaimed, "No, this is absolutely cold." Then he called some of the watching colleagues to come and put their hands in the water, those ones just look at their six colleagues wondering hope nothing was wrong with them, this is just ordinary water at room temperature that anyone can conveniently drink. But the six experimental pupils insisted no it is hot… it is cold…. they argued in a chorus.

Great mind do not live like a thermometer that rides on the temperature of people's opinions but a thermostat, that jump starts a new course of findings and thinking. The world is filled with point of views that point in many directions, great enough to form a flux of confusion for anyone who chooses to ride with the crowd. You are only preparing to live until you discover what you can die for, often not what lives before.

Your passion may dwindle, your vision may be cloud covered, your method may crack, your pressure may be off measure, and you must give in; let it be your goal of the time not your dream of a life time. Escalator unifies all on aboard to the same rising speed, but remember, your legs are still there; if you must miss a flight use it, give no room for the common. Do not let common situation generalise your will with what is obtainable. Do not let anybody dwarf your dream; refuse to let them cut it to their comfortable size. Joseph's dream was not welcome, even his father and mentor tried to hush him. David's king and mentor—Saul tried to hush him. His brother tried his wife tried but he thrived despite all. You can.

Champion your opinion

Great minds are full of many thoughts they never talk about but work over them, small minds are full of many talks they never thought about that over work them; they leave their ideas as general topic for the crowd to take decision. Goliath was not the first and greatest enemy that the young, ruddy good looking Hebrew boy fought but the last enemy. When David approached the valley of battle between Saul led team and Goliath led team, he was faced with the first word war. His elder brother accosted him, what have you come to do here? You are a lazy wanderer, you are not meant to be here. It is not your turn; it is not your level; go back to the wilderness and tend the sheep; you can't make it here; you are not fit; it is genius affair; you do not have the qualification. But David won the first war, he replied "What have I to do with you, is there not a cause?" He left him to be right of his opinion.

Then as if that was all, the second word war came up between the young good looking psalmist boy and the king of Israel. Saul called for him to disarm him of his opinion, saying you are not able to go, you are a little child but he a man of war from his youth. You do not have the experience or the skills, or the talent, or the ability. You are not fit; it won't work like you thought. Just like people will tell you, you are too short, you do not have credentials nor potential, you do not have the financial base, your colour is a barrier. Let the sleeping dog lies. But David left to be right with his own opinion. Then the third word war was with Goliath, he shouted, "Am I a dog," that you have come out to me with sticks, come and be messed up. With such a bully oration David still held on to his opinion, my God is able. The forth war was fought victoriously.

~Those who only have something to say
should not hinder those who only have
something to do~

Neruda, Pablo Chilean poet, diplomat, and politician who was awarded the Nobel Prize for Literature in 1971, was perhaps the most important Latin American poet of the 20th century. The son of a railway worker, his mother died within a month of Neruda's birth, and two years later the family moved to Temuco, a small town farther south in Chile, where his father remarried. Neruda was a precocious boy who began to write poetry at age 10. His father tried to discourage him from writing and never cared for his poems, which was probably why the young poet began to publish under the pseudonym Pablo Neruda, which he was legally to adopt in 1946. He entered the Temuco Boys' School in 1910 and finished his secondary schooling there in 1920. Tall, shy, and lonely, Neruda read voraciously and was encouraged by the principal of the Temuco Girls' School, Gabriela Mistral, a gifted poet who herself later would become a Nobel laureate.

Do not complain an escalator is too slow like every other man on board will complain when you have your two legs. You do not need the world to believe in your idea you only need them to behold. Ideas are creators of inventions but many such potentially great ideas have been buried under the influence of negative opinions. Those who look differently and advantageously in every stage of adversity are never in lack of opportunity. Stack of continuous focus will multiply your strength despite the world negative look and lack of it amplifies your weakness; you may need to quench your association before you can re-fire your passion.

~Your eyes can't see what your mind has
not sighted; neither can your feet go where
your thoughts have not made a road~

Make room for your foot

God gave you a unique finger print, a unique height, a unique stature and a unique dream plus method. Your gift is presented in a rapper and as you know it is the duty of the celebrant to unwrap the gift and put it to use by creating room for its application. At a camp meeting, a Sunday school teacher was teaching the young stars how to let God determine their value. At the recession of the teaching he asked the young boys to dig a small hole and to fix a drawn measuring tape to the wall. He called one of them and measured the height. It read 1.5meters, and then he asked him to stand in the 0.5 meter deep hole. He asked them, "What is the new height of your friend with reference to the tape on the wall?" They did little math and said one meter. He asked them to dig the hole further to one meter and told the boy to jump inside. When he asked for his height they said he should measure 0.5 meter. Again he instructed them to dig it up to two meters and asked the boy to jump inside. After that he asked for his height again they said there is no need, it is nothing. Then the teacher asked one of them to take a measuring tape and jump in to the hole with him.

After joining him and he was asked the height of his friend, he bent down, measured his height and announced to the rest above his height is 1.5meters. The teacher called them all together and said in life do not let people conclude your value, because they will weigh you with their own scale, they will view you from their own reference point, they will judge you from their own view and your present state. When they are highly placed they see you as a nonentity and when they are lowly placed they see you as a celebrity; if you listen to any of the crowd you will either end a victim of pride and stagnation or self-pity and inferiority complex. Your true value is best measured by someone who is standing with you at all-time who will be with you when you walk through the valley of shadow and when you climb up the mountain of obstacles or you are dropped in the pit like Jacob's eleventh son—and that is your creator, the author of your time. Your Maker is the only one in the same shoe with you in the pit who can accurately tell you your real worth and height, no other person.

A path is for the few a road is for the crowd. On the path, you can trace the footprint but on the road, every print is in confusion. That is what happens when you travel with the crowd. You may not be right until you are left behind to think. Wings are grown on a spot, in isolation, in space above the ground. The bird in the lonely sky places the nest; the butterfly in the lonely suspension stages the cocoon. Be ready for separation if you are in need of transformation.

When you ask a pessimist to describe the dawn, he had say, this light is dark, and you can listen to optimist that says this is brightness of darkness. I wish you do not try to impress anyone who will clap for you; I hope you do it to those who have no time to live as spectator. Do not walk yourself out on those who antagonize your dream just walk away from them—forget their comments. You cannot change everything in the world neither should you change with everything in the world. In life, we are often so focused on what we need to get hold that we overlook the more important thing that is holding us back from getting them; those things we need to let go. Succinctly put, if you are always available to all people and comments you cannot be valuable for long.

~If you can't change the whole world,
leave a mark that you begin~

Think more, dream more, work more, and you will live more despite the men's comments. Do not let men's given titles push you to battle, only pursue the problem you are equipped to solve. Life is short, but living is not shut out from full expression, just take time to live out your best per time so you can out live your life time.

Awake that dream

Dreams get you awake that time is at stake, and a need to go ahead to wait for it. What you have in head today is limited if you have no dream ahead. Dreams make us live maximally. It is the sixth sense of wise species of mind. Until you begin to think you can, life will not think you count. Dream makes us restless to our present comfort, it makes the past distasteful, incomplete and incompetent. When you have the shadow of your past before you, it shows you are backing the light of tomorrow.

~The past is to commence today not to
compete with it, neither is it to complete
tomorrow~

Where there are no dreams reality and futility reign, since there is no room for possibility. The purpose of dreams is to keep us awake. Dreams without pursuit are wishes. Dream what is achievable not what is available; dream what is required to make the world better not just what to acquire to make your worth bigger. Start low, start slow, to start not at all is the enemy of the going. The little walk of beginning is a room to make your entire mistake and still move on; it is a fearful thing to get to the top and drop in error. Fly safe as you dream great things; to be great is to be delicate; those who fly do not fall down they drop off!—they crash land unlike crawlers.

Butterflies are beautiful in the sky; they are more beautiful when they choose to fly than to be at rest. On a spot they fold their wings, hiding the beauty of nature but when they flap and fly, the sky is adorned, like a soaring rainbow they ski the atmosphere.

Your best is in your test, you cannot change your altitude without demonstrating your dream aptitude. It is dangerous to have wings without legs, no birds ever down look its legs at tall altitude. They start with the legs and land on the legs. Dream will help your pursuit to take off and will help to determine your safe ending. Future without dreams is like wings without legs. Some dreams can never be caught while you are roaming the street, you can only get catfish and the rest in the flowing river. Deep calls on to the deep, rivers are everywhere so they are ever shallow; sea stays on a spot and ends so deep. You cannot be everywhere and yet be a man of deep insight. Sharks and whales are not found in the streams but the sea. Take time to conceive dreams so big that you lose your sleep. Dream better dreams not just bigger ones.

~Better to be bigger but it is bigger to be better~

Point the search light to your face

Your shadow can become bigger, taller, and longer than you but can't run faster than you, likewise your dream can be bigger than you, your vision can be longer than you, your aspiration can be taller than you but you can run faster than your character which is the ladder to the peak. Jane was a young kindergarten getting prepared for a day out with her mum. When Jane got in to the dressing room it was dark, the bulb just went off as she opened the door. Being almost late for the Christmas party, she concluded no need to tidy up anything.

On getting outside, her mum said, "No Jane, you can't do that, go back and comb your hair." Then she exclaimed, mum, the bulb just went off and I could not see the mirror again. His father reached out to the drawer and gave her a search light. She collected it and rushed back to the dressing room. She quickly put on the touch and pointed it at the dressing mirror. To her surprise, she could not see her image in the mirror rather a blurred dark pattern; to worsen it, the mirror reflected the rays back in to her eyes that she hardly saw the doorway as she left the room with disappointment.

When she got to her father she exclaimed, dad it didn't work, come and fix a new bulb in the room. The father asked, why? It should work! He said how did you make use of the search light? She said, "I pointed the search light to the mirror." Her dad said, no! You were wrong; you should point it to your face. She retorted, "But I want to see my image in the dark mirror hence the need to light up the mirror"

After seconds of argument, she agreed to go back and point the light to her face partly. When she did that she saw herself clearly in the mirror and everything she needed to adjust. As the young girl sprang out of the dressing room to joyfully report the success her grandmother came in. Now looking cute and radiant, she joyfully went to her grand ma and narrated her experiment. The old woman said, "Jane, did you learn something?" "Yes, she cut in—that anytime I want to see how I look I should point the search light to myself and not the mirror before me."

The grand mum looked at her, eyeball to eye ball and said, "When you succeed to shine light on your heart and search your deepest part you will see your weakness and strength clearly as you stand before the mirror of relationship. Do not point it to people or circumstances or situation, you cannot get your real personality, flaws and ability. People are not to be responsible for the comments you need to polish your character; sometimes they could be wrong, selfish, delusive, undecided, ignorant and critical, and so point the search light to yourself and let them be a mirror to reflect your discovered insight as you display them before you in relationships.

When you point the search light to others for your attitudinal description, you will get a blurred and confused image like the young girl. Learn to remove the log in your eyes before you can remove the speck in others eyes. Do not wait until people tell you who you are rather explore yourself as you face the mirror of their actions, reactions, and inactions. Moreover, you cannot see your own weakness when you point the search light to others weakness. You will rather look perfect and better when you are not. Think beyond people's comment either good or bad, enlarge your mind to believe what God conceived about you, to feel what God thinks about you, to hear what God says about you and sieve your motive per time.

CROSS THE FINISHING LINE

~The most important thing in life
is not to compete but to complete~

Your dreams may not go at the same pace with your colleagues but one thing that is important is that you are moving forward and toward. When she started struggling halfway through a 10k, Lt. Gregory jumped in to help. On its own, Asia Ford's story is one of the most inspiring ever heard. However, coupled with what one determined police officer did for her, it becomes something else entirely. 474 pounds, Ford knew she had to make a serious lifestyle change. She enrolled in a boot camp and managed to lose 25 pounds. Nevertheless, she wanted to push herself even more, so she signed up for a 10K run.

At Louisville's Rodes City Run, Ford managed to push through about four miles, until she started feeling sick. She thought her dreams of completing the run were over. But that's when Lt. Aubrey Gregory did something truly remarkable. He jumped out of his patrol car and started helping Ford finish the race, one-step at a time. He helped her stay motivated, talking about her children and sharing how his own mother had died from diabetes. "Your heart starts to fill up, you get those goose bumps and tingles all over your body," Lt. Gregory said, "When I watched her approach and I started to hear people scream and I let her go right there before the end and to see her raise her hands, there are not words to express the way I felt seeing her being successful."Ford finished last in the race, but to her community she's the biggest winner. Photos of the inspiring pair were shared thousands of times on social media.

This inspiring news was tagged Cop Helps Exhausted Runner Cross the Finish Line. When you are determined to finish God knows how to help you mine all resources available. He will race helpers for you like the cops showed up once your focus is His race. The first to finish is nothing compared to the last to vanish on the track of time. The only thing that will make life a worthy adventure is for it to venture in to all the possibilities. Remember, the Master said the first would be the last while the last will be the first. You may be the least now just maintain the list of your dream.

Chapter Three

THINK YOU CAN AND YOU WILL

~A wish is the cart, a will is the horse~

The gunman signal to the lion tamer for the last second readiness, at the trigger of the gun, followed by a sound, the lion was released and the runner picked up. This is a scenario at a time in history when men of goals dared to conquer the four-minute mile. Many athletes have unsuccessfully tried to the point that they resolved to using a lion to chase a runner that he might attain the set record. However, all proved failed. All concluded it is extremely difficult if not practically impossible to achieve the world set goal.

For years, so many athletes had tried and failed to run a mile in less than four minutes that people made it out to be impossibility. The world record for a mile was 4 minutes and 1.3 seconds, set by GunderHagg of Sweden in 1945. Despite, or perhaps because of, the psychological mystique surrounding the four-minute barrier, several runners in the early 1950s dedicated themselves to being the first to cross into the three-minute zone.

In Oxford, England, 25-year-old medical student Roger Bannister cracked track and field's most notorious barrier: the four-minute mile.
Bannister, who was running for the Amateur Athletic Association against his alma mater, Oxford University, won the mile race with a time of 3 minutes and 59.4 seconds. Roger Bannister, born in Harrow, England, in 1929, was a top mile-runner while a student at the University of Oxford and at St. Mary's Hospital Medical School in London. In 1951 and 1953, he won British championships in the mile run. As he prepared himself for his first competitive race of the 1954 season, Bannister researched the mechanics of running and trained using new scientific methods he developed. On May 6, 1954, he came to the Iffley Road track in Oxford

for the annual match between the Amateur Athletic Association and Oxford University.

Conditions were far from ideal; it had been windy and raining. A considerable crosswind was blowing across the track as the mile race was set to begin. At 6 p.m., the starting gun was fired. In a carefully planned race, Chris Brasher, a former Cambridge runner who acted as a pacemaker, aided Bannister. For the first half-mile, Brasher led the field, with Bannister close behind, and then another runner took up the lead and reached the three-quarter-mile mark in 3 minutes 0.4 seconds, with Bannister at 3 minutes 0.7 seconds. Bannister took the lead with about 350 yards to go and passed an unofficial timekeeper at the 1,500-meter mark in 3 minutes 43 seconds, thus equaling the world's record for that distance.

Thereafter, Bannister threw in all his reserves and broke the tape in 3 minutes 59.4 seconds. As soon as the first part of his score was announced–"three minutes..."–the crowd erupted in pandemonium. What limits us is not what stand before us but what stand within us shouting aloud to our subconscious environment what may befall us if we dare the feared before us. Nothing limits a talent like lack of furnishing training. Name your limit and I will show you men who took it as platform. It is better to work to stretch your mind first than to stress your muscle because your body cannot work where your mind never walk. Like Bannister did research before he rehearsed for the race.

A boy saw a little gold fish in the water at his arm's length in the bucket decided to touch it, but to his surprise, his hand could not reach compare to what his head calculated. When his father came around, he stretched his hand and touched it. The boy easily understood that his dad's longer hand assisted him. So he turned and asked him why was it that his hand could not touch it as perceived with his eyes? He was not aware of apparent depth due to refraction of light. Your dream will take you more than you project or envisage it will; what you picture as task is apparent the real cost will surface when you begin to pay the price. Be ready to go extra mile for the extra smile you dream of.

~Life shrinks or expands at the proportion
of one's courage~ Anaisnin

I like the timely counsel and choice word of Charley Young to the young boy who was about being let out of school. The clergy told schooling Billy Graham a life changing sentences that reshaped the course of his path. "You have a voice that pulls. God can use that voice of yours. He can use it mightily." How many lives could have been changed and pushed to their destiny if they had heard some choice words of courage to run with. You need people to make you feel you are able and not unqualified. Like the choice of voice and creative word of Mary kay ash mother, often she would echoed in her hear you can, you can do it. Growing up, Mary Kay did more than embracing this empowering, can-do spirit—she lived it.

When faced with new and daunting tasks in caring for her father, she would call her mother for guidance. Along with the guidance, her mother encouraged her by saying, "You can do it, Mary Kay. You can do it." As an adult, Mary Kay would pass this spirit on through a remarkable company that would inspire millions of women for generations to come. Mary Kay Ash earned a place in history when she stepped out in a man's world to blaze a new path for women. Recognized in her generation as America's greatest woman entrepreneur, Mary Kay created new opportunities for women around the world. Her revolutionary move led to a multibillion-dollar success. In the process, she earned a place in the hearts of millions for her giving spirit, unwavering values, and inspiring belief in the power and potential of women.

A High school football coach on taking over the new school football team looked for a way to build the confidence of the newly selected football team after the several defeats and humiliation of the prior one. The students have been so used to defeat that they have lost confidence in the future success of the team. The new coach quite aware of the challenge before him invited the new set into their dormitory, sat them down and told a story of an experiment carried out on a group of birds. Twelve sparrows were captured and put in captivity, in a big wooden cage with a glass as the top cover.

Eleven adult ones were able to fly freely in the big enclosure why the twelfth one was still very young—newly hatched, so could not fly but perched on the floor watching. At the beginning of the limited freedom of flight given to the birds, all of them quickly flew up to the top thinking that it was an open space for escape. As they reached the top one by one they hit hard on the transparent glass, dropped and picked again. The young one did not bother itself much as it watched older generation unsuccessful escape trials. After several attempts, some became so weak that they gave up the exercise. Some got their wings broken. Some became frustrated at a point and they all stopped trying as it became a threat to their existence, rather they all resolved to flying up keeping a good distance away from the topmost top to avoid hitting the glass. After some days they all became used to the new maximum safe horizon of flight. The young bird was looking and learning. Due to the injuries they had all sustained and the factor of time and age, the eleven grown up birds died one after the other.

> ~If you think you can, you can and
> if you think you can't, you're right~
> Mary Kay Ash

At the death of the last, the young bird began to make its first series of flights but incidentally, it too kept the same maximum horizon like the older dead birds. Meanwhile, the glass cover has become weak due to the several collisions from its older generation. A day came that there was thunderstorm, which hit the covering glass and shattered it; the pieces fell into its place of abode. The cage now with no covering at the top was exposed to the drizzling of rain in to its interior. The bird began to fly as the rain touched its feather but it dared not flew above the everyday flying height boundary—the decimated heights its older generation had kept after their failed attempts. The rain fell and beat it so hard yet tried not to escape though the cage was now open at the top but it seemed sealed with the glass.

After some days it rained again, the water in the enclosure rose and the young bird was getting drowned in it resolving to fate. The water level rose and reached the top of the enclosure; following this development, the young bird struggled to paddle and accidentally floated itself out of the cage almost dead. When it finally regained its consciousness it found itself out side free at last, having been pushed out of its limitation, though through the help of the prevailing challenges. The old minds sometimes are not aware of the platform they have built though they could not reach the goal. They through their stressed and unsuccessful attempts blindly close the possibility page and open the impossibility diary. Challenges force us to use our reserved potentials.

The fact that others failed does not mean the door is closed. We should learn to take advantage of opportunity, which may come as hindrance. We pay greater price for our ignorance and old time assumption, as the young bird almost died for its ignorance. We should learn to unlearn our experience; the old generation could after all be wrong or never tried enough. We should not fail to take risk again. Those old birds were not outright failure they at least weakened the glass; that is, our failure in life are still pregnant with seed of little success. There is no absolute failure for those who dream in purpose nor is absolute success. He said further that the old team had left behind a legacy of seed failure. Attempts are potential clues for us to learn the winning skills against the opponents. As those birds were hitting the glass cover unsuccessfully, they were actually breaking it gradually.

Learn from the past pains and build on the lessons. Dared to approach the fear, dare to risk the avoided. Many wealthiest guys today were those who took a bold step to buy up bankrupted businesses, revitalized and grew it up in to an empire. The fact that Moses could not get the Israelites to the promise land did not make the journey impossible. It does not make him a failure out rightly for his shortcoming achievement was a prelude for Joshua's success.

THE POWER OF ATTITUDE

~Some birds can't soar because the
wind roars, but eagle's spirit glides
with tides~

Come back spirit

Paul Vincent Galvin was one of the two founders of telecommunications company—Motorola. Founded as Galvin Manufacturing Corporation on September 25, 1928, Motorola is now a big name in communications equipment. Galvin invented the first car stereo, which spearheaded Motorola's start out business, which later crash-landed. At the peak of a failing career, it was documented that, Paul attended an auction of his own company. He was defeated but not deflated! With his last $750, he bought back the department, which later became Motorola. It is not everybody that stay to the end that wins but everybody that wins stays to the end. What you are left with, is just the right thing to start with. Attitude is everything when it comes to doing the impossible. Mind you, do not have to win always but be willing always, wining is not every time but willing must be every time. It is a greater thing to be the better of you than to be the best of all. Go back to the basis if need be and do not put on the easy mask of imitation. Two young stars were given instruction by their grandparents to fill a bottle with water using a big spoon. Then the old woman placed the two bottles in the taller bucket each and asked the boys to begin work. But she did something abnormal, instead of opening the cover of the bottle she choose not to but rather used a tiny nail to make a hole on the cover.

After she was done, she asked the kids to start the chore. The two of them were surprised at the old woman strange attitude and discretion. But before they complained she hushed them and asked them to work it out. Then they started transferring the water from one bucket to the bottle in the other bucket but with no apparent success as the water ran over the hole in to the bucket. After some turns, they felt disgusted, but one of them that used to be smart was quick to stop the fruitless labor. When the other kid which seemed to be a slow learner and low IQ saw his brilliant friend turning away from the exercise; he presumed that as usual, he had floored him as he used to do in the class—that he had finished using his gift again, so he tried to continue in other to reduce his shame—that, it is better to be least and be on the list than to be out of records.

However, the effort was not yielding as the water kept rolling off yet he refused to stop until the bucket was filled. Then something happened to the water in the bucket, it rose above the height of the bottle and without effort if began to percolate in to the bottle freely the young chap never realized it as it was getting dark. He based on the grandmother's instruction not to leave until the bottle was filled by the night. But he had to stop when the water in the source bucket got exhausted.

~Better to be least than to be out of the list~

Not quite long, the old woman returned from her outing and called the two boys to bring the bottles of water. The smart one went in arrogance to bring his empty bottle, ready to confront the old woman of her foolishness and ignorance of an impossible task when the other boy got to the bucket and try to lift the bottle it was heavy, surprised by what had happen he had to call his friend to help him lift it. The two were curious of what had happened to the bottle. Who filled it up? In the midst of their curiosity and amazement with his humbled friend wide-open mouth the old woman smiled and told them, "My son you filled it because you chose to go extra mile." When he got to understand how the magic happened, he smiled—extra mile births ultra-smile.

Not everybody was born a genius but we are all born with something: diligence, patience, determination, will power, perseverance and opportunity. And at the end we can all make a difference and influence by what resources we feed on from within. According to Wikipedia's definition, persons with genius tend to have strong intuitions about their domains, and they build on these insights with tremendous energy. But I will rather say energies, what are they: determination energy, passion energy, joy energy, zeal energy; just as anger and fear drain energy so do the positive attitudes supply energy.

~Genius is a talent for producing something
for which no determinate rule can be given,
not a predisposition consisting of a skill for
something that can be learned by following
some rule or other~ Immanuel Kant

BE STRONGER THAN FAILURE

~Your problem is to announce
you stop announcing it~

She told that privileged audience. "You might never fail on the scale I did, "But it is impossible to live without failing at something, unless you live so cautiously that you might as well not have lived at all—in which case, you fail by default." The author did not magically become renowned overnight. Penniless and raising a child on her own, she wrote the first Harry Potter book on an old manual typewriter. Twelve publishers rejected the manuscript! A year later she was given the green light by Barry Cunningham from Bloomsbury, who agreed to publish the book but insisted she get a day job because there was no money in children's books. J.K Rowling, the author of *Harry Potter*, quoted the above while addressing the graduating class of Harvard in June, 2008.

She did not talk about success. She talked about failures—her own in particular. There is no living thing, man, animal or plant, even the biggest of trees, that won't float when placed in water; no matter the height, weight or volume; this denotes a life lesson for us that life storms are not designed by the Creator to submerge us. God's plan for you is to arise and shine despite the gross darkness of the situation.

Sometimes we fail, not because we did not plan enough, or passionate enough, or not knowing enough, not because we want it but because we need it. Success never trains anyone only failure does. When some people fall they do it on their face but some rather fall on their knees. They have the long-term insight that the darkest night reveals the faintest stars. There is no other platform for success like the compressed failure not that it serves as foundation for it but it makes its story fantastic.

A man was standing on the third floor of building with his daughter and son, he had two balloons with him; he blew air into one, tied the mouth, and left the other empty. Afterward, he threw both balloons down, the empty specimen fell down straight to the bottom of the building why the other air filled began to be tossed here and there in the wind, dangling zigzag in the air, hitting the branches of the tree and landed some yards away from the base of the building. The man looked at them and said when you choose to be empty of dreams and aspiration life will give you little problems—you will face little challenges, the journey will be so smooth, you will have no cause to hit anything nor anything obstructing your move, but at the end of your life you will land at the base of your starting point.

You would have covered no miles of success, but when you choose to be filled with dreams and future you will subject your time to the storms of challenges, drifting you here and there, sometimes hitting you with the branches of rejection, failure, disappointments, but at the same time you are been pushed toward your goal, you will surely never end where you start your life, as you choose to release your talents and potential within under pressure like the air in the balloon.

~Every dreamer fights more,
loses more and wins more~

Life adversity is an advert of opportunity. On a sunny day a man was looking for opportunity; as he was passing through a deserted road he saw from afar a sign in front of a building with front door widely open; he increased his pace gasping for breath but on getting closer, on it was written 'ADVERSITY', at the door of the main entrance was hung a placard displaying "Open For Now," so the man afraid and disappointed paced up and continued with his search.

After covering miles, tired and bathed in sweat, he got to the end of the road and had no choice but to turn back late in the evening. Journeying through the same lane, he got to the same bill board now with the other side directly facing him and on it was written 'OPPORTUNITY'; at the door of the main entrance was hung a placard displaying "Closed For Now". Those who take a step in fear usually take it sideways not forward nor toward. Isn't it correct that the hardest substance shines most—such is diamond, a crystal rock and such is life; hard times will make something dies in you for something to live but it is not for everything to die with you.

God has promised you a table set before you in the presence of your enemies not friends; that your best will be encountered in the presence or amidst of challenges. Like the four lepers in the time of drought when the enemies laid a siege against Ahab and the Israelites. God promised through His prophet that by this time tomorrow there shall be surplus. These four lepers almost starved to death told themselves if we stay here at the outskirt we will die; if we go into the city the famine is severe and we will die; thirdly, if we choose to face the army besieging us we have two options: we either obtain mercy in their eyes and get meals or they choose to kill us. So they went for the third option. They choose to face the adversity which had already been planned to make them celebrity.

They got there and behold a table of abundance was set before them; they had so much that they were able to deliver the city from famine. The adversity was indeed an advertisement of what God was set to do. Do not run away from that masked opportunity, all you need do is to stay in the ark of promise, when the flood increase, it will lift you above mountains you can't climb ordinarily. Like the order of Noah, the flood was a great challenge but at the end when the water of trouble subsided, the ark was resting on the mount of Ararat. Technically and humanly speaking, there was no way Noah and his disciples could have placed such a magnificent ark on the mount but God used their storm for their rising.

~My great concern is not whether you
have failed, but whether you are content
with failure~ Abraham Lincoln

Fail wiser and better

Fobes reports that the world's richest people, money comes and goes constantly—it's not uncommon for the wealthiest individuals to make or lose tens or even hundreds of millions every day, yet they kept on taking risks upon risks. Nobody walks by taking the right leg alone we as well take the left leg, in other word we take both the strong right step and weak left step to move forward but it appears to us as a wrong step when. We call it failure. But like the two legs of man we walk on the two together—you have to take both the right leg and opposite together. Life runs on the two legs of failure and success. There are no inventors with a hybrid brain they just learn to trade their shortcomings for their long going through having the never quit spirit; in fact, some like Albert of relativity suffer retardation of growth. He could not read until he was seven and had earlier been written off by his tutors as incompetent for mental world. Thomas Sir James Dyson's whose company is now a worldwide success shares the same drama, selling bag-less vacuum cleaners in over 50 countries. It made him a billionaire. He created 5127 vacuum prototypes, all of which could be considered 'failed attempts'. He spent 15 years perfecting his product before taking it to market in. The vacuum worked on hisown patented principle of cyclonic separation, that's why it doesn't need a bag. He said, "By the time I made my 15th prototype, my third child was born. By 2,627, my wife and I were really counting our pennies." By 3,727, my wife was giving art lessons for some extra cash. These were tough times, but each failure brought me closer to solving the problem." With such relentless drive despite failures and hardships, how could Dyson not be a billionaire? Success pulls us forward, failures pushes us forward—both carries inertia but you are sitting at the driver's side.

~Failure is success under construction,
do not abandon the site, do not please!~

Thomas Edison famously put it; 'I have not failed. I've just found 9999 ways that won't work.' Sir James Dyson, the founder of the Dyson

Company really took this principle to heart. His wealth ended being decimated in ten digits of dollars. Are you failing or you see yourself trailing the path to the success? Although Washington never gained the commission in the British army he yearned for, in these years the young man gained valuable military, political, and leadership skills. He closely observed British military tactics, gaining a keen insight into their strengths and weaknesses that proved invaluable during the Revolution. Washington learned to organize, train, drill, and discipline his companies and regiments.

From his observations, readings and conversations with professional officers, he learned the basics of battlefield tactics, as well as a good understanding of problems of organization and logistics He gained an understanding of overall strategy, especially in locating strategic geographical points. He demonstrated his toughness and courage in the most difficult situations, including disasters and retreats. He developed a command presence—given his size, strength, stamina, and bravery in battle, he appeared to soldiers to be a natural leader and they followed him without question. However, Washington's fortitude in his early years was sometimes manifested in less constructive ways.

~Failure is only the opportunity to begin
again, only this time more wisely~
Henry Ford

Everything is a change both success and failure, none of these anyway should change our personality. Success makes you happier failure makes you stronger. One of the evidences of life is detection of pain. It reveals you are still alive and can feel something but much more that you can be filled with the gain. Face the light of future and back your shadow. If you fall roll forward, and do not first run after what falls down from your hand but what falls you down to the ground. Often, when a man falls he is conscious of what befall him more than what stands before him. Some people tried it once and succeeded, some twice, some seven times and at the end, all have the same title —successful. Neither success nor failure reveals the limit of our strength both events conceal still our possibilities. Every success comes with a greater challenge; every failure comes with a lesser challenge.

This is why, when you succeed people expect something greater to come out next, which you have no idea yet of how to discover and deliver, but when you fail people expect same target from you which now, you are equipped with the dos and do nots of the process—for a righteous man falls seven times and rises again—rise up in pain for the gain you deserve as dividend. Note that the just and not the sinner, a man in pursuit of God's path and not a wonderer. Just like Jesus told His disciples about their friend Lazarus, this sickness is not unto death but unto the glory of God.

Your failure is not denial but a trial ahead of triumph. It is a blessing to fall on the ground than to fall to the ground. Success opens to bunch of keys; there is no master key to it, but mastered keys. I know you do not want to live like matter that has mass and occupy space, but want to matter, lead mass and dictate their pace. A winner is never known until the race is finished—one event can't make you a life time loser or a life time winner.

~People fall forward to success~ Mary Kay Ash

> You may render your dime
> You may tender your time
> But do not surrender your goal
> Not crime to fail when frail
> But as the just, just fail better
> If you must fail again
> Fail higher, fail farther, fail focused
> If you must fail again
> Fail wiser, fail stronger, fail closer,
> Fail smarter, fail happier, fail learning
> Fail mastering, fail further, and fail onward
> Above all, fail growing!
> Fail succeeding!!

Be tough like a weed

I once read of an elderly woman who enrolled in a university to study as a young girl, but due to financial constraint, she had to withdraw. After 64 years she saw an advert that Government is re-enrolling all university drop out. On hearing this she made a move even though she had earlier angrily thrown away all are necessary document she was helped out by the authority to retrieve her old record in the institution. This woman now in her eighties is about to graduate as an artist.

Perseverance means to be hardened and addicted to a good course and with good deal of time. It means to be unendingly and unrepentantly bent to a choice less decision, just like weed. Weed takes no permission to spring up. They do not need special attentions of acceptance to thrive they only engage their power of resilience and perseverance. The more they are removed the more they spread.

Steven Spielberg is consistently being viewed as one of the most popular and influential filmmakers in the history of cinema. He applied and was denied two times to the prestigious University of Southern California film school. Instead he went to Cal State University in Long Beach. Now he's worth $2.7 billion and in 1994 got an honorary degree from the film school that rejected him twice. To date, the unadjusted gross of all Spielberg-directed films exceeds $8.5 billion worldwide. Forbes puts Spielberg's wealth at $3 billion. When people disregard your goal because it goes not in their direction, do not discard it. Not being elegant does not mean not being relevant. Your beauty is going to emerge from the cocoon of determination and persistence.

Mistakes are sometimes inevitable, we try either a new thing or a known thing, but to try nothing is mistake by default. Do not fail by default; fail better by defeat and you had come second, third or the least on the list but not the first out the list. If you ever have reason to quit make sure it is not because you have succeeded or failed at last. Problems looks for every one's addresses but some choose to address it like in a ring while some choose to dress it up like a king. We would live our best when we leave our rest and are leavened by our test; either you are ready to fight or not life is a battle, the stage is set, the line is drawn, you are born to be king but you are born on the ring.

A man used to collect different flowers for his little son. He returned from the garden all the time with species of flower plucked with short stem but there was a particular flower he plucked with a long stem and this happened to be the most beautiful of all and cherished by the son. This had been happening for a long time and the boy always have a question in his mind, "Why should my dad treat this particular flower specially to my hurt that I find it easy to play with the rest, to hug and embrace them but this my favorite always call for special attention in handling, its full of thorns at the base." One day he was bold enough to challenge his father why such a callous and unusual treat, his father laughed and said, "My son do not just give people a rose flower, pluck the stem with it, with such balanced love, they had understood this life in its reality. Good things come with great task. There is a price attached to every prize."

Top your effort do not crop it

Guilt is the virus from the past and worry is the one in the future. Have you ever been faced with the temptation of quitting? You are not having a strange feeling it is normal for anyone who choose to leave the comfort zone for the combat zone, but you can always choose whether to quit the foundation you have sweated to build because the bricks for the wall are taking time to bake or because the leaves to make the tad roof is scattered by the wind. In a little city located on the hill was a farm boy who lived with his uncle who was a farmer. Their hut was situated at the suburb of the city close to the steep side of the hills.

The young boy hardly had access to what his peers enjoyed in the town, no toys but squirrels to play with. No swing but tree climbing to substitute. One day, his uncle gave him a treat and surprised him with a gift of weaved ball. The boy was exited and rushed out to play with it. His uncle called him back, Mark, listen to this clause attached, actually the ball was rented, as you know we can't afford that luxury with our financial standing.

So be careful with it, do not soak in water not smashed in mud. Moreover, the duration of the rent is just for a day. So think of how to maximize your fun period. Lastly, before any sporting get water in the drum at the poultry half filled. I will be back in the evening. The boy was exited for such a once in a blue moon treat, kept the ball under the stark of hay and quickly dashed off with is pitcher to the stream. He never felt the stress of climbing the steeply foot path as he hurriedly fetch the water.

>   ~You do not solve a problem by thinking
>   about it, you think on it~

When the water was half filled he brought out his ball and began to play with it all around. Suddenly, the ball bounced into the half-filled drum. He shouted and began to lament—the woven ball must not to be soaked in the water; he quickly remembered his uncle's warning. In a rush, he snapped to the four feet tall drum, peeped inside, he saw the ball being tossed and floating. But his real ordeal is this. His hand couldn't reach the ball. He had managed to fetch the water in the drum by placing the pitcher on his head and pouring the water in the drum. He began to think of the way out. A thought came in to his mind, pushed the drum and let it fall to the ground, by doing that you will have the ball. As he was struggling to capsize the drum it dawned on him the implication. Firstly, he will lose the water he had fetched thereby subject to be seen as a lazy and ungrateful boy by his caring uncle and portrayed disobedience.

More over the drum is on a steeply side if I succeed to overturn the drum the ball will flood out with water and off it will run down the slope, and in the process it may end in the stream, possibly I might have to go far to get it if at all the stream has not carried it away before I get there. So he stopped the first resolution, then he sat down and thought again. Suddenly, he jumped up I have got it. He picked its pitcher ran down to the stream, came back with it on his head poured it in the drum. The first round, the second, the third after some rounds the water reached the brim of the drum. Based on the law of floatation the ball had been rising with the water level.

Since the water is now at the brim the young lad happily reached out, stretched his hand a bit tilting on his toes he picked the ball. Still have some time left to play with it. When his uncle came to retrieve the ball for return he was surprised that his boy had fetched the water not to half of the drum but to brim. He said Mark, "What a good boy you are. I am proud of you and greatly impressed. As a matter of reward to your extra ordinaries, I will not return the ball again today you can have it till tomorrow. I am going to the man to pay another day's rent." Does that sound like your case?

You could choose to stay by the life storm side and continue to watch your goal being tossed here and there by the waves of life, claiming it is unattainable, it is unreachable any more. You could become so frustrated and desperate and choose to take a rash decision that may cost you your goal or make it longer and more difficult to reach. I mean you can angrily throw the baby out with the bath water by trying to take a short cut like the boy thought first. However, you can take advantage of your existing labor and experience to go extra mile to work harder, endure, persevere, and at the end get your goal with such accuracy. You do not need to throw the baby out with the water, I mean do not dispatch your dreams with the storms of life. Do not because you want to excuse yourself from discouragement and discomfort excuse your dream along. Have a rethink like the boy, there is always a goal oriented way out.

Put in more effort and zeal, you will not only reap the reward of extras but also recover the past labor in form of experience as the boy finally had a drum full of water instead of half. Solomon said whatever your hand find to do it with all your might in other word pursue it with your today, thoughts, time, talent, treasure, team, tissues and tenacity. In addition, one thing about goal achieving is the reward that follows not about the expected gain of the adventure alone but other doors it will open for more outreaching and impacts. Your goal might be punctured but that should not deflate our dream.

TAKE ADVANTAGE OF THE WEATHER

~Where fear exists, people only
exist and exit from rear~

Just like in the plant kingdom that every season comes with a fruit, every life circumstances comes with a substances. Life is like a house with two entries of opportunity with one door of adversity controlling the two. When the door flings from one entry to the other, it opens the previous and shut the later. It cannot close the two at a time. In other word when a door closes it opens another. Every disappointment is an appointment in another platform. When the doves complain about the wind the eagles commence acrobatic flights.

Back into the slave trade, a cunning merchant called his slave boy and told him, you are dutiful just as if my family member and I wish to free you. However, I have one test for you to pass if you must be free. I will take you to the valley and stand on the mountain, without telling you I will take my leave, if you can see me immediately I turn to go then you can be free to go. This old man was wishing to let go but not willing. This seems simple to actualize but as one may think but it is not because this young slave dare not look up in his master presence he had to bow his head and focus on the ground while talking with him. Having realized how this will be difficult he said sir, "I wish to make one request from you just this one privilege I have never been given." "Why not, as a send forth ceremony for you," the slave owner said. "Sir, can we make the deal in the noon?" requested the slave boy. He nodded in agreement thinking what makes a difference. So the slated day came and the duo landed in the outskirt of their village, the young man stayed back in the valley and the old slave owner up on the mountain. After a while, the man turned to leave; the young boy who was looking down immediately turned to go in freedom.

The old man was dumb founded, he exclaimed, how did you know. This supposed freed slave replied, "I took advantage of the weather." Once you were up there, your shadow was right there in front of me on the ground. So as I focused on the ground in awe bowing down your movement was in my sight. Nevertheless, this man chose to be dubious he said, "I actually forgot to tell you, "I have two tests for you, now you have done well in the first hear the second." Take a basket from the backyard and use it to fetch water in the drum there. Once the water fills up the container and overflows in freedom then you can have your freedom finally."

This young man still looking down started to look inward what the way out could be. He said, "My master I have one more request I will like to make as well. Can we wait for the winter to carry out this?" The man replied, "Great! Why not," thinking that he had worsened his own situation by now having to trek miles to get the scarce water by then. Time rolled in and out and here came the winter. This young man took the basket and went out to fetch water.

The old man went inside to relax having presumed the end of the matter. After a while, he decided to go and check the drum and the fruitless effort of the poor slave, but was dazed seeing the drum half filled. He went to the window in haste to see the exercise in birds view. Getting there, he opened his mouth in amazement with what he saw—a boy coming and singing with a basket on his head full of snow.

Many business magnates in history happened to be men who walked on the wings of the moment when other only looked but never saw.

They choose to buy collapsed empire of business; they look out for liquidated investment and foresaw what was likely to be the turn of consumer's emotional trend, so plunged their race and resources in to the abandoned mess. George Soros emigrated to England after the second world war, graduated from the London School of Economics, moved to New York in the mid-1950s and began a career in finance that saw him enjoy extraordinary success as a savvy speculator, most notoriously as the so-called "man who broke the Bank of England" by making $1 billion during the UK's 1992 currency crisis. Soros is the founding chairman of Soros Fund Management and heads the Open Society Institute, a grant-making foundation. At age 80 his net worth was $14 billion.

~Adventurers look, opportunist sees~

John Paulson was another business mind that capitalized on the feared. New York-based John Paulson graduated first in his class at New York University's College of Business and Public Administration, and in the top 5 percent of his MBA class at Harvard. He worked on Wall Street, including at Bear Stearns, before founding his own hedge fund. Capitalizing on the recent insecurity in the mortgage and foreclosure market, Paulson & Co. made profits of $15 billion in 2007 alone.

Take charge not care

Life is like dropping from parachute if you just hang there and enjoy the cool breeze and the shade from the sun, it will take you to where the wind blows—in the ocean or forest; but you can control the flight and land at the expected end. You must take charge of your life or all you get is the change from the expenditure by time. Do not shiver to frozen on the roof top because your feather is wet, while waiting for men to heat the house, for when you fly the wind dries it faster than the heat from the chimney which may never flow. Often the help you need will come from taking a step of faith into the challenge, when God sees your feet in the Jordan He will part it.

Men can promise and can compromise, men can give their word today and forgive theme tomorrow, only God has made His word His name, only Him can't forget what He beget. Failure is an event from responsibility not an eventuality of ability. When you meet challenges on the way dressed in confrontation, do not change your address of desired destination because it was sent to lead you there. Tough time will either emerge you or submerge you; the altitude is your choice of attitude—up or down. Tough movement answers to tough moments. When life poses a question to you it has the answer on the next page though it may be inverted—do not close the book yet. Life is tough but do not live it rough, live it tough. Be quick to recover.

DEVELOP MENTAL TOUGHNESS

~Winners are not always the
strongest but the boldest~

If you finally fail or succeed, do not make it final. Failure is not a form of success but often a platform for it. Limitation is not where we stop at hand but when we stop in mind. In school, we were thought imitation and limitation. They gave us laws and theories, which sometimes are good enough to repeat history but never make new one. It is no news again that the world greatest inventors are mostly unschooled, because they never allowed their neurons to be soften and conditioned by those great scholars. Success is not the ability not to come over failure on the way but to overcome it by the way. When you fail in school for a number of times, they ask you to withdraw, so those guys withdrew so they can have enough room to fail to eventual success. Failure sometimes is not just part of the process but a path to the success.

Every success is a failure laminated with courage. We set our limit by our thoughts we break our limits with our thoughts. Do not stay too long on that spot no matter the temperature, move in head, and eventually move ahead. Any further stay in the cocoon can wreck a future progress father than the past success. Success that is not turned into process overtime is a future potential failure in its overtime. Feed on your success fruits only for a while before you turn it into a seed. Old age is a slow stage but still not blank page of life book. We have no control over the ageing of our brain but we have over our mind and dreams. Colonel Sanders, in 1955, confident of the quality of his fried chicken, the Colonel devoted himself to developing his chicken franchising business. His likeness continues to appear on millions of buckets and on thousands of restaurants in more than 100 countries around the world. He remembered his mother's recipe and went out selling. How many doors did he have to knock on before he got his first order?

It was estimated that, he had knocked on more than a thousand doors before he got his first order. A man in his sixties began to make history. Shadow doesn't leave a foot print, be real and dare the scary; people who live like people have easy way out but do not leave a trail that worth something. Keep your mind focus on your dream no matter the drifting of the storms.

Fight to update your thought

The mind is a battleground for the army of past thoughts that daily struggle with that of today. The imagination you fail to cast down will cast you down or in other word, make you feel down cast. You need to block your mind from relegating play back. Solomon said fortify your mind with all diligence, all your mental armor. If you have nothing you look toward to in the farthest future, you are not a leader to look forward to in nearest future. We cannot create a future it is already there but we can calve out its features. Dreams are a future in measures. To every sleeping dream, the past is already awake. The past—that is the only dead thing that can't be revived, you do not exercise hope in foolishness by dwelling on it. The purpose of today is not to repair the past but to prepare the future.

~You have lived your past; now,
let your past leave you~

Those who live tomorrow in worry will leave today in a sorry state and gather little harvest from their time investment. The past is like the backyard, though we need to visit sometimes but we must be careful not to hang our house address there, for visitors and strangers of life opportunities, walk through the front door. In other plainer mood do not replace your identity with your past picture, let your thought box be in front of your life for in it opportunities and ideas will be posted. There is lesson to learn from the past truly but we should not turn it to a classroom. Today is a present for the future do not present it to yesterday.

One thing about tomorrow is that it will come either we prepare for it or not and another thing about it is that it will go either we reap it or not. You cannot hold the present down but you can hold its presents down. Time is slow enough for you to think about what to use it for and it is too fast to be re-used or for you to think very slowly. Today is the fruit of yesterday and the seed for tomorrow.

The purpose of dreams is to take away sleep, it makes us restless to our present comfort; it makes the past distasteful, incomplete and incompetent. When you have your shadow of yesterday leading your real self, it shows you are backing the light of future; you are walking backward potentially. Dreams are like stars in the sky they must be appreciated afar off and reached out to, not to wish they fall like shooting stars on our laps, less they fizzle out like them in our eyes as we gaze in the sky of wishes. When a leg is broken the sticks can be used to walk slowly but when a wing is broken the flight is cancelled; that explains the power of the mind, a disable mind is the worst stage of handicap. A dreamless life is a horseless cart—it can't be managed.

The little walk of beginning is room to make your entire mistake and still move on, it is a period of fail safe. Assemble your will strength to push the start button, you will always have the good reasons to spend more time planning when actually you are abusing the resources needed most, meanwhile which is time. You have planned and strategized enough now break the shell. When a cotton wool fail to break at the required time it loses value. There is a season for every fruit the same for everything and idea.

Dreamers are not born they born their dreams. Dreams without pursuit are wishes. Dream what is achievable not what is available; dream what is required to make the world better not what to acquire to make your world bigger. The dead has past but no future, only those who are alive has past and future, but those who are truly living filter away the past to have solution for the future. Your past brought you here but can't take you further, any attempt to ride with it will take you farther only to the pit of past. The past is to commence today and not to compete with it neither is it to complete tomorrow.

Build a dream around your soul and build your life amidst the dreams. Dreamers live a timed life, at the end they leave behind a timeless life. Your identity is a mold, every other input from men and challenges should be poured in to this mold to fill your destiny and not for them to re-shape your design.

> ~Not everything that flies has wings
> some just make sure they are
> light enough to be lifted by the free wind~

Nothing weighs a man down like the load of depression; nothing clips his wings of thought like gum of anxiety. A wet wings makes no flight, joyless mood makes no sight. A wet wing makes no flight above, joyless mood makes no sight ahead. Birds do not fly in the rain; keep your dreams from men who can only shower on you the reasons why the tower is impossibility and from missiles of impossibility thoughts. Impossibility is sometimes an expression of laziness and not incompetency. Dream is not an event that will happen someday but that which is to invented. We may seem to be all the same today but tomorrow our dreams will separate us, small dreamers as the least and none dreamers out of the list.

Do not Quit, Doeth Queue
When your dreams fly ahead of your planned horizon
Do not quit, queue for fresh wing
When your goals are not scoring
Do not quit, queue new coaching
When your efforts seem aborted
Do not quit, queue for another brainchild
When your road seems rough
Do not quit, queue for another shoe and strength
Quitters are ever too soon to give it up; winners take it up

Give wheels to your will

What you do for interest—profit and what you do for interest—passion are not the same; and the latter, being the secret of success must be encouraged. We need thinking to establish the faith in the head, afterward, we let go of the thinking and let will go ahead. A strong will always dream all the way, even when I fall it will be in the pool of lessons, it will be a new way to dream. When you fall, it is an opportunity to view things from different altitude, to review your rung up the ladder and interview your wrongs for clues.

In a small town in the East Asian, there was a village in the remote part, which had the landscape divided in to two leaving the dwellers to occupy one side. The other though rich in resources was not accessible to the dwellers because of the dividing river. Not only that, the river was full of deadly crocodiles and carnivorous fishes. There had always been a debate on who will first cross the river but nobody ever tried. The bold men there would only come to look and turn back. Beside the river was a very old and tall tree. It had its roots half on the land and half tracing their way in to the river water. One day, a group of young men came to have their bathe at the safe zone of its bank. Then one of them decided to climb the tree to have a good look of the rivers length and the strange land terrain.

As he climbed up, he strained his neck to catch the view which he couldn't so he decided to move to the side of the tree branches which happened to be the side with the root in the river. Unknown to him, the river had eroded the soil holding the root to the ground, as he moved to the extreme branches his weight tilted the tree to side of the river, like a dream the tree began to fall off. All his colleagues shouted, "Tandy is in trouble, he is falling with the tree in to the river." Everybody fled in to the city to announce his death, meanwhile the young boy held to the branch of the tree he was sitting on.

As the tree fell gradually, with the root, which was as well gradually and slowly pulling out, the boy clung to the apex branch. By the time the tree will land, it laid across the river in its full width with the boy landing on the other side of the river. Not long, the city dwellers came and saw the boy alive on the other side. When the boy's dog that had been barking saw that, his master had landed on the other side it jumped on the tree stem and ran across it to the other side of the river using it as a bridge.

Then the observers came to themselves, as they watched the dogs strange adventuring steps, they told one another it is like our village dream had come to pass. We can cross now with the help of the giant cedar tree made platform. They all one by one crossed to join and celebrate the boy's achievement thinking he had planned all the episodes.

~Winners are not failure immune;
they are only success consumed~

Geniuses are souls who walk around monument of impossibility when others walk away, they continue to knock the door until the window shakes off, others give up on the ancestral door, but they, consistently and continuously knock the door and entered the room finally through the window. This was how ford handled the course when he gave his world the V8 engine. Henry Ford did not have much formal education. In fact, he did not go to school beyond the age of 14. Nevertheless, he was intelligent enough to know there had to be a V8 engine but he was ignorant and did not know how to build it. So he asked all his highly qualified, educated people to build one. But they told him what could be done and what couldn't. According to them, a V8 was impossibility. However, Henry Ford insisted on having his V8. A few months later, he asked his people if they had produced the V8, they replied, "We know what can be done and we also know what can't be done and V8 is impossibility."

This went on for many months and still Henry Ford said, "I want my V8." Shortly thereafter, the same people produced his V8 engine. Why did it become possible? They let their imagination run beyond academic limitation. When you get to a road and there are no footprints on the path, I think you should not go away, if there is a path someone made it and it must lead to somewhere great enough for them to have turned it to a road. Every road was once a forest created by someone who was finding rest beyond the restless city in another world. When God wants to expand a man, he first enlarges his limited mushroom mindscape. He enlarged the heart of Solomon as that of the seashore sand before He blessed him like no man had ever received. You cannot succeed beyond you dream successfully for what the heart has not conceived the head can't nurse nor can the hand receive.

Those who have nothing to do but to say should excuse those who have nothing to say but something to do. Sometimes you need to walk away in life and sometimes you need to work out a way. Impossibility is often a matter of time if the dream lives on it will come to say I'm possibility.

~*Im*possibility whispers *I'm* possibility,
I am what you say I am~

Your passing through becomes a path

If you are passing through it is a polishing tool, be pressing through that is how to be shaped through not just scale through. You cannot solve a problem when you are dissolved in to it. One day a mother eagle wants to take its eaglets to the source of food, and then she announced, "We are going to walk the distance since we are going in the night." They squared their shoulders and replied in pride, but we have the best of wings and can scale the highest of cloud; why should we be deprived? The mother eagle calmly replied, I know we could fly but if we soar tonight how will you come here tomorrow morning, but for my footprints. What, if God is using you, as generational prototype, of a new course of success adventure?

Some are recalled as pioneer of new insight but their uncommon labor and landscape is a price to be paid. What, if God wants to use your life to draw a new map of success path? All will count at the end just do not end it yourself. Paul recalled his life episodes and concluded that in me first Jesus Christ might show forth all long-sufferings, as a pattern to those being about to believe on Him to life everlasting.

God can choose anything to drive us past our limitation; He can engage a situation to launch us beyond our comfort zone so that at the end our journey will be a lecture note to refer to when training others. Today, God advises us to look unto Abraham and Sarah for direction because they had lived to pass through a wilderness to make a footpath; they have used their hope and faith to draw a map on the rock of their predicament. A life without a test will be void of testimony. God tested Abraham before he attested him as faith mentor and pattern.

Consider this proverbially story, hope it links you to your first hope. In the 18th century, there was period in the raining season that gave birth to continuous down pouring of rain that ended flooding the entire habitation of wild animals. All the animals ran for their safety. Some quickly dashed to the top of the mountain while some ran to another habitation. However, not all could achieve this, like the tortoise, it was left behind. The water level increased and it flooded the slow crawling creature away. As it was being dragged along, other animals began to pity it from afar.

The waves turned it upside down and made its hard shell in to a small canoe, but the tortoise was still helpless. At a point, the water rose so high that the tallest tree in the village was covered to the apex. The flood dragged the creature over the branches of the tree, which are several meters high, seeing it as an opportunity to save its life it clung to the branches of the tree like a drowning man will cling to a straw. Others thought it was all over for it. Some pitied. The rain stopped and the water began to recede.

The first day, from 50 meter height to the 40 meters. The tortoise now above the water but was afraid to jump into the water below. The second day the level reduced the third and by the 14th day, the water had returned to the ground level leaving the tortoise on the tallest slippery tree in the animal kingdom. The other animals had concluded that life had ended for the tortoise. 50 meters above the ground, the tortoise had no choice but to stay up on the tree. Therefore, it began to feed on the leaves of the tree and the dew that settled on them.

Gradually, the dwellers of the village began to re-occupy their homes after they all had fled for their lives. One day, after life and activities had begun fully in the village, a hunter trying to shoot down a bird from this dreaded tree saw the tortoise on it. Nobody has ever succeeded climbing the tree because of its height and shape—it was highly slippery and has no stepping stumps.

The man could not shoot anymore; he stood in awe and wondered, what a miracle he exclaimed. How come that a tortoise succeeded in climbing what no man can climb? He went back to the city and announced his discovery. Everybody came to see the amazing and extraordinary creature. The reporters came from everywhere with the camera flashing every second. The tortoise was surprised at such a honor, what special thing have I done. This sound like the case of Noah's ark, how could Noah and his eight men team have ever placed such zoo size ark on the mount Ararat? However, the challenging flood was intentionally used by God to achieve this. Do you know that many stars we celebrate today are that tortoise?

Their storms have carried them far beyond what they could ordinarily have achieved. What was meant for evil God turned it out for promotion. There are black spots on their sun but the shining light they finally fanned to flame has overshadowed the black spots. At the end, all your storms will count—they will account for your success.

Build the escape velocity

Your past is a ladder and you have climbed it these far, reach to the next rung not the past wrongs. Failure is a hot stepping-stone to success; the gain will cool the pain for those who do not take it as a stopping-tone. Just as the space shuttle had to jettison some expired take-off gas chamber components—attached parts, so it is in life, some bitter and better past must be jettison at some particular points in your live if you must boost your speed and height of accomplishments to break the limits of the sky. At the end of the earth distance phase, the space shuttle floats freely in space having let go of the load to gather the escape velocity.

> ~Those who succeed often fail more
> than those who fail; they queue when
> those others quit~

Do not just see your failure as a bad experience, see it as a good experiment at the end; it is how you receive failure that really determines the gravity. The leader in you is revealed at the face of loneliness and desertion. When it gets tough winners emerge quitters are submerged.

Mary Kay Ash faced a situation all too familiar to women in the early '60s. After 25 years in the direct-selling business, Mary resigned a position as a national training director when yet another man she had trained was promoted above her at twice her salary. Her response was visionary. At first, she started writing a book that would help women gain the opportunities she had been denied. Sitting at her kitchen table, Mary Kay made two lists on a yellow legal pad. One list contained the good things she had seen in companies. The other featured things she thought could be improved. When she reviewed the lists, she realized she had created a marketing plan for a dream company. So, in 1963, she put her plan into action.

With her experience, the plan and $5,000 in savings, Mary Kay Ash enlisted the help of her 20-year-old son, Richard, and created Beauty by Mary Kay. It was a first a company dedicated to making life more beautiful for women. It was founded not on the competitive rule, but on the Golden Rule, of praising people to success and on the principle of placing faith first, family second, and career third. It was a company—as Mary Kay Ash would say—"With heart." But she could have welcome the situation with weights of depression and rejection, like many who lost their job will do.

Sometimes we need to be harshly treated like Laban did to Jacob for us to put on the creative mentality. Many job seekers have become job sickened when they carry potential to become an institution. If you are sacked do not become slacked, you are only punctured you can choose to use the deflated air to inflate your dreams. Let go of the good memory of salary and begin from where you are, with what you have, with how you left and whom you are.

~When you handle failure as a project
you project it into success~

Start crude

When you depend on external motivation, the movement in life will be externally controlled. When you are bent on getting all resources you want to start you will be boxed. It reminds me of the Ford's early automobile, the transmission, consisting of two forward gears and one reverse, was of the planetary type, controlled by foot pedals rather than the more common hand lever used in sliding-gear transmissions. Spark and throttle were controlled by a hand lever on the steering column. The 10-gallon fuel tank was located under the front seat. Because gasoline was fed to the engine only by gravity, and also because the reverse gear offered more power than the forward gears, the Model T frequently had to be driven up a steep hill backward. Such deficiencies, along with its homely appearance, less-than-comfortable ride at top speeds, and incessant rattling, made the Model T the butt of much affectionate humor in innumerable jokes, songs, poems, and stories. Nevertheless, the guy started anyhow and ended in many wows. There are some mistakes you are expected to make as a toddler so your pencil has eraser at the bottom; there are some mistakes you are not expected to make as a scholar so your pen was denied a cleaner. Therefore, start raw in a small way, you do not need insurance fee in such magnitude if at all.

Some people want to change their personality but not their principle how hard it is. Every life pilgrimage has four wheels, a pair of wish and a pair of will, if it is a rear wheel drive of followership let the pair of will be at back and the pair of wishes at the front, if it is front wheel drive of leadership reverse it the order.

~Every dreamer possesses the wish passion,
every winner possesses the will power~

Insist to persist never desist

When excuses will not give way, a will is not yet your wheel. If you are looking for a way to excuse yourself you will find one, if you are looking for a way to execute your goal you will find. When there is a will, there is a way with time, when there is a wish there is a sway with time. When a system goal is in place, an order is invoked and time is multiplied, cost is minimized and output is in exponential. A man that refuses to dance to a tune of change is weak likewise; a man that is fused to the music is weak, for change should change with time track. No training is lost; it is a stem of knowledge as long as you live like a tree of focus you will bear the fruit. We talk through wire today because a man yesterday will work through the day, think through the night. When your idea is ripe, enough birds of men will come to taste the nectar and propagate the pollens of its seed. Idea takes time to grow, it takes time to glow, it takes time to show, and it takes time to flow.

~To fail does not make you the tail~

One of the secret of genius is power of endurance; where their intelligence wants to call it quit for the test their persistence queue still for the rest. Without persistence strategy, goals are exposed to offence tragedy by the critics and static traditions. When you succeed, you have nothing new to learn, when you fail you have something new to learn. When you succeed you have something to earn but nothing to learn, when you fail though you have nothing to earn but something to learn and that is your earning. Winners' mentality never loses, for even when they fail they learn more gain than the pain.

Live your life piece by piece with focussed energy so you do not die in pieces from diffused energy. Be a leader, holds the ladder for others to climb by starting. You are not awake from sleep, until you are at work on your dream. A working slave will soon be richer than wondering heir. Think and grow rich in mind, work and grow rich in hand. Records are set not as standard but as scaffold for higher heights. Purpose is the architect of our future; vision is the structural engineer and dreams, the surveyor while goal is the builder. So start the going. When is goes tough, go through. Failure is not a good end but not a bad foundation. Onetime success of a goal could swallow up a life time successive failures. When you finally succeed your failure becomes a teaching tool and your success reaching out tool. But you must be smart to start.

START WITH YOU

~You can be anything but you must begin
with what has been with you—you~

In a hut of an African outskirt, the young heart just finished his college education and with a great zeal, he arrived home to inform his father of his new achievement and his plan for their deprived community. His father asked, "What is your great plan all about?" He replied, "Think of changing the world," His old man replied, "But I too have a plan," the young heart asked, "what's your plan Dad?" He told him "Think of changing me." When he accused his aged dad of selfishness, why trying to change yourself when the whole community is in mess and urgent need of change not to talk of the globe? He replied, "I should have accosted you of your foolishness, for I tried to build from the roof like you but here I am today ineffective tool in the hand of time and Creator." I have failed to change my village alone nor my family as you can see.

The boy said, "Oh! I see my ignorance." "But if it happens we can't change the earth why not change our planet, I mean go to other world?"

becoming concerned, he asked. His experienced mentor replied, "The problem is not really about how to break the distance barrier of journeying to the Mars or Mercury, it is not with the container but the content." If the world moves to Mars as of today, it will mold its heart like the art on the earth. It is not about the geography but the ruling philosophy of man. The day man landed on the earth satellite—the moon, a flag was placed not of the United Nations but United States, the beginning of the process of 'MOON WAR I'. For when other countries would get there, then there will be a war of flags and later of race and color. So my son if the heart of a man can change the earth of the man will change."

Every change begins inward with a start and every start begins with a forceful range. Start small, start here, start now, and start with you, then yours and lastly your world. When the water goes up nobody sees, or hears it but when the rain falls everybody sees and hears it, the same with starting with you, it is so easier done than starting with the world. When Jesus was addressing the Jewish Pharisees, He charged the scribes and Pharisees—you blind Pharisees, cleanse first that which is within the cup and platter then the outside of them may be clean also.

Progress begins not in changing what you do, where you are, but much more who you are or think you are, by virtue of attitude. Gather all your resources including your mind and you will discover you had always had enough to start all this while."

Drain your fear

When your mind is sitting on the fence with fear on the left side and faith on the right side, tell hope to push you, I am sure you will land rightly. Excuse and execution are twin rivals of the beginning but you can always choose which to be loyal to, but you are to kill your excuse and rather execute you project. Do not let available choices cowardly determine, limit, or water down your decision and capacity. The greatest enemy of starting is not lack of money or men or material but mentality cultured on lack of ideas and stack of fears.

In Gen 1:20, God said let the waters bring forth abundantly the moving creature that hath life, and fowl [that] may fly above the earth in the open firmament of heaven. When God created the birds the primary purpose was that they might fly above the earth in the open firmament of heaven, but how come that some of them can't fly anymore and some only little height at a time above the ground unlike the rest.

Those that cannot fly I assume could be not because of weight. Aeronautically, considering the flightless Ostrich, which is 156kg, it seems, justified; but what of the inaccessible Island Rai which weighs just 34.7 gram, which also cannot fly? However, I discover that all the fish can swim, all the reptiles can crawl, and all the terrestrial animals can walk no matter their weights and sizes, but not all birds can fly. Is this not because of the trap of choice. The fish has no other choice of habitation, so they all can still swim up till today; the reptiles can still walk possibly because they have no other choice as well; but not all birds can fly anymore, possibly, because they have the choices of wings and legs—the choice to walk on ground or glide in the air.

~Options is often a limit to actions~

Be careful not to be fearful, there is tendency of fearfulness in too much carefulness. The fearful only live the life that the brave once lived, they go where the road leads and to no others place but the grave of the brave to cast roses. Their freedom is stopped at the proposal of the brave prediction; they dare not live beyond the braves' liberty. When fear pushes you to the wall you need not wish the wall collapse on you nor jump over the wall nor dig a hole through to escape but to peep and see what is beyond the wall—extinction of hope! This is more dreaded than fear; when you allow fear to suck hope out of you it has gotten more than it bargained for. It is better to face the fear you know that the fate you do not know. The aim of fear is to chase you beyond hope. It is better to face your fear than to feel safe in its prison of reasoning, because to be glued or caged in poses equal danger to your future. God makes a way when we refuse to make excuses. Greatness is in boldness. The beginning of courage is to step out to be you. Dreamers do not slip under the carpet while fear walk on it majestically. Things may fall apart but your dreams apart.

When God says, fight a good fight of faith the opponent I think must be fear and in the ring of hope. Put behind you fear and before you faith, above you hope and besides you love; resolve to incline your eyes ahead at 45^0—upward and forward then move on. It is either you sit in fear or you walk in faith, you cannot stand in neither; if you are not taking steps you are baking fear. Fear is only on errand you can bark at it or send it back. If you must fear, let it be the fear of allowing fear. Fear is magnification of lies and consolidation of deceits. When fear knocks at your door do not open the door but the window of truth for a peep and you had discover, no one present but shadows.

When a tree falls either to the north or south there it will remain but when a man falls should he remain there? No dreamer falls with so much energy that there is none to stand again. You are not a tree after all, so stand up only taller! The fear of mistake is the beginning of failure. Lead can float on water it depends on the shape of the art. Before you develop wings to fly develop legs to land, before you draw the length to go build the strength to cope which is nothing but majestic fearless faith.

A failed plan can still prosper it depends on the shape of the heart. Often people develop ideas from others failure while the victim is enveloped in the pit of pity. What some call mistake some see as a design, put some touches on it and make their way to the market. To a welder the scraps are good only for the dumpsite, to an artist they are good for museum, and they will make a great tourism. When you gather your mistakes together like the artist, you can build a monument of lessons and formula from them that generations will come to observe and learn.

A little more patience is often the beauty of patience, a little more push, a little more fight for possibility. To die without regrets you must have lived without wishes but wills. Wishes have wings but like penguins, they do not fly but swim down in to the depth. Wishes won't raise your altitude but keep it on the ground or drown it in the ocean of time. Failure is a definition of success from the back, when you turn it inside out, upside down and sideways you will have new view to success. In other word review your fallings and rise with the findings. Often many are so concerned about what fell them down that they forget about what fell off their hands meanwhile. It is better to surround yourself with people that have failed but are trying than with the people that have succeeded and retiring. You cannot soar faster than the wind speed but you can flap as fast as you wish.

~Nobody was born to fail,
we only fail to born~

NO ROAD, NOT NO WAY

A man working with a construction company was told by his boss, "Dave take the earthmover and take the road to the site. Driving a bulldozer, Dave got to point on his way to site, a junction, he saw a small sign post, on it was symbolized no road. Dave thought of what to do and seeing he had no alternative, turned back, based on his working experience about road blocking signs. When he returned to office, they asked him have you been able to get to the site. Have you done the job? He replied Sir, no road! His boss in amazement sparked at him, "That was why we sent you with the equipment." We wanted to take the road to the site. When you get to a point in life and you are told no road most of the time life is not saying you should get back rather that you should create a road. Do not make an excuse out of your mistakes; for excuses are greater mistakes. Life is like a convoy, the dignitary comes behind. Giving up is missing out after all the painful findings.

~Do not just live in path leave a path~

Clear your head, retreat and retrace

I love this story and I love you to read it. He just lost his entire business locally and internationally; thoughtfully concluded, he had no further reason to live again. He gave up the goals but worse still he thought of giving up the ghost. "Where will I start from, I have lost everything." He thought so much about taking his own life despite all the encouragements from his wife and family. The following month, he was still meditating on his ordeal when his phone rang; his wife had contacted his pastor. "Hello, Mr. Jerry, can we have appointment tomorrow to discuss?" The gentle priest requested. "Man of God; I hope it is not about my case, if it is, do not bother, it is closed. Tomorrow is the dead line I gave myself to commit suicide, thank you, see you in heaven or where about. Help me take good care of my family," responded the wealthy man as he hanged the phone. As he went to bed that night, still soaked in his termination thought, he slept off and had a dream. In the dream as he had much thought of committing suicide it happened in the dream that he attempted suicide. In his dream, he was climbing a ten story building in order that he might jump down. At the last floor, he discovered the place littered with signs "Beware of wild dogs."

He ignored the notice as a quick means to his mission he thought. So he opened the door to the observation deck. Immediately, two heavy and wild dogs banged on him, he tried to pushed them away and took to his heel but unfortunately they pursued hard after him. In fear and ignorance of the building architectural design he ran off the observation deck and down in to the sky shouting "Help I am dying." As he passed through the ninth floor, in a moment, all his entire life episode was quickly replayed at a glance, as he passed through the eight floor, he shouted oh my darling wife I will miss you what a gift you are to me, through your wise woman counsel I was able to build a great business empire, I could not imagine leaving you; as he passed through the seventh floor, he screamed Jack and Sarah what great kids are you, are you going to become fatherless at such a tender age? Oh my God; as he passed through the sixth floor, he lamented my parents how you have labored on me you will sure miss me; as he passed through the fifth floor he remembered the remaining two other business he just started to grow, who will see you to fruition? As he passed through the fourth floor, he remembered he had just become a grandfather three months ago, he cried of Sarah, your newly born twins, oh what a life filled gifts to you and our entire family; as he passed through the third floor he wished his wife could locate the document of the shares he had spent all the profits of the his business to buy and the remaining one in fixed deposit; as he passed through second floor, he suddenly remembered his first born Jack will be getting married in two months' time, oh how I wish I sit at my rightful place by myself; as he passed through the first floor he said Lord please help me, it is not worth dying! As he landed on the ground floor, he discovered the building was surround with a pool of water.

Immediately his body touched the water, he woke up from sleep. It was just 5am. He picked up his phone, dialed his pastor, "Hello," said the priest clearing his sleepy voice, "Have you changed your mind to come for the appointment?" He said, "No sir, I am not coming to your haven down there, neither am I going up to heaven up there anymore; life is good and cool. Thank you." He shouted and hanged the phone. When you do not think enough you will shrink in hope.

~Winners are not failure proof;
they are only failure proved~

What seems catchy to my eyes about the story of a young 'B student' during college and an avid surfer, a hobby which often times interfered with his studies was his decision to relax after hitting the boat with the bottom of the rock twice. Went on surfing vacation only to return with a blue print of what turned out to go viral. He was not born a billionaire. Prior to the advent of his widely known camera style—a brand of wearable cameras—GoPro, he was humbled and downed by market forces twice of his two consecutive establishments—EmpowerAll.com, an e-commerce site which was hurriedly shut down after a loss outing. Also, in 1999 he set up FunBug, an online marketing company.

This also crashed with the $3.9 million funding he solicited from various investors. The young heart was only knocked down but not knocked out of the business ring. He was defeated but not deflated. Countered but not conquered. He remained in admitting his failure, but two years after, he was able to successfully launch out. In Forbes report, he summarized his failure adventure that weighed $4 million dollars: He succinctly put it does "I mean nobody likes to fail, but the worst thing was I lost my investors' money and these were people that believed in this young guy that was passionate about this idea... you start to question: are my ideas really good?"

Following the dual losses he cleared his head from past failure shadow by going on a surf trip, a long one. On returning, he commenced the project—a wearable camera which can be used by athletes, named it GoPro. He said he was afraid to rise the third time like many feel as well, scared he might fail again like the first two outings but the rest is story. GoPro became fastest-growing camera company in America, listing him as one of the youngest billionaires with capital net-worth of $1,750,000,000 at a time. You always have something left to fall back on, either a physical asset or mental asset. Never fall on your back and stayed grounded. If you want more happiness, risk more happenings! Sometimes you need to throw the baby away with the water believing the baby will craw back. Sometimes you need to let go of your coat and your cloak.

~Sometimes you need to lose your
weight to gain your height~

Sometimes you need to leap in faith before you see the facts. You need to lose some emotional weights of anxiety, fear and the rest, to attain the height you desire. Let your birth be a prize to the world and your death a price to the world through your adventurous life style. You do not need two long legs measuring 6400km before you walk the earth. You do not need longer legs to walk faster; you need only a starting step and strong legs. Winners quit everything for their goals; losers quit their goal for anything that stands across their path, they stand for nothing and fall for anything. Fear is the problem around their solution.

Your relationship may be one of those areas you will need to retrace your time investment. There are moments of loneliness in life and there are moments of aloneness. The higher the mountain altitude the narrower the area; the peak things up, the apex narrows up, you will have to be very choosy in your relationship if you want to reach the topmost top. Some people are merely wants in your life and some are needs in your life, when you increase the rent of accommodation of your time they will be sorted out. True friends hold themselves in the hand not at heart.

The mother eaglet asked the eaglets what is our limit to fly the sky? The eaglets echoed, the cloud, and the experienced mother replied "No! Not the cloud." She asked again, and they chorused the wind, again she said, "No!" "Rather our wings, our fears, our sight and especially our ostrich friends."

Walk the sand of time with your footprint and not shoe print—be real, step out from behind your mask. You cannot matter when you live like a matter like you only have mass but no mind of your own; you occupy space but like a shadow of another life. As you sail through the day's voyage and have opportunity to look at the time, do not be concerned with how many hours are left but how many hours you live are right? How much have you lived? There is a thin difference between activity and productivity. Bees are not busy for fun, honey is the evidence.

You need to move in head before you move ahead. We celebrate today, people whose signboard reads success, but they have legs of failure concretized on the ground of their dreams. You are what you think. All you need is 99% of findings and 1% feelings to start. You can start from the scratch but not from the past. Sometimes you need to unlearn how you succeed to reach the next sky. Death is not the ultimate thing but the final thing, the ultimate thing is to live in absence and die for nothing. Never be intimidated from doing dreadful things that are needful to leave behind. Create a path, and if opportunity is not coming yet walk in the path yourself to look for its advert, and do not turn if the advert is promoting adversity. What you love, love it with passion and whatever you hate, hate it with passion, and love what is right—your dream your goal.

~The sky is not the limit for the stars,
only a platform to view them~

Chapter Four

BELIEVE IN YOUR TALENT

~Go for joy not job~

A boy needed a picture of a bird to be hanged in his room so he picked his drawing materials and began work. When he was almost done a bird flew close to his window and perched on the hood. Suddenly, he thought of how wonderful it would be if he could get three dimensional prototype. At the end, he did not like what he drew as it only provided him with a two dimensional image. He said to himself he wanted something he could hold in his hand and possibly play with like a toy. When he told his father, he counseled; you would need to get to the bush to catch a living one as alternative since we can't afford a toy bird as a farmer. So he decided to go look for a living prototype he could hold in his hand as alternative.

As he walked in the bush, he saw a tree with holes in it. Suddenly, a woodpecker flew out of the hole followed by another five. He waited and watched as the bird flew back in to their home some minutes later with food. So he taught of what to do to get the birds thinking at least these are good prototypes—though a living one. After much brainstorming, he told himself, "I could not climb the tree, I have neither gun nor snare, this is what I would do, I will quickly chop the tree down and catch as many birds as I want." Therefore, he went for an axe and in rapid successions fell the tree. As the tree was being impacted, the birds as well had sensed a danger and were afraid to go out. As the tree fell to the ground he was exited and quickly reached out to get a net for the catch, but he was a bit late, the birds also had perceived the feller had relaxed and quickly, they flushed out of their hole home.

As he looked up to move to the hole he saw the birds one by one flying out, he tried to rush close and catch at least one but he was not smart enough, they all flew away. He got to the hole, searched thoroughly but found none in the tree any more. Disturbed and disappointed he packed his materials and was about going home when suddenly a man approached him. He asked him, "Were you the one who fell this tree?" "Yes," he replied. Young boy, this is a good tree for my job, I have been eyeing this tree for long, it used to house some birds an indication of its good quality for my job, could you please sell it for me?

The exhausted boy gladly said, "Why not at least to compensate my effort; he thought." So the man bought it and as well made a request, he said, "My son could you please do me a favor, as you can see I am an old man, there is no way I could carry this tree all alone, could you please lend me a helping hand, my hut is not far away?" So the boy consented to help the man, cut the log in to small pieces and carried them one by one to the door step of the man's hut waiting for him to open the door and move them inside.

When the man opened the door the boy shouted, screamed, "This is what I am looking for!" The old man wondered, what do you mean, is there any special thing in my home that you want? "Yes, many things; everything! Sir, look at them, my dreams, and my desires all littered your compound"—the well-sculptured birds of different types, well designed and painted. This is what I have been looking for. "Sir, can you please give me one? I want a bird prototype that I can place in my room, to see and play with like a toy and that was why I went in search of living birds as alternative. I tried to draw one but was just two dimensional not handy or real, and my father could not afford toys either." The man said but there used to be some birds living in the tree you fell.

He said it is true sir, "But I have lost everything as I was cutting the tree, they all flew away." The man looked at him the disturbed boy and said, in that wise, no, for there are still birds in the tree. The boy said no, "It is empty, I have searched it carefully, nothing sir but a log of useless wood, merely good for firewood." However, the man insisted that there are still bird prototypes you originally wanted inside the tree. As the boy was about to argue further he said, "My son sit down a while." The boy sat down and in the next few hours, the old sculptor was busy hammering, chiseling, and carving the wood. At the launch time a beautiful bird emerged out of the tree logs he brought home, to further his aesthetics he painted it, put it in the sun to dry, all the while the boy was looking in amazement and wonder. When it was finally ready, he gave it to the boy. He said as you can see, there are still birds in the tree good for your dream prototype. As the man handed it to the boy, he added, you can have this as compensation for your kind gesture of helping me transporting the log down here. I will use the remaining length to make more birds for my trade, thanks. The boy went home partly happy and partly sad. Happy because he was given one prototype; sad because he could have had much more if he had known more of the hidden potentials in the tree. He could have taken the time to go for training on how to be a sculptor he once heard his father mentioned.

You are not empty because your past has exhausted you. You are not empty because you have lost and failed five or six times. There is still a potential in you to make you achieve God's best for you. You may need to go for training as the boy later realized. All you need could be some patience to let God take you to the next level of your potential. Sometimes we sell out ourselves because we thought we are not that valuable anymore, because life has had its time on us. We go about like a hopeless log of wood. We look for those who could employ us or engage us cheaply. We are desperate to get the least value of our self-image that our selfish world could offer us. The birds came to live in the tree and so they could be able to fly away but the inbuilt bird of the tree will forever stay with the boy. The world may give and take or down look your credentials, which they gave you, but your potential no one can take from you. It is yours forever—it is the Makers doing.

~Focus more on your potentials
than your credentials~

Do not end up having just one bird and having the rest sold out. Jacob had been selling out his potentials to Laban and all he could get was a household but nothing to provide for them. Then one day he chose to take charge of his potential, he chose to be self-employed, enough of selling my talent so cheaply to heartless employers. He ended up getting all the possibilities in him. Do not sell away your potential so cheaply, when time is dawning on you that employer will definitely dump you. Value your God giving ability and maximize it. Jesus said do not cast your pearls before swine lest they trample over it and turn back to hit you. You might have lost something but definitely not everything. The prodigal son lost many things but not everything. His potential of son ship bailed him out mercifully.

~Do not take up a job gift that will
make your giftings jobless~

The heart is very deep we cannot finish drilling out the resources but for a lifetime. Solomon in one of his proverbs said counsel in the heart of a man is like deep water and a man of understanding will draw it out. Little things in little way in little time, by a brittle man for a consistent time is the secret and strength of many folks in the hall of fame. He who discovers his potential discovers something. He who discovers his purpose discovers many things. He who discovers his personality discovers everything. You can't know yourself until you unmask yourself from the world's opinion and your own illusive conclusion.

There is no little man without a little mind about himself and possibilities of his potentials. If you want to be efficient in life be everybody, if you want to be effective be yourself. If you can't be relevant in your absence your presence has really worth little. It shows you have not offered something unique that will serve as your trademark. Your weakness can defeat your strength depending on which you focus. Show me any success story and I will point you to the bottom-line of the climb—a man who has enough gut to believe in his gift and in his God. Nobody can live with influence without courage to let be his difference.

Courage is the cart of talent that will drag it through the time of training and polishing, through the time of castigation and intimidation, it will pump it with hope and strength when deflated by giants' shadow. To observe your weakness you may need to reserve your strength when there is a need. After you have left what is right, you cannot be right in what is left. Do not be present where your gifting is not recognized as a present to them. If you claim to love me them you must love my shadow as well, I mean you must accept my weakness as well. My shadow is inseparable.

THE SEED OF DESTINY

~Privilege is sometimes a trap to
live less under a siege~

There are five battles of life: battle over possessor: who or what you surrender your existence to; battle over possession: who or what you acquire in lifetime; battle over personality: who and what people see you to look like; battle over purpose: who or what you are; battle over potential: who or what you can be. The number one person to admire you is God, the second is you and the third is you uniqueness. Do not let your judgment of value be attended to in the court of social opinions. Do not let the water of public echoes be your mirror to study yourself from time to time, the fish of men will stir the water and produce the blurred image of you. Rather view yourself in the mirror of God's mind—His word: you look inside to the best you can be that no man can deny, for you will secured within, your dream of larger than life.

Despite their reputation, pigs are neither dirty nor stupid. They are naturally clean creatures and are among the most intelligent of all domestic animals—even more intelligent than dogs but they are not found in the sitting room because of their outlook and where they look for food and choose to relax. Do not allow the way people see you to sieve out the seed in you as chaff. Do not allow where you are placed determine what is placed in you.

When you get to the bank, you will be asked to identify yourself, to get what belongs to you. The same when you get to the reality of life it will ask you to identify yourself by your potential to demand what your Maker has reserved in your destiny bank. Identity is the pathway of celebrity. It is the seed of destiny. Everywhere you feature in life, they issue you new identity card, when you get admission to school, when you get a new job, when you go for banking, when you become a national, when you want to be a voter, when you join a club, when you join an association and the list goes on; the same with life, everywhere you go in life beware, for people will always want to give you a new identity, they will want you to behave in their cultural attitude, talk like them, think like them and be like them. However, the choice is yours, to paint your face, take up a mask or just be you.

It is good to have a role model but here is the definition of abuse of a role model. The queue of men, young and old behind a star, celebrity or hero, the line is so straight that when the roll is given a front elevation view all you see is the front liner.

~Free things sometimes
take away our freedom~

The rest behind fall in line with the hero's shadow and they are out of purpose sight. Everywhere the train of these lives goes all the world sees is the front personality. There dressing, talking, looking, aspiration, dreams and character have become absorbed in the image before them—like queue of faces they live behind the mask. The highest freedom is not when your nation gets independence from colonization but when your nature gets independence from imitation and intimidation of others success—when are you through to be yourself; when you are bold to live the cocoon of men and face the cold reality of purposeful success; when you are ready to pay the price for your own unique voice and difference. Shoe sizes are all applied in approximation for no two men's feet are actually of the same size. But life should not be treated as such; people should not be generalized just because they are of the same color, race or national. Many who have sold their identity never realize they have actually sold their birthright. You cannot live life to fullest until you fall in love with yourself—until you can be happy with your picture, your structure, treasure, your features and your future.

Though in life, we can't escape the influences of the relationship we come in contact with, our parents will deposit a great portion, then our friends, bosses, mentors and leaders, spouses and siblings, but above all, the good we will finally absorbed from all this should be used as a paint on the edifice of our identity, it should be to garnish our gifting, to give feathers to our dream wings and not to replace our identity structure.

Do not let your life be built of paints, and decorations, have you seen a building that is built of painting and decoration? That is why some people only live as shadows, they run fast, they live vast but they exit like the never exist. Their identity was laminated all through their stay on this geographical citadel. They submitted their lives as scaffold for others to build their selfish ambition. So after the role models are done they have them discarded.

A boy just returned from hospital after collecting injection. He tried to figure out the exact point the needle passed through to deliver the drug but he could not see it. Yet he was convinced that there was a hole but so tiny through which the health officer had passed the needle. It was so tiny but could allow 10 ml of liquid. Do you know that it is the same way things are passed across to our mind by the enemy? Just a little careless hole is all Satan needs to pass into us all manners of negative thoughts. A little anxiety, a little fear, a little worry, a little depression, and a little anger; just a little is all required to keep the battle in your mind all day long. A mushroom is enough for Satan to make much room for his weapons needed for the battlefield of your mind. At the end, we can't really say where or when it started. So watch out for the injection of opinions that sneaks in to your life to take over the throne of identity.

~Give no room to negativity,
not a mushroom~

Sometimes you need to be your own first audience, your own referee and critics and appraisers. If you do not do this to yourself, you will be affected when others do it too little or too much to you.

Go back to yourself

~If you are looking for who to blame
for your failure do not use a telescope
just a mirror will do~

A young girl followed her mum to a choir rehearsal. During a recess, she found her way to the microphone stand. Sneakily, she spoke faintly in to the microphone and heard herself from the speaker but not as loud as she wished. So she decided to realize her goal and gradually moved towards the speaker raising her voice but she discovered the more faintly she heard herself. That is the case of many dreamers. When then want to get inner drive for the next set of goals they move towards the crowd for feedback, but often, the crowd have nothing encouraging to say. The young girl should have rather moved closer to the microphone and raise her voice and not the speaker. The same with you if you want to hear word of motivation do not get close to the crowd for comments rather get closer to your inbuilt microphone and speak to it. This is your conviction and vision. They will amplify back to you what you wish to hear loudly.

~When goal is imitation,
limitation is imminent~

Do not just consider the height of the ladder you want to climb consider your own weight as well, do not just jump in to open doors of opportunity consider your own dream continuity. Do not just fling in to opportunity of connection consider your own direction. It is not the color of wings that determines the height of flight but the strength and the length—your best is in your depth of discovery. You can fly beyond your length of knowledge and the strength of passion. There is no traffic in the sky because each flier makes his road. If you are held to a halt in life, possibly, you are stuck to the common sense. If you want to count the stars you will not live to give the account of your report, the same with those who live to discuss people, philosophy, places and personality, they end life without a reference. Change your topic, change your song to who you are and you will change your range of achievement and audience.

Not every employment employs your mental capacity to optimal; some will just keep you alive; spirit soul and body. You have the best hidden in you, and for you to market it you have to show that you believe in what you have to offer and look it. A sales rep with unsure and uncertain tone will of course find it difficult to convince potential buyer. Some analysts have argued, for example, that John F. Kennedy's relaxed and self-confident manner, as well as his good looks, aided him in his debate with Richard Nixon and contributed to his narrow victory in the presidential election of 1960, because of the potential impact and the enormous audience of the debates. Be confident and conscious of your God designed assignment from the heart more than man assigned employment on earth.

~You are born with something,
but you need to burn to born it~

Dare to live inside out

Genius are those guys who discover their work, then think on it, talk of it, wait on it, search on it, eat on it, sleep on it , fight for it, hide in it and then make it a wow and wonder to their world. The force of gravity can stop you from going up but cannot stop you from growing up; when you choose to build on your roots—originality, you can't but beat the limits. Why? Because you are growing not just going about as a shadow. The seed of self-discovery is heavy because it has life, when you throw it into the ocean of time it sinks to the bottom of competitive planet, not with a lost hope for it takes root, and begins to germinate sooner; though it appears raw, uncommon and longer. Your decision to embrace yourself will speak in time to come. When time fulfils its purpose on it, the truth shoots its stem and rises above the water level, at such appearance it catches men by surprise and before they interpret what has happened it begins to bear fruits of revelations and revolution. At that period the seed of fake lifestyle is rounding up its time as it rots away from the scorch of the sun of rising generations; the remnant is blown away by the wind of change. That is often the lot of fake lifestyle.

Our skin color is just like clothing's of many colors if we all remove it we discover we were born inwardly equal and with no anatomy disparity. He who wants to be free financially doesn't work for money but with money; nor live for monument but fulfillment. Physical slavery is when a man is sold in to bondage; psychological slavery is when a man sells himself for acceptance. Freedom is found in the terrain of knowledge of your inner value.

~The force of gravity can stop you
from going up but can't stop you
from growing up~

Let the world see the world in you, do not squeeze in to the mold of culture, mentors, tradition, beliefs, norms, philosophy or obtained ability; rather let your skin be the mold for your self-esteem and your dreams for your purpose. You need to separate your credential dreams form potential dreams. Until you are able to define your life apart from certificate you can't refine your capacity; until you can remove the mask you can't begin your own original task; until you can have right birth of self-image you can't discover your birth right of destiny.

This is how it sometimes starts when you are given a nickname base on your habit that was not your intention but the lost contention to the force of influence. Then with time, the same weak mind begins to tailor the outfit of his character and self-image in the measure of his definers and designers. Your aka should be checked before you check in into the mold if it's not a picture of whom you have discovered to be by purpose then have it stopped. What people call you often will calve out your behavior thereafter.

Raw talents litter the gravesite; refined talents litter the stage sight. It doesn't matter whether your talent is written in italic, upper case or lower case, it does change the message it conveys. People can complain about your life lettering but always know that the handwriting is still the handiwork of God and it is for a purpose and the message is unchangeable. Every talent is a gift and every gift is a responsibility. Raw talent has many times been treated as flaw.

~Your talent is your greatest idea~

GO FOR JOY NOT JOB

I once read about a woman who got engaged in more than 30 jobs at different times and locations before finally found the right one for her fulfillment. I mean the one she derived joy and contentment from. Joy and job are inseparable at the bottom line of every achiever's story. Many have remained at the low helm of endeavor because they had gone for job and not joy. The worth of your vocation should be the amount of joy it brings not the amount of money. If you see 4pm as an escape velocity each day at work, you may never experience the desired acceleration you wish in your carrier. I once came across a gardening fact about the honeybee that to produce a single pound of honey, a single bee would have to visit two million flowers. You can see that bee must be happy in the hive for honey to be available.

You cannot be joyless and not be jobless at last either commercially or mentally. One day a prisoner who had spent 30 years in the prison since he was sentenced to life imprisonment once asked the prison warder for the date. This inmate had been locked up in the underground cell, and hardly sees the sun making it difficult to know when it dawns and the dusks, therefore becoming impossible for him to know date and time. The warder laughed and laughed. When he was through the man who had been wondering what caused the laughter said, what's funny? The warder replied, you made me laugh, what do you want to use the date for? You are here for a lifetime imprisonment so what is the purpose of you monitoring the date?

The old man humbly said, "Young man, I knew when you came here—when you were newly employed; I knew it was the day I clocked 50years for I had only spent a day here. Ever since, I had wished a day will come when you will be liberated. All the years you have been here I have noticed your sad countenance about your job, the way you treat us and your assignment showed you were really doing what you do not like, and you are like what your life should not portray. You are literarily in the prison of depression and discouragement, coupled with you lamenting for the state of your finances. You often talked to yourself about your family, complaining that you have been leaving them every morning in sorrow of going to the work you had wished not be and retuning every night with burdens of the ordeals at work. You had never enjoyed a moment with your work.

> ~Everybody dies of something either
> of old age or otherwise but very few
> die for something~

Ever since, I have been looking forward to the day you will be free which never came, but I know when you reach retirement age you will be set free from this prison. That was why I asked for the date my son. I wanted to know how approaching your freedom year is. I want you to be happy as I am here. Every day I had prayed for your freedom. So can you please answer my question that I may know how long or short I will still need to pray until you regain your long desiring freedom?" The young man told the old man he was sorry. From there they became friends. One day he asked the man what brought him to the prison? The old man humbly began, "I was an engineer and I worked for the prison ministry. I was put in charge of constructing the prison structure and I hated the job like you too and this led me to delegating the foundational work to my junior. Out of inexperience they made a mistake about the design which led to the gradual sinking of the structure.

When the ground floor had finally sunk below the ground level the building stopped sinking and the consultant engineer finally confirmed it safe for habitation. As you know the law of the field, I was sued and sentenced to imprisonment. It finally happened that I was put in the ground floor where you met me and where I serve my term, this explain the inability of any one here not to see the sunlight and become ignorant of the date. From then the young man learnt the disadvantages of not being happy with your work. The old inmate added, this made me to learn to rejoice with my work and wish everyone I come in contact with to do the same. I am serving my term with joy now and I wish you serve your nation with joy as well."

Do not look for a job that you will be looking for how to escape from every evening and having to surrender to every morning. If there is anything you do, that gives you joy look for how you can turn it to job then you will have a lifelong vacation not vocation. The economy is full of employees looking for job; the problem is not unemployment really but unemployed mentality.

~Blessed is he who has found
his work. Let him ask no other
blessedness~ Thomas Carlyle

THE LATENT TALENT

It seems even nations are gifted as a race in a particular field of life race. As I came in contact with the citizenship of some computer geniuses in our contemporary world, with good chunk hailing from Israel as Jews—talking about brains behind Facebook, Oracle, Dell computers and Google partners; coming down to football as a sport you have country like Brazil mostly producing the world's best. Indian get good chunk of national income from her health skills; education and innovations are synonymous to South Korea, China keep dominating table tennis, etc I have a slight conviction of this school of thought. Down to individuals, we are encoded differently. No dual souls are repetition. The Bible said God fashioned out hearts turn by turn.

~He fashions their hearts
 individually~

You are fearfully and wonderfully designed, designated and delivered to this place. A parable was told by the Master about a servant who went to bury his talent in the ground. That is quite a safe place to preserve it—for the grave; like a wise mentor once humorously said that the grave site is the richest place on earth lavished with numerous untapped potentials and talents. The servant did it out of fear and ungratefulness to the giver. Many people as well do the same today. They are afraid of exposing their raw gift to harsh weather of competition and opposition. They prefer to keep it in a safe place. But you need to let the baby stamp its feet on the ground; to fall and rise, to rise and fall; to stagger and stumble. You need to be merciless with your potentials, let it face the reality of responsibility. So what is that thing that is unique about you that is lying fallow or fearfully buried?

A boy and a girl were given seeds by their parents to use as counter in solving their arithmetic problems. Over the months, they had lost some of them as they were out growing the usage of counters. Their wise mother who wanted to create a memory for them to pass on to their children advised them to plant those seed in the family garden, so that it can reproduce the same seed in volume for future use and as family memory treasure. The boy went out, dug the ground, put the seed and covered it with the soil. However, the girl was so emotional about the seed which she had used to solve a lot of problems; she would not wish them go like that. Therefore, she watched his brother planting instead of following the same procedure she deviated. After digging the hole, she placed the seed and refused to cover it with soil. She thought how can I burry such a friend wickedly. Moreover, it will be difficult for it to emerge having to struggle all the way through the earth crust. They left. After one month they went to the site and behold the brother's seed had become a seedling while his sister's seed was partially rotten.

Every seed passes through pressure into lime light. The same with our dreams and talents they seem to come buried and require that we water them until they push through the limitation of world opposition and discredits. The resisting soil is like the criticism; it is needed for your seed dream to emerge otherwise it lies rotten like that girl's. So do not try to avoid or run away from opposition rather let them incubate and germinate your seed, taking advantage of them as the soil required. Those who wish their idea is never opposed so hiding them in comfort are like the younger sister, you will have it rotten at the grave site at old age.

Let your seed talent pull out from the cocoon of small starting like the pupa of butterfly, which is what will fine-tune the beauty of future color and glory. The soil supplies the seed with nutrient and waters, the same with your dream some of the vitamins and energy you need to drive your dream cart will be obtainable from your critics and critical situation. Do not wish all the way for an open heaven when the rain comes directly on your seed, that it has no need to suck it from the soil, such will end up washing away your seed or over water it.

I once read of a wealthy couple who went dropping their kid who just gained admission as an undergraduate at the school. They dropped but not like common parents for he was checked in not into a hostel or two rooms rented apartment but in a $1.5m town home purchased for him around the school. Five bed rooms. 4.5 bath residence and with a butler service. A successful banker and wife just gave their child the best gift they thought ideal. Not only that four shipping crates were sent containing everything he could ever wanted. That is a great start and that is what we all desire from God. But what do we desire in life, a great start or a great end? God is a parent and a wise one in deed. He will rare you with love not luxury, with self-confidence not inter-dependence, with self-esteem and not self-ego.

~Water can wash anything clean but water;
only you can discover your best~

Do not be scared of shortcomings when you choose to be original. To dare to be oneself is to lose ones footing momentary, not to dare is to lose oneself to human commentary. Everything God created was first good but not perfect. Nothing, nobody and nowhere is perfect. For long scholars assumed that the moon is a perfect and flawless circle in shape. But when the science was upgraded and astronauts moved nearer and nearer they discovered clearer and clearer the imperfection. The moon looks perfect at the surface when viewed from the earth but when you land on it you will discover that it has a rough surface: just like the earth it is full of mountains, hills, crater and lakes. Jesus when called the good man reacted; no one is good but God.

All you need in life to build the strongest self-esteem is to have and know deepest that one person love you deepest and that person know you deepest and has the highest plan for you. We often wish that the cloud will lighten up before we shine our light, but it doesn't do that for the sun. The sun begins to shine at the face of the cloud until an opportunity comes amidst the cloud to reach out to us. The sun is always ready and so catches up with every opportunity the cloud reveals.

Rough diamond believes in its worth but do you believe in your raw? God created everything good but not all are polished. Every creature of God is pregnant of something new. The trees, the seas, the land, the sky and the man; inside of all are potentials to bring out something desirable but not available yet. Solomon said [It is] the glory of God to conceal a thing: but the honor of kings [is] to search out a matter. You are more than what you look outside; your container may determine your shape but neither your content nor capacity, for you shall expand to the right and to the left but it starts with inward explosion. No seed is too small to germinate; the power of growth is not being controlled by the size of the seed but the size of the field—your dream. The power of any talent is not concealed or limited by the size of the beginning but the space of the mind and resilience of courage.

Focus on your abilities

~A life without focus is never
distracted, itself is a distraction~

Riding in a car on the freeway my eyes caught up with an automobile workshop where a car jack was being used to suspend a trailer. The jack looked too small for the task but it accomplished it. Have you as well considered how you can use a simple jack to lift your automobile? Naturally speaking you cannot lift it with your human strength but this small device stand in the gap to magnify your strength somehow. The working of the system is not that it adds more power to yours as it involves just a thread around a rod. No prime mover. So what happens? Do you know that it is still your strength alone that lifts the car? What the jack does is to concentrate your muscle glucose to such a small lifting height of a thread length and like a converging lens, it focuses lifting the car in very small seemingly insignificant height per time. For every turning action of the device the car rises in very slight hardly noticeable height. The same with your resources: emotional, mental and financial. You can achieve more than ordinary by simply engaging the power of extra focus attribute.

A teenager named Paulo wanted to become a writer. Writing was his passion, and his gift. His parents, however, felt he would do better pursuing a career in law, and suggested to him that he do his writing in his spare time. Whatever his parents said, Paulo stuck to his guns, insisting that he would devote his life to writing. To help him change his mind, his mother and father had him committed to a mental institution, where he was submitted to electroshock treatment to "cure" him of his dream. In total, he was committed three times, and underwent electroshock treatment repeatedly. Was he cured of his desire to write? It seems not. Paulo Coelho is the best-selling Portuguese-language author of all time. His books have sold tens of millions of copies and have been translated into over 60 languages. Your developed originality, despite depravity, is the shortest route to stardom. Bees are always working and what they produce is sweetened not just sweating because they are at what they love to do and are created to do. When you begin to do what you love you will live it. The weather determines our type of dress, but what influence the color? Our choice! People may determine what you do per time but what influence what you think or feel about your person it is your choice of focus.

Do not let your responsibility detract you from your ability. To every life lived there are two basic abilities just like the energy terms—kinetic and potential. Some spend theirs to exercise and maximize their kinetic ability but never engage their potential ability; they are always on the move but never change heights or positions. They roam in the same altitude for a time like a plane trying to escape a threatening weather. Some live and base their life on their potential ability; they are full of proactive thoughts and unbeatable imagination yet they live like a clip-bird, they never soar. It is time to balance your potential energy with kinetic, I mean put your discoveries to work through focus. A physics teacher once tried to digress from the norm of science in motivating his students, so he took them in to a gym.

He asked them to mount the scale for their weights. They all have it measured. Then he asked them can you weigh more than that? They said in the future. However, he insisted that they should go and weigh again now not only standing on it but also jumping up gradually. The first guy stood on it and weighed 60kg. He asked him to jump up 6 inches he landed on the scale with a reading of 70 kg; again, he jumped up one foot and read 80 kg. When he came down the professor told them sometimes in life you determine your worth by the virtue of the combination of all your endowed ability. In other words, engage both your potential and kinetic talent.

Refuse to be trimmed

A woman just bought a house as she travelled down to the Asian side of the globe in pursuit of her career, which was well garnished with flower; the flowers were planted in pots and still in there tender stages. As a lover of flower, the woman began to prune the flowers, which were of diverse species with a particular one, which was meant to be transplanted as it had the tendency to grow in to a beautiful flowery tree. But the mistress was ignorant of the species of flower due to her native back ground as a westerner. As the flower began to grow she continued to trim them all to the same size to give a well structured aesthetic outlook.

Doing this, ignorantly limited the flowery tree from expressing its capacity. Two years later the particular flower's root began to press against the plastic flower pot while the woman continued to trim it to the same miniature size as the rest. A day came that the root forced itself out of the plastic pot breaking it in the process. After three months it had become obvious to the woman and her visitors. Being embarrassed and disgusted about the broken pot right there at her entrance and the splitting of water from the hole made to the floor anytime she watered it, she got fed up and thought of how better to handle the plant. She took out the pot and dumped it at the back yard.

When a neighbor who was from the same country saw the pot, she asked the woman do not you need the flower again? The woman replied, it is of no use to me, it couldn't meet up with my limited space. She finally gave it to the man who was well knowledgeable of the plants nature. He took it to his garden and transplanted the plant. The woman finished with her course went back only to come back after few years for continuation. She went to her neighbor to say hello and announce her arrival only to discover he was away. But something struck her sight a beautiful tree she had never seen in her life, laden with gorgeous flower with a naturally trimmed figure. Still in her wonder land, when the wife of the man came back from grocery store.

After exchanging greetings, she asked her about the flowery tree; where they got it and how she could get one. The woman smiled and said, "Do you mean it or you are just pulling my legs?" "No, I meant it," she said. The Turkish woman answered, "But my husband said you gave him while you were about leaving, in fact I was about appreciating you on his behalf when you just asked about it. It is a very expensive flower here and rarely successfully cultured. So when my husband got it as a gift we were so exited." Those who are ignorant of your value and potential in life will do nothing other than trimming every of your motive and pruning your uncommon move.

They will generalize your ability and try to limit it to what is obtainable around them. But men can place a barrier over your plans but only you can limit your dreams. As long as you continue to dream and believe, one day your rooted determination will break the barrier, they will become uncomfortable with your passion and get out of your way. You will be found by those who will appreciate your value and ability, and someday they will come back to admire you.

Remember Joseph, they tried to curtail his dream but when he kept on having dreams they were not comfortable with him, sold him out to the men who value his treasure with. Potiphar recognized his gift and grace and maximize it. Pharaoh also entertained his potential and through that he became a beautiful personality to desire and admire. His brother finally came to embrace his destiny.

David brother shunned him to go back to the sheep fold rather, he was determined to fight; he left his critic brother and moved on to those who have answer to his reward question until he got in contact with Saul that sensed the grace of God upon him and gave him a chance to manifest. Later the bible said his entire family came to him in the wilderness to seek fortress.

Body dimension of purpose

If you are naturally fat, thin, short or tall it is for a purpose; your anatomy dimension is for a purpose. You are purpose customized, intention design and a piece in a jig jaw puzzle of Master's plan. If you try to change your container, which is practically impossible but illusionary realistic, you will deprive your content a productive place to pour in to; and like piece of jig jaw puzzle you affect the big picture of your maker's master plan.

The first seven U.S. astronauts were chosen for Project Mercury in April 1959. They were selected from some 500 candidates, all members of the U.S. military. Each candidate was required to have experience as a pilot of high-performance jet aircraft and, because of the cramped conditions inside the Mercury spacecraft, to be no more than 5 feet 11 inches (180 cm) tall and weigh no more than 180 pounds (82 kg). The Soviet Union selected 20 air force pilots from 102 candidates for cosmonaut training in February 1960. These individuals also had to meet restrictions on height (170 cm, or 5 feet 7 inches) and weight (70 kg, or 154 pounds) because of the small size of the Soviet Vostok spacecraft.

One of these 20 young men, Yury Gagarin, became the first human in space with his April 12, 1961, one-orbit flight.

You can see that many basketball superstars are automatically limited to be an astronaut. For example, Michael Jordan is 6 feet plus. Your shape was customized to the purpose of your content. You can choose to accept your container and give the content express expression and freedom of manifestation or you listen to the crowd pushing you to panel beat your design orientation. Great men are born but not with greatness they live to born it.

~Little mind discus the product, average
mind discus the price, great mind discus
the process ~

The smart leaders had developed the capacity to take advantage of disadvantages. At 6 feet 5 inches (1.96 meters), Bolt defied the conventional wisdom that very tall sprinters are disadvantaged as fast starters. In 2007 he appeared newly dedicated to his training and earned a silver medal in the 200 meters at the world championships. He also persuaded his coach to let him try the 100 meters, and he ran 10.03 sec in his first professional race at the distance. In 2008 he lowered his best time to 9.76 sec, then the world's second fastest mark. Four weeks later in New York City, Bolt broke the world record, running 9.72 sec to defeat world champion Tyson Gay.

Do not let your body dimension deflects you to wrong mission, consider as well your soul reflection and heaven's intention. The world record breaker in 2008 Olympic 100 meters is just one inch shorter than the big don of Michael Johnson. Michael 6ft 6in, Bolt 6ft 5in. What people call disadvantage is the desired advantage in the heart of an optimist. At the 2008 Olympic Games, Bolt became the first man since American Carl Lewis in 1984 to win the 100-meter, 200-meter, and 4 × 100-meter relay in a single Olympics and the first ever to set world records (9.69 sec, 19.30 sec, and 37.10 sec, respectively) in all three events. His 0.66-sec winning margin in the 200-meter race was the largest in Olympic history, and his 0.20-sec edge over the second-place finisher in the 100 meters, despite beginning his victory celebration about 80 meters into the race, was the largest since Lewis won by the same margin. At the 2009 world championships, Bolt shattered his 100-

meter record, winning the event final in 9.58 sec. Four days later he broke his own 200-meter record by the same 0.11-sec margin to win a second gold medal at the world championships.

You have a secret fitness

In the North Africa there was an Arabian trader who makes sales exceptionally. He happened to have three animals: a goat, a camel and a donkey. Every trip the man would lade the donkey and the camel with goods to be sold while the goat will be merely dragged along the journey. On their return the man would have sold all the goods carried by the donkey and the camel. This happened all the time and the camel and donkey began to be proud of their being useful to their master. They bragged about it. The goat overheard their boasting and became discouraged. Every time I left home empty and returned without accomplishing anything. One day the goat refused to follow the man and the man asked for the reason, it explained but the man said that it was as useful to him as the other animals.

As they journeyed on the next trip, the goat managed to escape as they were approaching the market thinking, "I am tired of standing there all day long without contributing anything to the great and regular sales of my caring master." The owner began to look for it but to no avail. The goat had run back home. That day the man made virtually no sale, hence a serious problem for the donkey and the camel. They will have to carry the load on the return journey. When they finally got home they were almost dead and there they met the goat sleeping. The man moved in to the fold and shouted at the goat, "Why have you done this to us?" The goat pleaded and apologised. The man said look at the goods we took there, we returned everything. Your colleagues are dying. The goat asked "But why no sales, after all it has nothing to do with my ability unlike my colleagues with strength?"

In the presence of the three, he began to reveal the secrets of their unusual sales record. In the village where we use to take our goods to, there is no goat. So anytime they are opportune to see one they will go and call everybody to come and watch. This is what you goat have been helping us to achieve, once the people come around they come not just only to have a closer and longer look at you, in the process they buy whatever we have in return. You have been the secret of our great sales all this while. Meekness is knowing your value in the eyes of God and refuse to neither add to it nor allow the world to remove from it. What you are is greater than what you have. You have a secret potential that the world will miss despite all the invention going on around the globe.

Garnish your talent with your style

~Without effort talent is nothing;
without talent effort is something;
but with the duo are many things~

Emil Zátopek, known as the "bouncing Czech," didn't look like the picture of Olympic grace. Although he set a new standard for distance running, his contorted running methods and facial grimaces made observers believe he was about to collapse. Instead, he used his unorthodox style to build a stellar career. Zátopek had won gold in the 10,000 metres and silver in the 5,000 metres at the 1948 Olympic Games in London, and he arrived at the 1952 Games in Helsinki, Finland, poised to take the gold medal in both. Zátopek defended his 10,000-metre title with ease; his even pace annihilated the field, and he shattered the Olympic record. In the 5,000 metres he faced very real opposition in Germany's Herbert Schade, France's Alain Mimoun, and Great Britain's Christopher Chataway, but his epic final sprint secured the victory and another Olympic record.

To add to the Zátopek family glory, a few yards away, his wife, Dana, won a gold medal for the javelin that day. His best record in 1951 was for 20,000 metres in 59 min 51.8 sec. At the 1952 Olympic Games in Helsinki, he set Olympic records for the 5,000- and 10,000-metre races and ran the fastest marathon to that time. Zátopek's success owed much to an unorthodox training program. Constantly experimenting with his workouts, he developed interval training—a stamina-building technique of alternating rigorous activity (sprints, in Zátopek's case) with intervals of less-intense exercise (jogging)—which was initially scoffed at but which eventually became a mainstay in most athletes' workout regimens. Zátopek's success was based upon ground-breaking fitness routines. His tough, military-style training became the stuff of legends—sometimes he would run 50 intervals of 200 metres with just a 200-metre recovery jog in between. His preparation helped him develop a mental as well as physical dominance over his opponents. A virtuous and popular national hero who was also beloved by his competitors, Zátopek retired in 1958 with 18 world records and four gold medals.

There is something about you that is hidden and specially fit to some demands placed on the planet earth. You have a special feature that can stand you out amidst crowd. Your self-discovery is your priceless discovery. People may despise your style or term it unconventional, they may appear not to support your pattern but they are means for your shortest route to limelight and stardom. If in your work place you can be replaced by machine, you are under living your potentials There are some people that no matter the advancement of technology they can never be replaced by robotic automation, why? Simply in that they are behind the new waves. During the day God turns up the brightness of the sun so we can see more and work more in the night He turns it down so we can see less and think more.

~All men are born equal but not all die
equal, because we believe unequally
in our talent~

FIRST TO BELIEVE IN YOU

~Manure can't change the fruits
of a tree, it will only mature it~

The Alchemist was first released by an obscure Brazilian publishing house. Albeit having sold "well", the publisher of the book told Coelho that it was never going to sell, and that "he could make more money in the stock exchange". Needing to "heal" himself from this setback, Coelho set out to leave Rio de Janeiro with his wife and spent 40 days in the Mojave Desert. Returning from the excursion, Coelho decided he had to keep on struggling. Coelho was so convinced it was a great book that [he] started knocking on doors. Today president hang out with copy of the book to relax and retouch. The book is an international bestseller. According to AFP, it has sold more than 65 million copies in 56 different languages, becoming one of the best-selling books in history and setting the world record for most translated book by a living author.

Some people will not believe in your dream until you live and die for it; so wait not for consensus not universal votes. Let your life be like leaking vessels everywhere you go; whenever you go let your influence wet the ground often that the sun of time never dries. Not everything that makes you laugh is a friend and not everything that makes you cry is an enemy. Some things that will happen to you will not be what you plan but that which God plans for you. It could be a total rejection that God intends for your vital projection. Joseph is a good example of a man that believed in himself even when the person that served as his confidant and supporter disbelieved and shunned his potential. Jacob did not believe in his son's dream though he loved him so much.

Do not be disappointed if your best human resources will constitute your greatest opposition. They did it for the Master; Aaron and Miriam did it for Moses; Eliab, Joab and Saul did it for David and they will do it for you. But above all be the first to believe in you and last to disbelieve in your failing moments. The leader in you is revealed at the face of loneliness and desertion. At first Einstein's 1905 papers were ignored by the physics community. This began to change after he received the attention of just one physicist, perhaps the most influential physicist of his generation, Max Planck, the founder of the quantum theory, albeit, Albert first believed in his equation. Happiness is not in having all you want but more in getting what you need and most importantly in getting what you have—your potential.

~Those who walk away on you have just
left behind what they will miss in front~

Follow your passion

Invitations came pouring in for him to speak around the world. In 1921 Einstein began the first of several world tours, visiting the United States, England, Japan, and France. Everywhere he went, the crowds numbered in the thousands. Enroute from Japan, he received word that he had received the Nobel Prize for Physics, but for the photoelectric effect rather than for his relativity theories. During his acceptance speech, Einstein startled the audience by speaking about relativity instead of the photoelectric effect. Whatever can't rule your mind can't rule your world in your hand. Great old minds are sometimes the limitation of greater younger minds. Bold mind is needful for inspiration for idea rides on the wing of possibility that must glide on the wind of impossibility to the port of reality.

See rejection as projection

Hear this from well renowned literary agent. "At the Florida writers conference a few years ago we had a faculty meeting prior to the event. Each faculty member stood up and introduced themselves. The first turned and said, "Hi, my name is ____ and here is my new book….which Steve Laube rejected." We all laughed. Then the next person stood and said, "Hi, my name is ____ … and Steve Laube rejected me too." There were over a dozen published authors in that room who claimed the "Laube rejection." So when it came to my turn, I stood and said, "Hi, my name is Steve Laube and I'm the key to your success." Hilarity ensued" That was an answer a well renowned literary agent gave to a question of whether anyone they once rejected get published. To be defeated is not to be deflated. When people refuse to buy in to your idea or gifting you have different ways to interpret it: you could go ahead and burry it as a rubbish after all or see a message lining their reaction reading, "Not well polished to be published" and after all not that they rubbished it. Everybody was once disappointed but those who see what they seek within never stop until they see what they seek without.

~Sometimes rejection
is a direction in illusion~

The greatest insecurity is not lack of self-defense but self-confidence. There are two ways to move a shadow; you shift either the light source or the object in question. If you are holding a candle for the light the former is easy but if you are depending on the sun for the light the latter is applicable. It is wisdom to know what to change in life per time; either others around you; the order of your life; the leader you move around with, change your abode or your self-make up. Nobody will buy into you when you make yourself a bye product of general opinion. There are two things everybody needs and everybody has, yet still in scarcity of supply: appreciation and celebration.

Everybody wants to feel important and contributive. Like Mary Kay Ash said, "Pretend that every single person you meet has a sign around his or her neck that says, "Make me feel important. Not only will you succeed in sales, you will succeed in life." Move close to those people who shares your incompleteness, then move closer to those who wish to complement it and closest to those who which to help you complete it. This is the law of progressive relationship.

The law of motion says to every action there is an equal and opposite reaction, but the law of emotion says there is an equal and opposite options. Do not try to make everybody like you, you will live all through doing what you do not like, going where you do not like, saying what you do not like: it is your job to love others not your job for others to like you. I am different because I am me. I am not responsible for my being different but I am responsible for the difference. When you face the mirror, what do you see? A hero, a champion, a genius, a gem? You are right if you are not wearing a mask to the mirror stand but if not you are seeing a victim, shadow, a weakling and potential scaffold.

~You do not need to be on all fours before
you carry people; it sounds like humility
but resounds stupidity~

The nest of happiness

If you want to be happy value what cannot be taken from you—your choice to be happy and if you want to stay happy do not live for what you can lose. Happiness is what we beget when we forget what has happened, and choose to happen for our future.

CHALLENGE YOUR CHALLENGES

You got what it takes

I once read about a man who went surfing one day and came across a shark. Sighting his tail moving towards him in a circle he was confused and thought of what to do. "I cannot run nor swim as fast as the fish." Quickly, he thought of how to defend its attack, he was armless and looked hopeless. The shark was closing up its circuit to the man and his brain began to sweat for survival. He shouted out of humanitarian art to alert other surfers of the dangerous creature making all to run for safety and leaving him more prone.

If I asked you, what weapon is with him you could as well suggest his fist, which is of course irrelevant to fight a carnivorous shark? Suddenly, he remembered that his surfing board has a pointed mouth and he could swim, so he hurriedly jumped in to the river and used his sharp pointed surfing board as weapon of defense shoving it at the shark as it made advances. After suffering from the pains of the hitting object the shark gave up and left the man.

Life challenges are like wet clay or photo film or better still mirror. They provide you with a template to imprint your total being. In other word, events of our lives, laughable, palatable or undesirable are lavished on us by God to give us room to discover our hidden weakness and strength. The smart will finally use it as leverage to the next stage of their dream while it keeps some at average range of complaints, regrets, excuses etc.

Three boys living in hostel had the cause to go to the river for water to take their bath. Because it was unusual for such case to happen as they were used to being provided with water, they had no bucket for fetching.

Therefore, they went to the art studio where they saw three water pots made of clay by the art students and chose to go to the river with them not knowing that the pots were yet to be fully dried and ready for use. So they went. As they were emerging from the stream, the pot began to get soaked by the water and it began to leak as a result. One of them seeing the mess up decided to throw away the pot off his shoulder landing it on the ground with a big crack for the water to completely leak out; he said I do not want my cloth to become wet.

The other quickly poured the water back into the stream, saying, if I can't go ahead with it let me go back to the base. The third guy did something funning considering the distance they had come all the way and the dare need to take his bath before going for his birthday party gradually use one hand to unzip his pajamas and let it off leaving him with a boxer along the deserted bushy route. He handed it over to one of his two friends. The other two boys laughed at him wondering what was wrong with him as they return to hostel.

Along the way, he exchanged hands to rob his body stylishly walk bathing. When they got to the hostel, the water had finished. He reached out to his towel to dry himself. The others began to complain of the failed attempt to get water to their just waking up colleagues; how painful it was to go to that distance fruitlessly. However, when they saw the third guy, he was looking fresh having had a shower and preparing to dress up.

They asked him how come, why was it that your pot did not leak? He casually replied, "It leaked but I licked it back with my body." Look at the first boy who would not want his cloth to become wet, what was he looking for? Was it not water to take his birth, yet rejected the free flow water because it did not come from shower or in the bathtub. That is how many reject offers of self-discovery that accompanies failure, because it is not coming on the platform of honor. They throw away the pot with the water because it is leaking.

They bank or burry their idea because it is bringing them opinions of shame and not general poll of honor at the start. The second boy threw the water back to the source that is very close to throwing in the towel. The past will always welcome your return; it is like the attitude of bankers, when you succumb that you are bankrupted they welcome you to offer your collateral as unction than to reactivate you, likewise pessimistic on lookers.

Taking advantage of disadvantage

Beginning his career in 1863, in the adolescence of the telegraph industry, when virtually the only source of electricity was primitive batteries putting out a low-voltage current, Edison, an American inventor, who singly or jointly held a world record of 1,093 patents and in addition, created the world's first industrial research laboratory. Before he died, in 1931, he had played a critical role in introducing the modern age of electricity.

From his laboratories and workshops emanated the phonograph, the carbon-button transmitter for the telephone speaker and microphone, the incandescent lamp, a revolutionary generator of unprecedented efficiency, the first commercial electric light and power system, an experimental electric railroad, and key elements of motion-picture apparatus, as well as a host of other inventions. Edison was the seventh and last child—the fourth surviving—of Samuel Edison, Jr., and Nancy

Elliot Edison. At an early age, he developed hearing problems, which have been variously attributed but were most likely due to a familial tendency to mastoiditis. Whatever the cause, Edison's deafness strongly influenced his behavior and career, providing the motivation for many of his inventions.

See how he turned his partial deafness in to total revolution of the world of technology. Look for settled moment to settle issues of stagnation you associate with your weakness especially the night season. When you burn a midnight candle, it gives light to your eyes and to your mind to see what the light of the sun brightens too much to be seen by daytime observation. Silent night is the atmosphere for the mind to breathe right and breed light. Remember champions inspect others opinion as aptitude but respect their own as an attitude.

May need to change your style

A man once promised his boy who had been maintaining the 10th position in class; he said if you come first in your class, I would buy you a big toy. In that calendar year, the boy came 30th. The man wondered what could have happened, he expected the boy to have performed brighter and better. Therefore, he thought and just tried to change his pattern—he told him, if you can study very hard, read your books, do your homework, attend all the classes, then, I would buy you a nice toy. That term the boy came first. When his teacher asked him how he came about it, he said my daddy.

Two sessions ago, he promised me if I can come first in my class he will buy toy for me, but I knew over time I have been fixing for 10th, so I knew unless there was a magic it could not happen. Moreover, since I knew there was no magic here in school, I resolved to fate and never bothered to read at all. However, this term he told me, if I could read my books daily, do my homework, study very hard and give my best, for that he will buy me gift. I did just that, I put in all my best as daddy wished I unexpectedly came first, which I did not plan.

SUCCESS PROCESS

~Silver cannot become gold
because it lives in a furnace~

The larger the goal post the greater the numbers of goal scored, dream enough that you cannot but hit enough target. Extrusive igneous, which is also known as volcanic eruption, is a great way to describe outstanding success pathway. Under the earth crust, the materials are heated up until they form magma under high temperature and pressure. Molten state looks for a crack in the crust. Once gotten one, it erupts because it is less dense than the rock surrounding from which it was formed. Then it shoots out above the earth crust, quickly cools down in to an igneous rock that could exist for countless generation. Now think about monumental achievers—their foundational method.

Deep down in the hideout they conceive ideas from existing ones and fact around. Review the conclusion around it like that of igneous rock that produces molten magma under. Typically, one or more of three processes cause the melting: an increase in temperature, a decrease in pressure, or a change in composition. They like wise heat up pre-existing idea or vary the pressure of meditation and re-conception they place on it. When fully reformed they begin to look for opportunity to express it like the magma looks for cracks in the earth crust to escape. The magma finally shoot out because it is less dense than the rock or particle from which it was form, likewise, these visionaries at a time operate at different mind density than history, they appear to be more volatile in their perspective. Eventually, they launch out; out of un-satisfaction about status quo in the open space where their idea becomes solidified, and for centuries, their achievement stands the test of time.

When you are under pressure, you make mistake and when you make mistake you go under pressure but that with a choice. No mistake or past is strong enough to define your life like your choice power. Shortly after Anne Mulcahy took over the helm at Xerox in 2000, with the company facing possible bankruptcy, she had a blunt message for shareholders. "Xerox's business model is unsustainable," she said. Expenses were too high, and the profit margins were simply too low to return to profitability.

~If failure is eventuality do it with
responsibility and forward~

Wanting easy answers for complex problems, shareholders dumped Xerox shares, driving its stock price down 26 percent the next day.

Looking back on that dark time, Mulcahy says she could have been more tactful. "I thought it was far more credible to acknowledge that the company was broken and dramatic actions had to be taken. Lesson learned." Her advisers urged her to declare bankruptcy in order to clear off Xerox's $18 billion in debt, but Mulcahy resisted, telling them, "Bankruptcy is never a win." In fact, she concluded, using bankruptcy to escape from debt could make it much harder for Xerox to be a serious high-tech player in the future. Instead, she chose a much more difficult and risky goal—"restoring Xerox to a great company once again." As CEO, Mulcahy did not become paralyzed trying to assuage angry shareholders. Instead, she headed out to the field, where her first priority was to win over Xerox's customers by focusing on their complaints. She told her demoralized troops, "I will fly anywhere to save any customer for Xerox." On her visits, she got lots of advice. One major customer, worried about the company's bloated bureaucracy, told her, "You've got to kill the Xerox culture." Never lacking in loyalty to Xerox, she shot back, "I am the culture."

Meanwhile, the drumbeats for bankruptcy steadily increased as the company reported significant losses, used up its entire $7 billion line of credit, and watched its credit ratings decline sharply. Making matters worse, the company was facing a massive investigation by the Securities and Exchange Commission of its billing and accounting practices. Mulcahy didn't blink. She refused to cut back on research and development or field sales, despite shareholder petitions to shut down all R&D. Instead, she attacked Xerox's bloated infrastructure, sold off pieces of Fuji Xerox, the company's crown jewel, and farmed out manufacturing to Flextronics. She reached a painful settlement with the SEC.

Along the way, she had to eliminate 28,000 jobs and billions in expenses, but she saved the company. Looking back, Mulcahy says, "There were many near-death moments when we weren't sure the company could get through the crisis. In those days we would do anything—and I mean anything—to avoid bankruptcy." Today, she feels a well-earned pride in staying true to her values and the company's, rather than capitulating to Wall Street and the bankers. She has paid off the company's entire debt (except for financed purchases), rebuilt its product line and technology base, and installed a new management team. But Mulcahy has done a lot more than restore Xerox.

She has completely transformed it. "Companies disappear because they can't reinvent themselves," she said recently. Mulcahy's advice for other companies facing massive problems, particularly during the current financial crisis? "Do not defend yourself against the inevitable." In other words, face reality and get your team aligned with the new vision that will result in reinvention.

Quitting is one of the options and good advices men will offer you, but I think it is better to queue again like Mulcahy than to be a recruit of failure. When you are subjected to pressure and temperature of life, if you need to melt like the magma melt, but never evaporate rather take the liquid state to look for crack of opportunity in the surrounding condition to erupt out.

~The gain in failure is in trying again~

Escape the mirror trap

When you are original your worst is still the first, and your least will find a way on the list. God fashioned our hearts individually but not independently. Joel Scott Osteen is an American preacher, televangelist, author, and the Senior Pastor of Lakewood Church, the largest Protestant church in the United States, in Houston, Texas. His televised sermons are seen by over 7 million viewers weekly and over 20 million monthly in over 100 countries. Osteen has written five New York Times Bestselling books. He has been widely nicknamed "The Smiling Preacher". In the first few months after he took over from his father as senior pastor, Joel tried to emulate his father's preaching style, but soon developed his own approach. His sermon preparation involves memorizing his remarks and listening to himself on tape. He is living his best because believes in himself.

You can become anything as long as you are in your mold and not the mold of others. Starting is the greatest step of change. Be yourself you are to fill the gap here not to be a gap. Success defined is 90% of a refined failure and 10% of furnishing.

~Do not dye your life with others color,
 bring out the rainbow in you before
 you die~

Not everybody was born into success but we are all born for success and into the process. You might not have been born into a royal family with such glamour, having your birthing captured by tens of cameras and televised worldwide like some monarchs' princess and princesses, but you are born to a loyal destiny. So let your dream be your breadth if you want to live it. Genius spend their time on their strength that so amaze people and get them in discussion all time that they end up having no time to discuss their weakness.

Mark your weakness and market your strength. You either use your strength to bake your weakness by focusing on it or use your weakness to break your strength by focusing on it. You cannot but appreciate God when you celebrate your uniqueness. Have you been in this shoe before when you slot in an original document in the copier and have some photocopies rolled out? When done how many times have you forgotten to collect or pick the original copy from the machine? Quite once, twice or more—the same thing with life, many people have lived and used to the shadow of their ability that they forget their original potentiality in the machine of time.

They have allowed the opinions of men to reduce them to duplicate of themselves. Many people intend to win but few contend to defend their uniqueness. To champion a course you need to persevere and not only that preserve your opinion. When you finally become you true success will beckon you, for in life we spend our childhood up to early adulthood trying to act the script of back grounds and mentors, we rehearse and depicts the script our culture and acquaintances influences placed before us, and spend the latter years of our awakening seasons to dismantle this mask they have coated us with, a task that many never succeed to subdue before they proceed to the grave for they lived for the people and die like people.

To make a difference you do not need to behave different just be you, talk like you, think like you and live like you. We become what we believe not just what we conceive. To be the best you do not have to beat the best but to beat yourself daily. Do not try to surprise your friends just try to surpass your best yesterday, just supply your best per day, and you are suffice. Be sure you can but do not be surprised if you cannot once, just continue to reassure and retry. You cannot do everything if you try, but you cannot do anything if you do not try.

~You may not have a birth right but
thank God you have a right birth~

CHARACTER INTELLIGENCE

Talent without attitude is a latent failure. When you are first sighted all what people see is your head and cloth to identify you, but when they want to recommend you what they look for is your mind dress, which is reflected in the way you address people. A mother of two bought two set of flowers one artificial and the other a seedling. They both looked alike in color and specie. He told her two sons four and six years old, you are going to take care of these flowers. She asked which one of you would pick the artificial? The older of them said, "Mum I want the artificial, since by experience he knew those they have had before required little maintenance, the other was left with no choice but to pick the live flower gladly.

The following month happened to be their birthdays and both share the same day. She asked what do you want for your birthday gifts? They both said flower. She replied, "Ok, do you want those I bought last month?" They echoed yes, so she asked them to pick the one each of them was taking care of. As days go by the younger boy began to see his inexperience to have settled for the living one.

Every day he had had the cause to water it while his brother only had the cause to dust his own once in a month. A day came that he discovered that he would need to transplant it to the garden because it was out growing the container. Therefore, he moved it to the family back yard; transplanted it into a bigger pot in the garden. Few days later, the two of them went out and discovered a number of butterflies roaming about the flower of the younger; the sight was so beautiful as that would be the first flower in their family garden. When the sun shone on the flowers, they became so radiant that the butterflies flocked it the more in much number.

The younger boy was so happy that after all, my effort was not a waste. The elder, who also was falling in love with such a sight went inside, picked up his flower vase and brought it out in to the garden. The following day the butterflies came as usual, they flooded the artificial flower, roaming over it because the flower looked like in full bloom looking for the usual fluid. The younger boy's flower was waiting for the sun. As the sun began to peep from the sky, the flower began to stretch themselves and one by one the butterflies tried out their luck on the second plant since their first host could not benefit them.

Once they perched on the live flowers, they never returned to the artificial. One after the other the rest joined. For the rest of the day they flocked the live flower as more came to join displaying such rainbow like sight, while there was no single butterfly hanging on the artificial one. The elder brother was surprised and angry. The following day he brought out his vase to the exact spot of his brother moving his own to the extreme end of the garden in a bit obscure corner; thinking that it was the location that was responsible for the patronage. But the same episode was repeated—the beautiful butterflies swarmed in and began to look for where to get nectar. They sampled the artificial flower until the sun rises and they sighted the live one in the corner.

The boy went in discouraged and confused. When their mother came to the house and found him sad, she asked, "Why are you sad?" After he explained, their mother laughed, he said, "What mummy. I said I am confused why those beautiful butterflies will rather flock John's flower and not mine after all both are equally beautiful." Their mother said it is not only the beauty that keeps them coming but the nectar they enjoy. Nectar is a very sweet fluid that is found in living flower. They have the ability to synthesize it.

In life, your charisma may attract people as well as your beauty for the first time but what will keep them coming back is your character and chastity—what you are ready to offer them that will make them feel happy. You must be ready to be a giver of good attitudes not just a show aptitude and altitude. But it takes a price as you can see the younger going out every time to water its flowering plant. It was not about position of where the plants were placed, but their composition. No matter where a man of virtue is relocated, the butterflies of responsible mind will locate him. Moreover, the flower of the older kept their full boom either indoor or outdoor but his own required the sun. Good character will cost you your comfort; you need to go extra mile to be a better and lovelier individual. You need to water your attitude with water of godly principle and people. Talent without a tailored temperament is just like the boy's artificial flower.

Redirect the search light

~Your best friend tells me your strongest attitude; your worst enemy shows me your weakest attitude~

When you enter your dressing room in the night with a touch and you desire to see your image in the mirror, where do you point the direction of the light? I know you will first be tempted to point it at the mirror since it is where you wish to see yourself, but you will soon discover that you have pointed it in the wrong direction for you will see nothing or at best a blurred and faint picture of yourself like the girl in the story above. But when you point the light to your face you will see the image clearly in the mirror. This is contrary to the common sense but that is what reveals your image. The same with life, to know who you are do not point your attention to the mirror of your outward reputation and fame. People only comment on your paint not structure—they are hardly accurate.

When Jesus asked the disciples who did men say that He was? They began to give the views of people; some say you are Elijah, some say you are a prophet, some say you are John, not one of the details is accurate; only Peter got it, for God revealed it to him. The same only God can reveal who you are to you when you point the search light inward, your potentials and faults will be discovered. Your true identity will be shown to you. People can talk you in to ambition, hail you into the shadow of yourself, and pressurize you to live behind the mask they have designed for you.

Water has no color, no taste, no odor yet it is the king of juice, the crown of quench. Stick to your un-commonalities and you will be in unavoidable demand. Accept yourself and people will respect you. What you lack in stature or nature you do not need for your future; the talent you do not have will make you the least on the list when you pursue it; it is only your gift that can lift you to be the head—God said it would make room for you. When what you think about is the same as what people talk about you, then you need both the vote of your friends and enemies to succeed in life, which you will never get anyway. Life is full of excuses for him who is fooled of imitation. He who gives excuses and he who takes excuses are potential victims of fate.

~I dream my paint and I paint
my dream~ Vincent Willem van Gogh

Break the cocoon

Failure is a fertile soil; you have labored to put the manure of experiences and lessons, but it is a pity that many only leave the soil without planting the seed of success. When you are climbing a ladder and a rung break what do you do I think you come down no matter the height? No! Rather you simply remove your legs from the broken one and place it on the next rung if it is yet to be your target height. This is the law of failing forward. If the rung under your leg failed hold on to the one in your hand gripping by all means, do not let go of the climb, do not give up to fate. When we do not live by faith, we live for fate. Faith helps you determine what the end will be from the beginning it is the evidence of the things hoped for.

With faith, nothing is impossible but without hope in God the stocked creative power of faith is impossible. Rise beyond your limitations by believing beyond your imagination; God is able to do just that. Failure may roughen you but when you are positive about it, it toughens you. When you learn from mistakes, you earn your dividends. Nothing is a waste, gather your fragments, and let nothing be wasted. It is your approach that makes it to look or not look like a reproach. Those who ever succeed failed in something, sometimes many things but they did not fail in everything and that explains why they become a celebrated hero.

Do not be tired even at the seventh time it is the season of perfection and the eight times will be a new beginning for you. Fight your fear first not your enemy, fight your ignorance first not your hindrance. Failure may embarrass you but embrace it, not that you love it but because you want to collect your dividend; it is not an expectation of your trials but not the expiration of your triumph. You are only passing through you are not passing with it. Sometimes failing through is a process of passing tool, a broken rung did part of the climbing after all. In the journey to the top, part of the route is fire: part is water but in all God has said He will be with you. Do not opt for what is left hope for what is right. You might have lost your title but do not lose the battle no not everything, I mean return with lessons and strategy that will now work. There is something that is worse than failure and that is closure. What you let go can yet grow.

~Do not just try few times,
 try until the due time~

Court yourself

Spend time with yourself that is how you can discover yourself the way a man discover his spouse by spending time together. When others discover your talent before you, it is as betraying when an outsider first gets to know your spouse's secret before you. You should be self-contained at least for some times to explore your self-content. Those who will go for the crown do not throng with the crowd. Those who are in the midst of the crowd cannot see the front or the back, like a leaf in the ocean they flow where the wind blows. They are like a mind lost in the sea of heads. You need to come out from the crowd to see the path to the crown. The crown is never for the crowd. You need to observe your nature to be able to serve humanity with ingenuity and sincerity. What people tagged a weakness could actually be your peak strength, for their view is often emotion oriented.

Two servants of a great king were given two leaking pitcher to water a bed of flower that linked the river to the palace. When they got to know they both were dazed and in lamentation went to king that this is impossible; how can we use such leaking vessel to water a garden of flower? Your majesty should have a rethink about it. The wise king replied, "My good servants, I have given you the tool you need go ahead and water my beautiful garden before it is sun dried." One of them went out and began to think about how good their master had been in the past.

The king cannot just become suddenly wicked much more when we have not done anything wrong. So he went to the river dip the pitcher in the pool and head for the garden as he proceed an idea struck him that why the complaint in the first instance the king had really made the job a lot easier by given us a leaking vessel. I need not pour anything just move around with my leaking vessel and the garden is getting wetted. When he was through, he went to the palace, thank the king but do you know he met his colleague there still logging and lodging his complaints and excuses.

That is what we do; we sometimes only see the negative, so blinded by it that we are grounded. All we see is the weakness in us and we engage in complaints to God that we wile away precious life moments. Whatever God places in your hand as potential take with thanksgiving, knowing well that God cannot mismanage your life.

~To be unique could be all the change
you will succeed to give this world~

Do not dress in another man's costume do not let the culture of men robe your destiny in traditional attire. No matter how big a ship is and the waves it causes in the ocean current, it is a matter of time the little boats coming behind will soon wonder whether any giant ever thread this path of the sea. If you want the coming generation not to doubt whether you once lived before you leave or you just exist and exit, live like you, live inside out, live purposefully, live intentionally, live constructively, and live like a living, blow like the wind on the sea that ever generates waves.

The great white light

It is a bit outstanding to know that it is a unitary sun light that spilts into the seven radiant colors of rainbow when passes through different clouds layers and atmospheric density layout. So Just as different colors come together to form a majestic and ultimate source of energy—the sun, so is our success in this world. We are here to complement each other and make a rainbow of success. What is a bridge, it is nothing but a road at the top, like any other road as yours in the valley; do not envy the guy at the top everyone is on the road, the road to success. You are not a failure until you are today and tomorrow and to the tomb. The distance between success and failure lies not really in aptitude but attitude.

Our numerical quantity as a race could be census by our color which may differ but yet infer not a deal, but our mental potentiality is likened to the color of our blood which is constant. No race is a unit to measure other in Creator's mental design like we do with currency; it is with the plan of absolute equality. Truth changes time and season but does not change with time and season. Learn about you and earn above your now. Understanding your basic nature is fundamental to launching beyond you and living after you.

~There could be a multipurpose
giftings but there is no multipurpose
beings~

DANGER OF STRANGER

~We are all strangers to ourselves, each man to himself~

Sometimes you have to lose some friends to win some limiting enemies. Not everyone that wants you that you need. Anyone who does not want you is not a need—to force yourself on a fellow man is a suicide mission of self-image. Some people live as a visitor to themselves all their lives—they have lived masked life. Do not dream your size, dream oversize with God to regenerate your eroding talents. The tree has leg of stem to rise, a foot of root as the stability, with that it grows up tall into the sky, its fruits fly to the height of air; a tree has a branch of hands, a palm of leaves, a finger of veins, with that it rhythms with the wind, to the left and right in the air. The day tree tries to walk on the soil, it starts to starve, dry and die. The day it starts to fly above the ground it starts to be left of birds and right for fire. Something dies gradually in every man, who strives to be every man; something lives in every man whose motive is just not to be himself. You can live like anyone but a copy; you can talk like anyone but an echo; you can think like anyone but a figurehead; you can walk like anyone but a shadow. What you have is not really what makes you different but what you are. If you cannot beat them, you do not need to waste time to judge them, or your lifetime to join them; channel your strength of time to dodge them and jug on with life. One of the ways to make a difference is to be indifferent in the midst of them.

When your output is negative like a photo film, you have two choices to go to laboratory of desperation and determination, till you print out your true picture from it or pin the negative film to your memory.

To be you is the greatest responsibility, to be you the greatest possibility, to be you the greatest potentiality. We are all strangers to ourselves, each man to himself. You need to meet the unique man that lives in. The world is like a mould and true men like a gaseous water, we must not exist as an ice cube that is self-cage within fear and unending procrastination, grounded in the school of life making decision but never graduating in to action; so living like a fenced opinion nor must we exist as a liquid that flows a while only to take the shape of the mould saying if you can beat them be then, if you can't mend them blend with them; but we should be like vapour that finds its way out of the mould to condense outside the world standard.

To reach out to heaven as cloud and be poured on the earth as rain refreshing lives. To feel at home in life, just free yourself, be yourself, and feel yourself, for when we try to be everybody we live like a visitor to ourselves; we will need to take permission from impossibility to utilise our potentiality; we attempt things with trailing consciousness of perfecting a photocopy; when opportunity knocks the door of our life we go in search of the original fellow to open the door while the talent key is buried; we become object of evaluation by those who choose to be indifferent about the crowd opinion.

You can't become anything when you want to become everything, likewise you can't become somebody when you want to become everybody. The best you can be the rest can't be, you are a customised part in God's global rehabilitation machine. If you do not like the way you look change your dress, if you do not like your weather change your country, if you do not like your job change your boss, but if you do not like your structure change your thinking. Whatever you can't change in life teaches you to change in return.

Being a black man is not a blank mind, being a white man does not make you a wise mind; as a man thinks so he is. If the great white house should be painted black, I believe that does not change the interior composition and decoration nor the activities that go on within; so is the black or white skin does not implicate neither superiority nor inferiority of mental, spiritual and emotional capacity in the least of common sense.

> I wish you were you;
> I wish your life is more than existing but exiting.
> I wish you will break out from the cocoon of second class colour.
> I wish your race never hinder your race in the track of life;
> I wish you die for something and with nothing
> I wish you live while you are alive and after you leave

Release all

Strive to die empty, pour yourself into lives like a drink offering—Paul proclaimed. In a little town, there were two farmer friends, having heard about inevitable future draught, which would be preceded by heavy downpour, decided to build a dam in their farmyards to store the rain and from the sea build channels to the dam to source water for future sustenance. One of the farmers was rich while the other wasn't. The distance of the sea to their small town was quite long several miles away.

The rich farmer within couple of months dug the river channel and began the laying of pipes deep down in the ground. In the next couple of years he had laid the huge pipe network from the sea to the town while the other farmer only succeeded in digging the surface channels to the town, he had no resources to install pipes. They went back to their village farm and constructed two very big dams individually and separately. Then they linked the networks to the dam from the river channel.

The rich farmer locked up the two outlets for the mean time to finish constructing the dam so that no animal could crawl inside the pipes to abode. It took each of them another several years to fortify and reinforce the dams outside. Meanwhile, the unexpected happened, as against the report of weather forecasters; it began to rain earlier than predicted as they began to reinforce the exterior of the dam. Before they would be through the dams were filled up, the extent of the rain was unprecedented, and yet the fortification of the dams was yet to be completed.

Time and age had told on these two friends due to the stress and rigor of the lifetime project. When they realized that they may give up the ghost anytime they sent for their two sons to come and inherit what they had lived to build for their coming generation. Few hours after the two sons had the properties willed to them their fathers died. They had little knowledge of the history of the project only that the rich told his son that the pipe network was locked up at both side, while the poor farmer told his son that he was unable to lay pipe network like his friend. They never knew the extent of the project where it started from nor where the channels stopped. So the two of them went back to the city where they came from. Meanwhile the draught has started in the land as predicted while the two of them were away.

~Where you are born and how you
are born is not as important as why you
are born and when you are born~

One day they received a distress call that their dams were cracking and beginning to give way because their fathers were unable to complete the reinforcement. They quickly rushed down to the town and discovered that the famine was so severe in the land. Confused on what to do about their inherited dam and the content, the rich farmer's son quickly remembered what his father told him that the pipe was locked on both side. So he thought to preserve the water from watering the town farm yards by reason of possible collapsing, he resolved to open the pipe at the dam side and let the water run in to the deeply planted pipe network, with that the water will be stored in the pipe.

The other boy thought of what he could as well do to preserve the legacy water. After so much brainstorming he realized that there was nothing he could do but to release the water so that the dam won't finally collapse. But doing this he knew that the water will definitely be of no use to him anymore. So they both released the water in to the two channels. Months after months the water continued to run through the pipe and the open channels. After two years the water stopped flowing and they both decided to trace the route of the layout.

As they went, the poor farmer's son was surprised to see people coming to him exited, cheering, singing, full of jubilations, hailing, praising him at every village they reached. And every time he inquired why they were celebrating him they had replied you saved our lives from the draught. The water you released from your dam kept on irrigating our farmlands as they flowed by. One elderly woman said, "My son, you are a gift to your generation, and you are a hero and messenger of comfort, a sent deliverer to humanity."

Meanwhile, no one came to meet the other rich young man only few that knew his father just said hi to him. At the end, they reached the end of the lay out at the extreme of a remote village. As they were about getting to the end of the pipe and channel layout information reached them that the two dams had finally collapsed despite all efforts to sustain them. More so, to their endless surprise the pipe lay out and the open water channel both linked up with the endless sea. The rich man son burst in to tear when he discovered that the only place he could finally release the water he had stored in the pipe was the endless sea staring at them where it was absolutely useless and will serve no benefit to humanity nor him anymore, neither is it useful again in the city that was already being bathed in rain. This happened to be the only option as the water was no more needful in the city since the two years of predicted draught had come and gone.

~If you do not make people laugh
while you live you won't make
them cry when you leave~

The other young man as well discovered that the water finally stopped just at the boarder of the sea, at that point it stopped running; not a drop escaped in to the sea, because along the way, it had watered, softened and soaked the grounds it passed through. As they both returned to the city the dwellers had arranged a big honor party for the poor farmer's son, there they honored, celebrated and immortalized his achievement. Do you plan to die empty?

Do you desire to pour out all of God's investment in you to your generation and benefit humanity here on earth or you want to carry it to heaven where it is not needed? Your talent is useless at the other side of life. Let men feed on your inbuilt resources; that is why you were freely given like the water in the dams was freely given to the farmer and their sons. You have nothing to gain by not dying empty. Like Paul said, "I have finished the race—" I have been poured out as a drink offering, I have released everything God gave me to my generation. I have emptied my potentials and delivered my purpose. And so I am ready to depart.

~I like this about **LIFE**: "Live It For Eternity"~

Chapter Five

HAVE THE FAITH OF GIANTS

~Winning is an attitude not just an aptitude~

A group of youngsters went on gaming catching funs with a water gun as they chased the geese and other slow moving land animals. At a spot, one of them saw a small wild pig making a close move as it surfed the leaves littered parcel of land. Immediately, his body chemistry release more adrenalin to his legs as he took to his heel to meet the rest. As he approached them, he shouted, "Run a pig is coming!" but instead of running they began laughing uncontrollably while he continued to run along the narrow deserted path. They retorted, "How dare you running away from a pig?"

After few seconds, the wild pig appeared with its noise and terrible rocky movement. Soon they discovered why their friend was running, it was not a domestic pig but unusually wild one. Without telling one another what to do they all took to their heels after their long gone friend. After covering few distance they met their friend running back towards them. They chorused, go back wild pig is still in hot chase; but he did not listen. Closely approaching them, they began to envy him for his boldness and doggedness—dumbfounded about his newly found courage to return to face what he once ran away from.

As they meddled with this in their minds he was already by their side about to pass them behind; them he exclaimed, a lion! a lion!, like a specially designed break system they all halted as if a troop on parade ground was given training instruction. Without mutual discussion, they all turned and changed the course of their journey. They ran behind their friend towards where they were coming from—the territory of the pig. When the pig saw the dreadfully fearless young muscles running with stout determination not to look nor turn back it also changed his direction back in to the forest giving the boys ways of escape as well.

You can't say what you can do until you do have a faith you can have. What you are running away from understands where you are going but do you? The first thing is to define the feared. If there is anything you need to fear in life, it is fear not mountains; if there is anyone you need to fear in life it is God not devil; if there is anywhere you need to fear in life it is heaven not hell; if there is anytime you must fear in life it is eternity not now. So define the fear.

~Consider this about **FEAR**
—Fake Expectation Attacking Reality~

Define the feared

Faith will always separate minds from minds and dictate the leadership; he puts the bold ahead of the old, making the young strong and the age wrong. The life battlefield of the mind is a picture of the Israelite and the Philistine at the valley. Let's picture it that the side of the philistine's army is made up of armies of discouragement, back biting, failure, past, criticism, risk, loss, betrayal, disappointments and the rest. This camp sent out their champion—fear, to bully the other camp of promise. Fear is the anchor of the ship of success enemies, as long as it is holding on to the bottom of the sea of life the storms prevails. It is the billboard that is written in the boldest ink on the path of success. When Goliath—the champion of the enemy's camp was brought down by David's faith what amazement that the rest of the philistine fled the scene, were they not warriors, well equipped as the Saul's army? Yet they fled at the face of the once timid Israelite. When fear is killed, the hidden potential of a man is released. The armies of discouragement, backbiting, failure, past, criticism, risk, loss, betrayal, disappointments will flee with their master—fear. The same army that was handicapped for forty days now roared like a lion at their mountain. When fear is conquered the battle is halve won.

When fear is killed the rest of the success enemy fade out while the counterpart of faith joy, happiness, boldness, positivity, encouragement, loyalty etc. will rise up in action.

~Fear is a virus of the soul; it feeds on faith,
latter attack the program of hope and eventually
crashes the system of dream~

Fear makes a mess of experience in the hand of the experienced since they sometimes have prevailing situation and new standard. Saul was described by David as being strong as lion and Jonathan as being swift as eagle with both having great victory record, but at that captivation of fear they became incapacitated.

Everybody who knows how to succeed knows how to fail; they came across it and crossed over to the dream world. Failure may seem to reduce your worth, but if you trace it back, it will introduce you to your world. It is better to have a small idea and a big courage than to have a big idea but a small courage. When a soul looses fear into operation it is no surprise that it soon loses hope, for either now or then our beings' nature develop the eye of fear, the ear of fear and mouth of fear and ultimately life of fear. In your vehicle of life, let faith be the passenger and hope to be the driver; for when faith is tired, hope drives on.

Faith bakes big dreams, big dreams build great people, and great people builds great place. A life without dreams and equal faith is still an isotope of ultimate failure. The aging of your walk is inevitable but the aging of your works after your departure should be preventable by the virtue of its landmark geared up by the earth shaking faith. Your dream is your voice when you learn to amplify it with the force of courage, it attracts generational audience and influence, for your duration of life is limited but the durability of your life should be unlimited. Having wings is not all it takes to fly, it takes faith and boldness to leap into air than to stamp your feet on ground to walk.

Dreamers fly, wishers stand and watch. Birds can fly not just because they have wings but because they have undergone faith training from the hatch; they grow bold. If today lion should suddenly grow wings and is taking to the top of Mount Everest to jump down I tell you, you will see another side of lion. The king of the jungles will cowardly turns back and chooses to descend the slope. Training impacts boldness, eaglets were not born special but were trained special.

You must spread your wings and your thought if you must fly across the oceans. Your imagination is the current to carry your dreams. The wing is useless in the cocoon, dreams are useless on the bed. Sometimes you need to jump out there in to the sphere of impossibility before your wings find expression. Like the working of a parachute, it is a burden when you are carrying it, as it never opens full fledge capacity on the spot but when you jump out in faith in to the open sky it spreads like a wing to sustain your journey and like a canopy to shield you from the scorch.

Give no room

Fill a bottle with water and leave just a little space at the top. Take it up and give it a shake, you will discover that the water will be trouble with bubbles springing up and the water will become unclear until you stop shaking it and it settles down. If you put a piece of broken glass inside it you will observe that it becomes difficult to sight it. Now add more water to the one in the bottle and fill it to overflowing, afterward cork it and try to shake it.

You will discover that the water will practically remain with no bubble and whatever particle you put inside will be clearly sighted. When you allow a mushroom size for the element of the enemy to inhabit you will be surprised that it can trouble your entire life that it becomes difficult to see what you once believed God for. Jesus thought us that a little leaven leavens up the whole lump. Do not entertain negative emotions they will turn the mushroom to much room ill motion and notion.

Dream dreams that will scare you to pursue alone, dreams that will interest God to invest His bigness. Dream dreams that will brace up your weakness and embrace your strength. Limit sometimes implies what your exposed weakness cannot overcome but which your hidden strength can turnover to a platform for a new summit if you can awake the hero in you. Those who want to go fast do not grow fat; those who want to go far do not grow fear. Let go of anyone who has no idea of your passion to fight through. Make friends on the way that can make you in a way.

Those who will make new history must quake known history, they must be ready to challenge the fearful conclusion of culture. No matter the speed of the wind, it can lift when the wings are clipped, and that is what fear does—it makes you to fold your tail in between your limbs. Boldness knows no gender and courage knows no sex, he who finally starts is bold. If you can hear the ladder speaks it had tell you, you can rise with me to any height as long as you have where to prop me—which is courage. You are here for the change and you must first be changed by the force of courage to be there. Those who walk away on possibility create room for those behind to walk over impossibility.

Those who are successful are like iceberg if they will be truthful; the success the world sees is the tip of the iceberg of failure, frustration, disappointment, discouragement, hurts but they chose to float above all. When life tells you to sit tight it's not talking about sit belt, is talking about adjusting to hot seat. Storm is to test your stamina not to set your terminal; if you pass through it you won't be normal to some of your weakness but it will normalize some. You need 10% courage to dream and 50% courage to start and 40% courage to continue, dreamers are potential stars but eventual stars are found among starters. One of the ways to maximize your strength is not to magnify your weakness before opportunity.

It is either you decide in faith or fear decides fate for you. Thinking makes things possible only action makes it happens and faith guaranty action. When the storms of life blow at you, like a string of a bow you might be force to be pull back but do not let your attachment to the bow be strapped off, if you keep the chord of faith intact you will but be release like an arrow shot off into the future and up in the sky when the storm is over. Freedom is not just to be able to walk outside unchallenged but much more to be able to lead inside against challenge. You must learn to obey the inertia law of life, when you fall back it is an action you can chose a reaction forward, when the bow is pull backward the arrow is about to be launch in to the future. Every star is truly shooting stars; they keep falling and glowing but never grounded.

EMBRACE CHALLENGES OF LIFE

In a botanical garden was a fruitful tree that stood alone. Being directly and lonely exposed to the wind, it was often forced to bend and be shaken by the wind. The son of the botanist who had their house located in the garden usually felt sorry for the tree. One day he asked his father, why the wind used to blow the tree mercilessly all the time. His father replied, "Because of the numerous and clouded leaves on it." "Why can't we reduce the leaves so the stress be reduced?" He pestered. "Why not," said the father, "But just a little." He added, asking him to do the job. The father went on a research journey the following day and the boy went to trim the tree leaves. To his surprise, the other day it rained and the tree was still being blown by the wind. When the rain stopped, he went and trimmed it the more. The wind blew and to another extent, it bent the tree, he again went and pruned the tree. The war for peace episodes continue until the boy removed all the leaves on the tree and the wind stopped disturbing tree. The rain stopped a while and the sun began to shine in its strength. The beautiful fruits of the tree were now beautifully expressed and the boy liked staring at and feeding on them. However, to his amazement, they began to dry gradually and the flower began to dry off as well since there were no leaves to shelter nor provide photosynthesized nutrient for them.

Within few days, the tree was left bare like a dead tree. Then his father returned and met him unhappy about the tree. He said Dad, "I wish I had left the leaves on the tree, though it will have to be struggling with the wind, yet it will be preserved and relevant that way." Sometimes we which our lives are free of storms but forget that it comes before the rain, we wish the road is so smooth without friction but forget it will hence become slippery, we wish we are let alone by the obstacles of life forgetting that God has only prepared a stair case for us to the next story of our life.

~God did not promise us a smooth
road but a straight one~

The water is deeper than you see, so you could be wrong by looking before you leap; rather walk by faith and not facts. Take time to breathe; do not live your life gasping for grabbing, at the end there will be many gaps in your unwritten biography. May your diary become your autobiography; may you touch all your thoughts; may you act all your dream scripts, live while you are alive. Your product is the conduct of your faith. Those who look with their eyes do not see. Do not fool yourself thinking your challenge is the greatest, even if it is so there is no trophy for the first of complainers.

The best way to avoid mistakes is not only to follow the footsteps of great lives but to much more to walk in the great light; it is no use following a map in darkness. Even if I do not have a roof at the top, I will still lock my door when I am going out for idea breeding, though I may be at risk yet I won't entertain impossibility visitors. No matter how a big the door is and no matter how small the key is, it is the power to open it. All you need to move the mountain is the mustard seed size of unwavering faith.

Stretch the elastic limit

Courage takes us to our elastic limit, faith takes us further to if I perish I perish. Courage will either shrink or expand your ability. Like earlier said, life is sometimes like a parachute, you must often have to jump before it opens up, and look before you leap is not always timely jump. Plan in purpose, look in hope, jump in faith and dive in love. Do not build happiness around your possession but around your possessor.

~People who say a thing is impossible
Should always complete their sentence
…with us~

If you do not have faith, fate will have you. Fear makes things happen; faith makes things happens, yours the choice. Where some people wish and pray to get out, some people wish to be and pray for it. Know that your worse sometimes is somebody moment dream, your obstacle is the miracle some are aiming for; whatever side the life turns to you remember it is simply your turn and that you need not complain, if you can't explain it just trust in God and keep thrusting.

We wish the rain to fall, but we want not the sunshine to be darkened, but can the cloud be pregnant of vapor and not spread a canopy of blackness on the horizon? Can we have a rose and fail to hold a thorny stem, adversity is life equation balancing factor, you are only passing through not failing through, pressed not crushed no matter how long the tunnel is light marks the end. God seems to be taking you through the mess but he is rather baking a message.

The law of saturation

Dare extra mile for a desired smile. In the eastern city of west African country there was a great king who has a beautiful daughter every young man desires to marry. In the same city is a young wise boy who could play flute very well which made the king to like him and occasionally invite him to the palace to make music for him. This made other young men to envy him. The land was known for its scarcity of salt as they depend on the Arabian travelers to supply them at a very high price, only the rich could afford.

One day the town crier came to the town square and announced that the great king of our land has decided to give out his daughter to a young man who can provide the king with a drum of dry salt within 24 hours of the day. The young men in the city began to see how to meet the target. This young man also began to think of the way out. Then he quickly remembered what came to his mind in the previous day, that each time he goes out to bathe in the river and the water dries up on its body there are always particles of salt clinging to his body.

Could it be that water contains salt? Therefore, he decided to try something nobody has ever done. He got water in a basin and allowed it to dry in the sun. When the water has evaporated there were particles of salt left in the bowl. So he repeated the process several times until he could get a bucket of salt. He went there the second day, the third until he could get a drum full. After he proceeded to the palace and told the king, "I could supply you with a drum of salt within 24 hours." When the other youth heard, they became jealous and planned to disrupt his task.

The D-day came and everybody was hanging around the city square. The drum was set and he began to carry the salt from the river to the drum. He was to go in six rounds to empty the drum to fill the other. But his critics decided to pour water in the drum when he was on his third trip to the beach. All the salt in the drum became dissolved as he got to the drum to pour the third round, he saw the solution of salt but he still poured it in to the drum since he has no other place to pour it. But something happened, as he poured the third round in to the water, he discovered that the water level did not rise. So he thought, "Though the water did no increase but my salt is still inside, in other word let me pour the rest and I will tell the king, though I can't give you a drum of dry salt, I can provide a drum of salt solution."

"I will not let my past effort to be in vain, it is better to be late than never, it is better to be average than to be leverage for failure." Therefore, he went for the fourth round, the fifth; but he noticed that dry salt has begun to appear in the drum by the time he poured the six one all the solution turned in to dry salt it became a saturated solution. He was ignorant of the law of saturation but it had worked for him. However, in your own case, I will call it the law of perseverance and persistence. Your effort may look life useless but the truth is that your reward is still lying there. The solution looked like water but it still contains the salt.

There is nothing like absolute failure, your labor is not a waste but on one condition—be ready to pour more salt for it to precipitate like the boy. Be ready to try repeatedly—again and again, then your latter effort will draw out the reward of your past failed attempts. Like a wise man once said that many of lives failure are men who never knew how close they were to success before they quit. Sometimes our efforts look as if nothing happened; we put more effort yet get less comfort. If you will not give up you will reap all your past effort. Do not stop in 999th, the light is just after the tunnel.

Goal addicts dream again

A leader once said: "I have to intentionally stop and dream again. What can I work on next year that makes me smile? Then my mind automatically moves from the strategic to the tactical. In detail—how can I organize my work and my life to do the things that cause that same smile?" He who gives excuse and he who takes excuses are potential victims of fate. Life is full of excuses for he who is fooled of it. We become what we believe not just what we conceive. Live today with due responsibility for you cannot live your past in reality anymore.

There is nothing like perfect mistake but there is something like perfecting mistake. If the tree is panted horizontally the stem will still grow up and the root down because they each know what they wanted the latter water and mineral, the former light and air. If you are distracted in life, it is either you do not know what you want or you do not want it enough. Dream again; harness your emotional energy.

KárolyTakács was a sergeant in the Hungarian army and a Hungarian athlete. He was a member of his nation's world championship pistol shooting team. At age 28, however, a grenade exploded in his right hand while undergoing training with his squad, leaving him without its use. It seems his dream of Olympic championship is gone. Depressed but not deflated, he taught himself to shoot left-handed. No one knew his training, what he was doing. In the spring of 1939, he showed up at the Hungarian National Pistol Shooting Championship.

Other shooters approached Takacs to condole and console the one time hero of his fate and having come to witness the occasion. However, all were caught dumbfounded when he said, "I didn't come to watch, I came to compete." They were even more surprised when the legend won! The 1940 and 1944 Olympics were cancelled because of World War II. It looked like Takacs' Olympic Dream would never have a chance to realize itself. Ten years later from the day of accident, he set a world and an Olympic record with 580 points to win the gold medal at the 1948 Olympics in London. He won a second gold medal with 579 points at the 1952 Olympics in Helsinki, again using his left hand. At age 46, Takács appeared in his final Olympic Games, finishing in eighth place at Melbourne in 1956. Do what everybody only read about, act what everybody only talk about.

Be not fear fooled

~Do one thing every day that
scares you~Eleanor Roosevelt

Worry wears and tears the system of heart; it is like putting your right leg on the throttling and left let leg on the break and choosing to press the two at the same time. Our lives is like the bank of time each day we withdraw from it and deposit it in to bank of eternity, so when we finally run it to red here we proceed up to cash it. Many pass through life in a hurry and in a worry that they forget to live before they leave. Take time to smell flower, take time to believe God, take time to smile, as you take time to breath.

You can always take the time from time; out of no time take a time out. Sometimes you need to be out of your mind to be right in your dream. There are three ways to get fruit from a tree: you can wait for the wind to blow it off, you can throw sticks at random wishing for luck and you can climb the trunk embracing the work, that is how it is in life—some wait for time of opportunity, some waste time guessing and hopping for luck, some chose to think and work it out.

Sometimes our mountains are nothing but mounting fears. When your earth is shaking and your heart is quaking, just finally leave the driver's seat and to the passenger sit, do not even try to act a co-pilot, let God carry you along do not carry God along. Your flaws point you to the law of success; your errors point you to the path of Heroes

~When you remember you are not
the one in control, then you will begin
to control your worry~

Fear will keep you from what you can do and but will not keep it for you. When you have enough failed attempts to form a sea a fish of success will emerge in its depth. Failure is like creating room for success to inhabit. All you need is a net of courage to catch it. Calculate your risk and get a rough estimation of the total cost before you are sold in to it or buy in to it. Sometimes some things we fear in life are like a child running away from a lion drawn in the paper.

When you lose keep trying when you win keep trying, let nothing occupies you that you see nothing to occupy again. Everybody wants to know how to win but few cares about knowing what to win, where to win and when to win. When it gets hot, losers halt but winners are only hurt. Humility is sometimes the attitude of seeing what is left as what is right for you.

Winners are never found at the starting point nor at the midpoint but at the end point. If you have never won and you have ever worn, you choose to queue than to quit, then you are an uncommon hero. Nobody will celebrate you until you elevate your strength above your weakness. You can choose to sing your past failure on high key and your future melody on low key, stream of pities will come to your concert but you will never sell any album.

When you win everybody celebrates your output when you lose wise people celebrate your input. When you win everybody celebrates your output when you lose let somebody celebrates your input—you. There are some failures that are must celebrated and elevated than success, the difference is in the heart size of the dreamer that influences such a big adventure that naturally advertise the braveness even though failed.

~It's like nobody succeeds
more than he fails. ~

Manage your excuse to execute your program. Explore your refined excuse for a defined exploits. There is nothing too small that cannot become big, and there is nothing big that cannot become small—attitude is the multiplying factor either on positive or negative scale. If you want your dream fame then let your passion be aflame. When you do not have a target, the world is a magnet. When you do not have any intention, anything gets your attention. Sometimes what we are holding on to is what is holding us down. The comfort you would not let go because of fear is the limiting combat you have never won. Master your feared excuse.

~Sometimes end winners are the bold losers~

MOTIVE POWER

Be critics proof

~Your attention is always available
when your intention is not valuable~

The purpose of light is not for the eye to see it. It is for it to shine on the target for the eye to see the target. When light is directed to the eye, the eyesight is useless and can go blind. The purpose of your dream is not you, the fruits is to be in the direction to better your world and those you rob time with; when they are blessed they reflect it in upward glory to God for your life.

Those who want their vision to live for them are often being blinded by selfishness and pride. It is not that you begin to live for people but let people live through you. Critic will soon join you if you won't soon stop. Today lies between yesterday and tomorrow but let your life lies between today and tomorrow. When faced with critics or critical situations dialogue but be deliberate, negotiate but do not depreciate, to avoid them is to be shy and to afford them is never to shine.

That is why you do not answer all their whys. If the time is right but the feeling is not ripe go ahead, and if the feeling is right but the time is not ripe glow ahead. Thinking is the action of the mind, choosing is the action of the heart, and doing is the action of the head. Critics are like camera, when they focus on a target, they capture a thought that is negative, when an optimist collects the negative films, he develops it in to positive. A pessimist complains the heat is much in the day to work and that the light is too dim in the night to walk. If you are caught in an argument with one you still have a choice to cut it.

We learn nothing when we argue because everybody is a teacher. When we define our weaknesses, we can begin to refine it. Deliberate about your weakness and be deliberate about your strength.

~Sometimes silence is the strongest
action and wisest sentence~

Life victory site

This is how unreal fear is; when Moses rod swallowed the rod of the magicians the size of his rod did not increase that shows you that fear is like magic—it is fake. When you stand and walk in faith, you discover that dark hunting monster is just a shadow. When you fall on the ground in a mud and as a kid your peers mock you and laugh you to scorn, I think you stay there in the mess and cry till your mum comes looking for you; no you stand up and go home for a cleaned up. The same with when life slips below your feet, not that you are careless or that God care less but like the need of champions and soil for the seed of success you can't but stand and confront your failure. You are not a design of failure so do not resign to it.

Sometimes the purpose of true love is to keep us together sometimes it is to keeps us apart. You need to discern when to say if I perish, I perish and when to throw in the towel both are expression of courage. When you love someone, you will not deceive her that she belongs to you. When we fall in love our heart leads our head follow, when we walk in love our head leads our heart follow. You only need feelings to fall in love you need findings to walk in love. The same with faith and fear you should be able to demarcate your head from your heart.

Be able to know when your hearing is wrong for fear comes by hearing as well. You need not follow your heart when your head is right. Emotions can err your motion. Let your decisions be based on your findings in the dictionary of faith—God's Books of promises and not feelings in the diary of past. Do not just be concerned that your journey is half-uncovered; concentrate your joy in the fact that it is half covered. Do not fear what is to happen fear Who makes things to happen.

~Fear knocks faith answer, when the door
was opened nobody was there~Anonymous

Desperation with inspiration

A hunter caught a large hare and put it in a cage. The cage is built of a net with a wide grid holes but not wide enough for the animal to squeeze through. The hunter went on gaming and suddenly sighted another small hare, immediately he let loose his dog for a hot chase. The hare after tiring dash observed the cage afar off with another hare and called out to his big friend the large hare. The large hare in the cage sighting the oncoming small hare also called out for a help. The small hare shouted please let me in through the hole, the big one cried out open and let me out!

The small hare's thought was that just let me escape from the dog's fang while the big one was to go out and preferably face the dog in a race challenge rather than being used for soup which the small hare was ignorant of. Such is life, what you are letting to slip off is what someone else is dreaming to start with. What you call end point is what someone else is considering as a starting point.

What you dump as failure of a dream success is what someone else is looking for as manure to fertilise his dream success. Something always comes before desperation and that is determination and something also comes before determination and that is resolution. To be resolute is to be determined, to be determined is to be desperate, to be desperate is to be toughened. You are not fit for success when you see every opinion to befit you. When you want to fix into every mold you will have to live shapeless and homeless.

Fear can't take you beyond your past; it can't lift you beyond your height. When a man thinks fear he will hear fear in every news; he will see fear in every good, he will feel fear in every touch and he will smell fear in every flower. If all the time you know a thing won't be possible you have demonstrated it rather than advocating it you will have disappointed yourself so many times, because you could have by chance done it. Every idea is a bold guessing and surprising ending.

How far you can imagine is how far you have drawn your margin of limit. Our thought is like the radius of a circle with our heart as the center of the circle; our life is the circumference we draw with the ink of time.

The longer the radius sure the wider the perimeter of life influence and attainment covers. Boldness is not in face, it is the pace the heart is ready to take when the ground seems to disappear. Anyone that tells you, you are not qualified to win could as well have said you are not qualified to live. To the living alone is the hope to win.

When you fall to the ground do not use your hand to dust yourself, the dirt is there too, rather get a handkerchief from standing hand to clean up, I mean when you fail it shows you need more than your wisdom to make things right. Do not use the same failed method to correct your falling. If successful people do not surround you, you go around them, the people you are close to determines a lot what you are next to. Do not lend me nor rent me your stair to climb up, rather give a ladder that I can use anywhere. You can't climb beyond the last rung of your ladder, there is always a time to drop good idea for a better one.

Life does not wait for you to be birthed, it won't wait for you after you are birthed, it is a flowing river that favors those who chose to swim not just in the direction of its course or where it carries them to but the channel they dig into their future. Every today comes with its own time allocation just enough to tidy up yesterday, try new things today and think new thoughts about tomorrow.

Those who feed on the past are never filled it only creates a feel of sweet memories and sweats of failed theories. Do not limit yourself to what you are best known for, or what you can do without fear: you can't know your total capacity until your weakness is betrayed and built up. Every man is average of his strength and weakness, but not all live average life; while some magnify their weakness others maximised their strength.

Mistakes are the broken rung of the success ladder; you need it after all to step higher, mend it and do not end it or push it away. If the roof top is your limit you need a tall ladder, if Mount Everest is it, you need a tight rope; if the sky is your limit you need a dream wing. Life is climbing a ladder no one can really hold someone else hand while he climb, all of four hands and four legs must be on the rungs.

Winners stick despite the kicks

The first woman in the United States to graduate from medical school; undertook the study of medicine privately with sympathetic physicians, and in 1847 she began seeking admission to a medical school. All the leading schools rejected her application, but she was at length admitted, almost by fluke, to Geneva Medical College (a forerunner of Hobart College) in Geneva, New York. Elizabeth Blackwell, months there were extremely difficult.

Town people and much of the male student body ostracized and harassed her, and she was at first even barred from classroom demonstration. She persevered, however, and in January 1849, ranked first in her class, she became the first modern-day woman doctor of medicine. When you attempt the uncommon you draw a battle line with common sense romantics. You can use your fall like water fall to generate power like it is dam stations and you can use it to wet the ground as in rain drop, or make noise like the rest or turn it to tourism. But you can use it to generate power for news.

The birds are epitome of faith lesson, they sow not nor reap yet they are not hungry. They jump from the tree every now and then never doubting if they will crash on the land. They sing all the time even when no concert organized in view for them but it is obvious we end up their delight audience, they rock on the tender branches swinging as if it will yield to breakage under their weight yet not once has the branch disappointed. They perch on high-tension cable where no man can dare yet they have not gone in to extinction because of electrocution. Little wonder the Master Counsels us to consider.

Deflating the common fear

There is no hero with zero fear; these are rather trembling minds that fear above their battled thoughts what humanity posterity will be void of; so they jumped in the torrent despite the foments. Let not your heart be at the mercy of fear, it is a fearful thing. Without challenge life will be too smoothly dangerous. A very little and feeble mind fear what people will think if he dreams his dream; if he ever dreams then he fears what people will say if he discloses his dream; if he ever does he begins to fear what people will do if he dares his dream; heroic and valiant mind rather fears what posterity stands to lose if they die with their dreams.

Not that we do not have faith at all but this fear comes so suddenly at such a speed that knocks off floating faith out our unprepared soul. Fear is a responsibility we take up to bottle up our ability within. Ignorance creates the room for fear to occupy, so the real enemy of faith is not fear but ignorance.

~Do not be fair to fear, be hard;
be heartless! ~

The chain of past

~When I have learnt I have won~

There is no warrior who feeds on worry to become a conqueror. Glance at your past but glue to your future. The longest path to success is series of decisions, the shortest path is action! There is no empty future but empty mind. Your future is not as far as you think for it ticks with the clock. A young engaged lady just received a jilt letter from her fiancé. Since then her life runs in to shamble. Every day, she thought about how they had enjoyed each other's company and how they had planned. She kept on failing her exams as she kept on living in the past relationship and the future she had always dreamt.

Her psychology professor, who was a bit close to her called her for discussion to know what was wrong. Before then he had contacted her parents for clues and he was told all she was passing through. When she came he asked her what the difference between today and yesterday(y)? She said yesterday is gone forever (gf). He said what is the difference between us and the dead(d) people? She said they are gone forever (gf). Then he said if $y=gf$ and $d=gf$ what can you say about y and d. She said automatically they are equal. $Y=d$ that is yesterday is dead. He asked further, where do we keep the dead? "In the tomb," she replied. He said, what can you say about those living in yesterday? She said they are living in the tomb.

He said the same with future; it is a newborn baby in the womb about to be born. He said those who live in the future could as well be dwelling in the womb. She said yes. He asked, what is the consequence? She said they would live in limitation like the fetus that is restricted to a position. Then she asked sir does that mean I was living in the tomb because all this while I have been thinking about my past relationship? The professor said yes and that with evidence.

You have recorded a DEAD progress academically because you dwell in the past and limited advancement because you have enclosed yourself in the womb of future as well. You have not been able to secure another relationship because you are not available to those single men who are living in their today. These are the two places you have been living interchangeably and refuse to live your today. . .

Discouraged, but determined to preserve a record of their aeronautical work to date, Wilbur accepted Chanute's invitation to address the prestigious Western Society of Engineers. Wilbur's talk was delivered in Chicago on Sept. 18, 1901, and was published as "Some Aeronautical Experiments" in the journal of the society. It indicated the extent to which the Wright brothers, in spite of their disappointments, had already moved beyond other flying machine experimenters. Whatever thing that compete with you understand where you are going but do you picture the trophy? Just as learning only stops when living stops; fighting stops when breathing stops. .

GO BEYOND YOUR ABILITY

~Doing it through God is doing it through odds~

Determination ends termination, because others fail does not make failure the order. Losers are often beginners, finishers are often winners. Take advantage of challenges to find your real range and to trace your lost faith. A farmer who desired a tree in his yard sent his son to his friend in next village to go and get a seed of mustard for him. The seed was very small and almost difficult to see on the ground. As the boy ran home in excitement papa, papa, the seed fell off his hand on the ground of their back yard. The boy began to search for it fruitlessly. When he narrated to his father his ordeal the man said, "Show me the exact area; he took him there."

Then the old man took a shovel and began to spread soil on the area. The boy shouted papa that will make it more difficult to see. You are making things difficult for the seed to be found. The man only whispered be patient. After the exercise they went inside and continued with their daily life. After few days the boy ran to the father, Papa! Papa! I have found the seed. The man said where? He said where it was lying. The seed had germinated into a seedling; in fact we only need to transplant it now. We all have gifts that seem too difficult to discover. But God will allow challenges to spread over our lives sometimes for the potential to react and finally emerge to be aware off. The boy did not find the seed but a seedling. The seed was already germinating. The same with us, by the time we will look back in the tunnel of challenges we will discover we have not only had our gifts discovered but as well polished, springing up to bearing fruits to grace humanity and eternity.

Worth gives birth to will; will gives birth to war; war gives back to ways and ways give birth to wow. Faith is just our responsibility that measures out our ability per time in God. God won't show you the source of your problem without having on ground the resource for the solution.

In God is your ability

Without God life should be avoided because it is void, without purpose life should not even be imagined. To know your God is the greatest knowledge the second is like it to know yourself and the third is to knowing you can't know it all. World is changing but His word is not changing and this is why there is gap between man and His maker.

No matter how great your future is you only need one architect and structural engineer: God and His ways. Do not let loose your passion until you get used to God's instruction. Zero your zeal until God clears your particulars and approve your mission. God sometimes allows storm to blow us away toward Him and upward from our comfort..

~God is calling you to do what
you can't do with the ability you
do not have~Rick Thomas

In God, we trust, in Him we thrust; outside God we rust, we thirst like we are dust. Those who want to reach the sky must learn to let the One up there to hold the ladder for them. You are alive that is why you are qualified a candidate of that situation. Thank God in all things and for all things; He is working behind the scene toward making everything sum up as good as you walk through the tunnel of obscurity. When you sail through the storm spread your wings of faith and God will be right there to steady the flight. I had rather settle for the time of storm with God by my side than crave for a moment of peace without God in my ride.

Be flexible to be able

The sign of cross is a sign of plus, no matter what you lose at the foot of the cross, it never reduces you. Water finds its way through the rock because it is flexible and claims no shape; to live by God's standard will be easy when you are devoid of your own human will, ways, self-worth and wants. As we walk with God, we should know that we are tending to be impatient. We want God to run ahead so we can run in to our future, but the walking of God is such a giant stride that each step He takes we will need to breathlessly dash to catch up, so if God should hurry up and run, then we will be lost in confusion. Scripture says a thousand years is like a day in His eyes.

~God is taking His time but we
see it as if taking our time~

Create room for God's size

This is how God does His things; He puts up bigger dreams in our mind just as we wind up on the level we are. God had a friend who was an old man with a dropping grey beard, wishing he could just have a child and be at peace. He believed God for a seed to carry on his thriving merchandise. His wife also could be quite comfortable with quick and obtainable alternative; her mind is smoothly relieved if she can get her fruits in apparent image—a son from a maid is suffice. However, God thinking of not to give him village population, a town, a nation not even a continent but the entire globe.

No matter the size of your dream, God's plan is to exceed it. The bible says, He is able to do exceedingly, abundantly; above all we could ask or think. Your life begins to follow the line you stretch in your mind. Jacob told the young Egypt ruler who happened to be his 11th son, I have not thought to see your face but behold here are your children before me. He was not able to comprehend that Joseph was still alive but not only that, he saw Joseph's sons. God surpassed his imagination. Dreams are the windows through which we peep into our futures; goals are the doors through which we enter in to them. Either you dream or not you will live, but you will by fate not faith.

A young adult teacher once asked one of his students, "What is the size of your lung?" The boy replied, "Just the volume you can see." So he gave him a balloon to blow: the first, the second, the third, he asked him again, what is the size of your lung? The boy kept quiet and later said, it seems to be bigger than my tummy. Then he asked him to continue until it got to a point that the blown balloons full the entire room. He asked him again, what is the size of your lung? The boy exited and curious said I think as much as I can blow. Your size in life is figuratively the size of the dreams you can intake and blow up to fill your world.

~Dream beyond your strength
if you will interest God~

Dreams give birth to dreams. Our mind is not a dream storage tank but its operational machine to create, culminate, and deliver, then ready for another operation. The young Hebrew boy is now gone for over 3000 years, but his dream and achievement is worthy of acknowledgement. Jesse's youngest child cannot stop aspiring for greater thing. Killing the lion, the bear were all processes to killing Goliath, and eventually tens of unending victories is his lifetime. David always dreamt bigger. First, he was anointed in his father's house, then over Judah and ultimately over Israel.

On his way Jesus told the woman give me water to drink but the woman was cultural. So Jesus told her, but I can give you endless springs of water? Now the woman sat tight and made a demand. She could see her drawer was useless and her water was temporal. God does not need your drawer neither is your small and temporary ambition moves Him.

He has something bigger in mind—something that only Him can accomplish through you, with you and in you. So stop bragging with your mushroom ambition, let it go and let God sparks His unimaginable dreams in you. Joseph dreamt that his family was going to bow to him back in the family house but the magnificent God is a magnifying God, at the end the whole world came to bow before him.

The ladder of dreams whispers further, I am as long as the measure of the ends of the earth, you can rise up the sky as much as you raise me high to climb; you can climb further depending on your wall of imagination you prop me against. Wherever you are today, is either the answers from the dream you had yesterday or the questions of a dreamless past.

Dream does not create a new future it rather discovers your unknown features to achieve your destiny. There is no man that leads ahead that did not dream ahead of others, it is the signature of leadership. Dream not what is sensible, dream the incredible, after all it is your faith, it is your life and it is with your God. Life without dreams is boring and a slave of fate. Before you finally go to sleep wake your dream to reality, let coming seeds know you were once planted. Let not your fruits die with your tree. Dream as big as mustard tree that spreads its branches to all for shelter; dream big dreams that can contain your world ahead.

~Tough times doesn't laugh but
tough people do at last~

People who succeed as much as possible failed as much as possible, but they tried as much as possible. We deliver our strength and discover our greater strength in our tough times. Dreams are like pregnancy—they are conceived in the womb of mind and nurtured, in the bosom of time.

~Let your dream be so big that
it becomes too heavy to throw it away~

The gentle lightning

When you follow what God speaks to you, it leads you to your peaks. A lizard unknowingly entered a house and when it discovered it was in danger looked for a way of escape. It saw a glass window and tried to crawl through thinking it was an open outlet. On getting close, it pressed through the locked window but could not pass through. Fully convinced that it was an open outlet, it persisted, making noise in the process. When the owner of the house realized the crawling creature, she opened the next window to it, to avoid contact. She opened the door as well for the lizard to escape but to the reptile, all of the openings look just like the close window. At a point, it became weak and stopped struggling. After then the woman came and used stick to push it to the open window, not wanting to push it down to the ground outside she left it there to escape on its own. However, when the lizard regained strength, it stared at the open window and never made attempt to escape thinking it was still like the closed glass window.

A while after, the woman came back and saw it, with the stick she hit the wall to alert the lizard. On hearing the shocking sound, it headed for the outside without thinking about the close or open glass. Sometimes we get stuck to what we think is right. We struggle from stories we have heard about people treading the same path and so we struggle. There is a way that looks so perfectly ok in our eyes yet it is absolutely close to our advancement. Just besides our thinking is the door God has prepared but our thoughts what seems bright must be right. God allows us to struggle in our own human strength until we resort to Him for strength and direction.

Even when God is now in charge, we refuse to have a change of mentality. We would become so used to the limitation that we assume everything else as a bunch of limitation. When we insist to desist out of fear of another failure God organized how to push us pass beyond our doubt and fear through the passage of storm. God allowed Jacob to be down paid and short changed several times by his master to the point that he could not provide for his household. Then he came to his creative senses that led to his financial freedom from the cruel employer.

~Sometimes what we are holding
on to, is what is holding us down~

Sometimes when we get the worse, we get to see the good in those bad. Keep the world in your hand and keep His word in your heart. Let the world be loosely held so you can let go whenever it becomes slippery; that your heart may be free and open for Him to come in and dwell for the next assignment. Have a heart of flesh, a mind of hair and a head of bone—so your heart might be soft for God to mold and write a memo of His plan and peace, that your mind might be flexible, dynamic and aired with ideas and that your head might be hollow of worry yet strong to hook on to a decision. Be grateful to God either you see everything happening fast or slow know that God is at work. Gratitude comes from an attitude a mind generates in solitude when it puts its aptitude to work—you will realize the altitude God met you and where you are today.

As you die for your course through the passage of the journey of life remember to live a balanced life, for you were given your breath for both comfort and combat. It takes peace without and much more within for a bird to sleep off on a dry, tender, dangling, branch of a tree, they believe God for their feed and now for a suspended bed. They must have been inhuman, not to have been turning on the air borne sofa with a consuming thought of what and how tomorrow will be.

Be aware of how movements express emotions. Life is not symbolically about correcting our mistakes but making the best of the residue. Inflate your faith every time and you will deflate your fear anytime. Kill the anxiety before it starts to fill, peel it off your thought before you begin to feel it. People who succeed possible failed as much as possible but they tried as much as possible. If you plan but eventually fail, you will still be different not in result but in next performance.

If anyone chooses to bang the door at your acts, do not be so emotionally down driven; take your heart back though—in pieces but not a fragment left behind. Some people operate their brain like the partitioning of the system hard ware. They gave the past 80% and let today and tomorrow share the remaining 20%. If you are to take a shot at a target in the night I think you had done it at random and that is no mistake. It is better to try when not sure of victory than be defeated without warring. Do not be afraid of stepping out; just make sure your footing is on purpose. Failure recorded in pursuit of purpose is part of the race. The end will justify the starting, success will justify the process.

Give thanks in all

A little lad once saw a lion cub in zoo and was so fascinated about the beautiful creature. When they got home he prayed his father to buy one cub for him as pet. His father laughed and ignored him. He became so persistent that he felt disappointed by his father. When the boy was a teenager he went again to the zoo with his father and incidentally the lion now a fully grown king of the jungle. Right in there presence a life goat was dropped in to the caged ranch as launch for the lion, after a brief chase it caught up with it, tore and fed on it.

The boy looked at his father in amazement and fear how the lion captured and incapacitated the goat. He then said dad, thank you for our pet dog, it is rather friendly and play with other pets at home. His father asked would you like if I get you a cub for a pet to grow it up, the boy replied dad you must be kidding. When we grow up our mind maturity and spiritual understanding, our prayer point will naturally change. We will see life in a new way; see why we must be grateful and not play great fool about the kindness of the Creator. Meekness is when you accept yourself, accept what you have, being content with your content. When you can lose anything money can by without losing your enthusiasm in the mean time before it comes back then you are among those who have mastered the secret of life time happiness.

Anything can be sold for money but money can't buy everything. Money answers all things, but only the things that temporal; at least Peter told us it can't buy the gift of God. How people value you does not affect your value in God's eye; you worth the apples of His eye. Appreciate God for the breadth you have, the bread and butter you eat, the bed and bed room you sleep, the butter fly and the sky you see, the bitter and the better taste, the best in the test, and the bright future you have as birthright.

~As we grow our wants becomes
our need and our need becomes
our wants~

Chapter Six

LEVERAGE WITH YOUR RELATIONSHIP

~In lifting people you build
your capacity~

A college teacher and a coach brought a bundle of keys to the class and asked the pupil to begin to pick it one by one and look for the one that can open the class book cabinet. The academic has carefully duplicated the keys to the book cabinet and mixed them together with the wrong ones though all looked alike. One by one, they began to locate the ones that can open it after trial and error. As they discovered it individually, he asked them to write their name on the holder. After the fifty of them were done, he asked them to bring the keys belonging to each of them. He then threw all the keys in the bucket close to the cabinet. He stood in the front of the class and said I want all of you to open the cabinet as a team as I am going to lock it now. He said, "I give you just 30 seconds."

Then they all rushed to the bucket rowdily each struggling to locate his own key he had tested, tried and trusted before in opening the cabinet. For the next 30 seconds nobody was able to find his key talk less of opening the cabinet. Then he announced, everybody stop and come near. He said how many of you picked the wrong keys during the search and how many did you pick? They all raised their hands, some said, I picked ten, some five, then he said ok.

He said further, "Do you realize that the first key everybody picked could have opened the shelf?" Then it dawned on them that right there in the presence of all, everybody had spent time to locate the key that could open the shelf and carefully written his name on it. In other word, all the keys could open the door. He said, as a team, you should learn to make use of each other's ability to achieve the common goal. You do not need to be bent in using your own strength and wisdom learn to leverage with the ability of each other as a team to achieve the mutual goal. He said further, "If I give all of you a candle each making fifty how many stick of matches will you need to light all?" They were about saying fifty when the lesson dawned on them. They chorused we only need one. Once one is lighted, we can all light others from the burning one.

I wonder how Neil Armstrong would have felt if Edwin E. Aldrin, Jr., and Michael Collins, were not there, he could have felt alone and lonely unlike Adam who did not feel such before Eve came. Adam was alone but was not feeling lonely because he has never tasted what it means to have somebody around. He did not see it as bad to be in such situation it was God who saw it.

You cannot really appreciate relationship until you imagine you alone on mars just for a day. Relationship is the food of time and the hope of growth. The earth is as small as our love for fellow occupants is as big. When there is enough love, there is always enough room. Love contracts to accommodate contacts. When love is absent, I tell you the whole universe is not enough room to accommodate two souls without a report of stepped toes. The whole universe can live in a room when the walls are built of love. Love is the largest room in the world. It is impossible to make it in life without relationship.

However, how we handle relationship will determine its leverage manner: for higher heights, keep us average or worse still take us backward. Friendship takes time to form, so we can take our time to consider if to conform. We dream in isolation, plan it in solitude and pursue it exodus. You do not need men to capture a dream but men are means to your dream and the ultimate meaning of your dream.

~When a sheep flocks with a lion
for so long at one day it will scream
if it can't roar~

RELATIONSHIP INTELLIGENCE

The weak and the oil are good specimen to remind us that God founded life on the platform of relationship. If you light a weak without oil in it, it burns so fast and that with little light. Moreover, if you light oil, it burns so much, but in a little while, it goes off. In both case they are useless for application. However, when the two are combining to make a lamp they burn intelligently, gradually and lastly. Relationship keeps us from burning out so fast and dangerously. The same with a reinforced concrete; when an iron framework is used to construct a bridge it gives up with time as it gets to bend under continuous living load.

Likewise, if a concrete alone is used, it cracks under load, but when these two are combined together they form a formidable strength that can sustain great loads for great length of time. Considering Sodium and Chlorine that come together to form salt. Individually, these two pose danger to consumption, but when they relate together they form the table salt that refreshes the lives of humanity. Of a truth, we need relationship to succeed, but the first and best is to thyself among your mortal dust. Know that you are world on two legs. You are an institution walled in a skin, a universe in human vase. Until you can pull off the world mask from your mind eye you will love like a gambler. We are all born a champion but not with an opinion but choice. The best way to know others is to spend time with them but to know yourself you need to invest the time by self-development.

A coach and great leader who had just retired called for his son who had just graduated and was set to take over from him. He said "My son, I want to talk to you about life on how to live as if you never die and not die as if you never live." He asked his wife to get him two candlesticks. After he was given, he asked the boy to pull out the thread weak of one of the two. He told him to light the other one and let it start burning. Then he asked him to light the thread weak that was pulled out and as well the remaining solid wax.

Therefore, the three began to burn; the thread burnt rapidly producing smoldering fire for few seconds while the wax melt down and caught fire. It produced huge flame but so rapidly and wildly, gave so much illumination and called for attention but also for few minutes. While the second candle continue to burn out steadily for the next six hours. Then he said, "The weak alone is like a man who has great picture, plans and people but no passion, pursuit and persistence. The great crowd, picture and plans will soon all fizzle away when the man passes on because what surrounds him was never ignited.

The other part of the candle, which is the wax, is like a man who has great passion, pleasure and pursuit but he has no picture, people nor plans. He too will create so great attention with a great fame only for a while as that which glitters will fade off in the nearest future when he passes on; because he never passes the touch to anyone. But when you strive to combine passion with the great people, pursuit with the big plans and persistence with the big picture, you will be like candle that has been burning all this while. Your dreams will live on longer than you lived."

Creation of Help

To come out of the womb we need help to enter the tomb we need help. We need help at the beginning and ending of our life. Life is all about giving and receiving help. Sometimes the opportunities you need are the people you meet. There are some people you must mix with in life and there some you must miss in life. You are a creation of relationship. We are species of relationship.

There is no absolute freedom, it is self-bondage. Freedom does not mean independence. A certain selfish and rich man wanted to live a selfish life and unrealistic life, he wanted to ensure nobody communicate with him for help or friendship. Therefore, he decided to build a three-story building at the center of 10 hectares of land expanse with no staircase nor lift, nor escalator. He told the contractors use crane to start and finish your construction.

When building was completed he asked them to help him construct an equally high ladder to be used by him anytime he wanted to go up or come down. To avoid possible overhearing of his neighbor he decided not to accommodate anybody to the second and third floor only the ground floor was occupied. So he started living his life like that. Every day, he would let down the ladder while going out and asked his children to pull it up when he has reached the ground. When he comes back, they would do the same procedure.

Meanwhile, his little cat and dog use to follow him out and while waiting for the ladder to drop his pets had developed friendship with the neighbors' cats and dogs as they come together quickly to play. The pets were so fond of one another that they became friends; a relationship the man deprived his neighbors.

One day as he was climbing the ladder with his cat clinging to his shoulder the other cats too began to ascend the ladder presumably trying to follow their friend to its house too. When the man reached the last floor, he looked down and saw some of his neighbors' cats climbing after him, he was furious, yelled at the cats but they were too desperate not to stop following their friend. Getting frustrated he began to think of how to avoid these creatures in his house. Then he began to shake the ladder to fall off the cats but they clung to it.

When he got to the last floor with unsuccessful trials to stop the cats seeing that they were almost reaching his veranda he angrily pushed the ladder away with the cats. He screeched you hell that serves you right. As the ladder tilted off, the wall some of the cats jumped off while some quickly climbed down, in the process some were wounded. Satisfied, he surprisingly got inside to meet his children battling with fire outbreak in the kitchen. He joined them to quench it but the fire went wild. Before he knew, it was out of control.

Thinking of what next to do, he realized there is no way to get out his goods except throwing them down, since the crane had been disengaged. So quickly, he threw all his valuable goods down, and as they landed, of course, they became valueless. When he was done, he quickly took his two sons, his dog and the cat to escape down the ladder. The emergency of the outbreak had overshadowed his memory of what had happened to the ladder.

On getting to where he used to rest the ladder he suddenly remembered it had been thrown down in his anger. So now is the time to swallow a big chunk of pride. He had always boasted to his two sons, "I do not need anyone's help, I am self-sufficient;" restricting his cat and dog from playing with neighbors. Emulate me my sons and be independent of men. He has nobody's phone number among his neighbor. Left with no other option he cried out to his neighbor; help me with the ladder, help! But it was difficult to hear him any way by the virtue of the distance and height to his next neighbors.

As his little dog and the cat began to feel the heat, they began to scream with distress while the dog barked non-stop, not before long their friends down on the ground joined to scream and bark. With such chaos, the owners were alerted who finally came out to the situation. His pets' sense of relationship bailed him out of its stupidity. You are born alone, you will die alone but you cannot live alone. God created everything to be interdependent for help.

The solar system is a good example. Consider the ecosystem and the body system. Everything was to assist one another. Consider our anatomy how the fingers work together, the tongue and the teeth, every cell connected to the other to form organ and organs to form system, which despite the complexity never imagine surviving the man without interaction.

Celebrate others weakness

Your relationship ability is best scaled by your reactions management not others action. Anyway, growth will reveal your strength but will not conceal your weakness. If you want to see a stain on a balloon, you will need to blow it first then as the size grows the strength mounts up and at the same time the stain is revealed likewise your weakness.

One day, the eaglet's summoned courage to ask their mother about their way of life as the mother eagle came in to the nest with a chick in its claw. They asked, mother, why is it that the hen cannot fly like us? The pride drown mother said, "Though I can really say only God knows detail but I can guess why," she said there is one major reason—"they are lazy."

When the eaglets began to fly, they descended so low and parched on the ground among the hens. As they began to watch their way of life; how they struggle with their claws to get food from the ground; how they fight off little creatures that come to disturb them; how they relate with men friendly: the eaglets having reasoned with themselves went back to their mother in the nest. They said mother, we think you are wrong in your bold guessing. We think we choose to fly because we are lazy; we want readymade food that we can descend and steal away. We think it is because we are unfriendly, that we are hunted by men. We think it is because we are proud that we try to isolate ourselves as special breed on high mountains. We think we are fearful that we can fight any of the small creatures so we chose to live in secret. We think we are…its okay, the mother eagle cut in, "I think I have heard enough." It is pride that keeps us away from others and the second is selfishness. Embrace the weakness of others as well as their strength, their weakness may one day be the strength you need.

When David was raided of his wives and children like wise those of his servants, he asked God for direction and instruction. On his way to recover the captives, his servants found a sick weak and left behind Egyptian servant who had not eaten for three days. They choose to take him up and brought him to David, he ended up assisting the sense of their direction, becoming a vital instrument they needed for the recovery.

On his return after victory the servants who were strong enough to go for the battle fully, said, those who were weak and could not go would have no share in the spoil. However, David refused he said as the lot of him who went to the battle so shall be the lot of him who was weak to go. He was a leader who understands how to manage the people weakness to continually bridge the potential gap in communication.

~First appearance in life is full
of delicate parameters to judge people~

Judge your mental spirit

It has being said that you do not have the second chance to make the first impression but we need to reconsider that first impression could be a false impression. You cannot weigh people base on a shallow interaction and hollow time together. A group of youngsters in their 100 level were teaming along their school walkway to the school amphitheater for the exhibition of their frame works in celebration of the school art week. Each of them had been studying foreign language as their discipline. As they got to the venue, they were surprised to see an elderly woman also coming to exhibit. Possibly one of the parents or guardians they had thought. They all were curious to read what she has done and displayed for the occasion.

They found out that it was written in English language with funny grammatical errors. They began to giggle and make jest of the woman. One of them was so arrogantly bold that he stepped forward to ask the woman her age and whether she had attended school at all. The woman greeted him just like her display, her sentence composition made the boys to finally burst in to laughter, which could be barely hidden from the well-composed and undisturbed grey-headed calm mistress. She told them her age and said, "I have been to school from childhood just like you." Then they thought and talked among themselves; "She must be a dullard."

The exhibition started, and everybody displayed his/her write up. The school art faculty dean mounted the podium and greeted everyone— the students and the outsiders that came to grace the occasion. "Right now, I am going to invite to the podium, our chief judge for the exhibition. She is a woman of multiple talents. She has mastered 50 different languages success fully and she is now beginning to learn her 51st language which happens to be our own official language, English. Join me to welcome professor..." he addressed them. Right from the front row stood up that same old woman, coming to the podium for her welcome speech."

After the introduction was over, she began to inspect the displayed work. When their turn came, she read the entire boys' frame works write ups, of different languages from German to French to Greek and the rest. At the end, she corrected errors in each of the boy's write up. The old scholar has chosen to communicate with the boys in English when they met on the way since they asked their question in English. She chose to swallow her pride by communicating poorly in language she has not mastered just to make the boys feel at home.

The uncultured boys fell embarrassed and self-humiliated for their untailored mannerism and sought to apologize. People can say anything about your first appearance or first outing but do not act based on their conclusion.

THE POWER OF TWO

~From the womb to the tomb you need help~

Mount Everest is not the highest mountain on earth but the highest point above the sea level. How did it come about it? By leveraging with the terrain around. There is no great life without a great relationship. An important influence on Einstein was a young medical student, Max Talmud who often had dinner at the Einstein home. Talmud became an informal tutor, introducing Einstein to higher mathematics and philosophy. Influence is relative, it may appear static but it is dynamically impactful.

Maximize your relationship

A teacher in kindergarten class once asked her pupils if you are playing ball in the room and you mistakenly throw it up and getting the ball hanged on the ward road top; what will you do to get it back?" The first one said he will take my table and climb it. "What if your daddy is sitting on your table what will you do?" the aunty said. He replied, "I will ask him to stand up." The teacher said, "Perhaps after climbing the table you happen to still not be able to reach the ball what will you do?" "I will jump." He replied with confidence. The teacher put it to him, "But in climbing you might fall and injure yourself or break the table." "In that case I will wait until I grow taller and tall enough to take it," he submitted. "By deciding to wait till you grow will deprive you of your toy in the childhood time when you need it most. More so, by them the ball could have become useless." The young lady told the boy who felt sorry for the limitation.

He then turned to another pupil, asking what will you do? The next smart kid didn't waste time; he simply said, "I do not need to climb the table, I do not need to jump, I will just ask my father to stand up from the table to pick it for me." The first boy said contemptuously to retort him, "What if his hand can't reach it what will you do?" He looked at their teacher, shifted his gaze back to his classmate and said "I will ask him to lift me up on his shoulder then I had pick it up."

Many of life opportunities ride on the cart of relationship. You will need people to commend you and later recommend you. The smart way to see farther than history is to sit on the shoulder of the history makers. But you will need them to lift you up on their shoulders wish you can only achieve through intentional relationship. You do not need to look for how to construct a ladder to climb when you can sit on a shoulder of a giant. You do not need to wait and grow up like the first boy before you can achieve great thing. Time is not a permanent gift.

~If successful people do not surround you,
you go around them, the people you are
close to determines a lot what you are next to~

Filtered lifestyle

If you want to change your look what do you do, I think you make up your face, the same if do not like the way your life looks like make up your mind. No matter how people look at you it can't change your look, do not lament over people's comment; likewise your past can be a passport for your future without your password. They may have right to say but you are left to believe or leave. Sieve your relationship and let some fall on the past list. It is easier to make friend than to unmake them, for though they depart not their impact both positive and negative. The more you discover yourself the more new friends you make and the more old friends you drop, for when things change in you there will be reaction from outside.

You know when put on weight you have to change your wardrobe, some outfit will have to be replaced, the same when you will have to lose weight you will need to trim off your cloth size, the same to attain, effect and sustain some changes you will need to change some friends. Like an adage in west Africa says people are my clothes.

There are some people you move with that you multiply knowledge there are some you move with that your ignorance is multiplied. Filter your thoughts to have clear words; filter your words to have clear actions; filter your actions to have clear habits; filter your habits to have clear character; filter your character to have clear relationship; filter your relationship to have a clear destiny.

The hardest currency

In a village, there was a man of great intelligence that kings come from different cities to book appointment for his counsel. One day he desired to do some adjustment in his house, which required the assistance of young men. He reached out to some young folks in the village and asked them to work with him. As they worked the smart among them use the opportunity to ask questions that had been bothering them. All along they discussed, interact and reasoned together while they engaged in the physical exercise.

At the end of the day's work, he called them together and began to reward them. He paid some in dollars, some in yen, some in pounds and some in euro being a wealthy old country man. When they were about going he asked them "What was the greatest payment I paid you today?" They began to mention the currency one by one and they agreed that it should be the pound. The man said no, "But the attention I paid to you." The greatest currency we pay in life is attention; it is the hardest currency we pay people. Kings hardly have the privilege of spending a quarter of the time we spent together today. You have taken part of my life no money could buy. Sometimes it is better to pay money than to pay attention and sometimes it is better to pay attention than to pay money. It is wisdom to know what to do per time.

Be open headed

*~Our world changes with
our friendship ranges~*

An old king called together his chiefs and the prince. He told them, you all can see how great this kingdom has become in my hand since I came to the throne of my father. He said what makes the difference between kings and ordinary men is wisdom. He then removed the crown on his head and asked all of them to remove the caps on their heads as well. He asked them, "What is the difference between my crown and your caps?" They all began to say the crown is golden why the caps are cotton made. Some said the crown has design on the head while the caps have none.

They continue to say many differences. After they were done the king said you have all tried but the major difference is that the cap is sealed at the top while the crown is open at the top. Kings rides on the advices of counselors that surround him; their minds are open just like their crown and this is what make kings wiser than all. There is a rare smartness in applying external mind. At a time in the construction of Eiffel tower the lifts to the second platform presented a more complex problem, because a straight track was not possible.

No French company was willing to undertake the work. The European branch of Otis Brothers & Company submitted a proposal but this was rejected: the fair's charter ruled out the use of any foreign material in the construction of the Tower. The deadline for bids was extended, but still no French companies put themselves forward, and eventually the contract was given to Otis in July 1887. Otis had been confident that they would eventually be given the contract and had already started design studies. Nobody knows it all.

Team pursuit power

*~To the bird and pilot the tail is as
important in the sky as the wing~*

Among all the animals that walk on the four limbs, there is a particular one that has the capacity to stand conveniently on the hind limb. Kangaroo makes use of his tail as the supporting stood to achieve this. It did not see or treat its tail as something to overlook. It gets to develop the tail's muscle from tender age by making use of it to do the task. The weakest part of a chain determines the overall strength of the chain. Every member of your team must be treated as important and well developed, not being engaged as occasion permits. When David was on the mission to recover his family and properties, it was an Egyptian, a servant of the raider that hooked up David for direction.

Because the young man was sick, his master left him and went away with the strong and healthy, he ignored his weak link on the chain and sidetracked it. But their gallant victory was turned down to defeat through the weak member of the team. When David came across the man, he took care of him and made him feel at home to extract information from him and this led to the discovery and conquering of the band. I perceive David must have learnt from the mistake of the enemy that came to raid him. Therefore, when he returned victoriously with the captives, he treated his servants that were left behind from following them on the recovery mission because of their weariness, the same way he treated those that were strong to go to the war. They all had equal share from the bounty. He went further to make it a statute in his army.

Try Every Available Mind—TEAM

It is a great leadership skill to entertain the potentials of others in a way that gives room for their leadership ability to be polished. A good leader knows when to lead from behind like the duck and when to stay in front like the hen. The sun knows when to withdraw for the moon to glow; knows when to hide behind the cloud for the rainbow to reign; knows how to rest above the storm for the lightning bolt to flash to visibility; knows when to sleep for the farthest stars to conspicuously shine; a good leader knows when to let others live themselves at the expense of his pride. You should know when to hide your ego for your goal to prevail on the platform of your investment in your team. You should know when to deliberately delegate and refuse to interfere at the expense of your perfectionisms. You cannot lead your team beyond your playing theme.

Men before the means

Insulate your dream but do not isolate it; dreams need people to be fulfilled, it is fulfilled with people and it is fulfilled for people. An officer who was assigned with the responsibility of light house maintenance discovered one day that the oil for the emergency fire was about being exhausted. He had already contacted the off shore station for refuelling and they had promised him but delayed in the supply. Around midnight he perceived a ship was approaching from afar and by experience projected that it will head straight for the formidable mountain which had claimed many big ships' journey. He thought of what to do, he reasoned that it was of no use to shout, and if he decide to use his specially designed slow pace paddle canoe to reach out, it will be too late.

After much thought, he resolved to set the boat that was meant to convey him to the land on fire using it as fuel so he could divert the impending disaster. Though, he was well aware of the implication, he may have to be starved for the period of time he could be reached from the station. But he concluded it is better for me to starve for days than for lives to perish in the sea. So he set it on fire. As he had correctly predicted, the ship headed straight for the rock but sighting the fire the sailor got aware of the obstacle and safely sailed the ship off by the side. As they passed the mountain and the burning boat, the captain of the ship got angry and wondered what his officer could be doing that the newly purchased boat carelessly got set on fire.

The ship, unknown to the lighthouse man was taking his boss and family to another continent. Right there, the captain drafted the query for the lighthouse man: he wrote, "You either pay up for the burnt boat with your gratuity as you were due to end your service or you spend your retirement in prison." While doing that, the lighthouse man was as well writing the report of what had happened. After three days, the fuel supplier came around with another scheduled fuel. When the starving officer accosted him why he did not bring the fuel as scheduled, he said the captain asked him to bring the fuel that he would help him to deliver it since he was passing the route.

The officer quickly reasoned he must have been in the ship he burnt the boat to redirect. Meanwhile, the captain delayed unaware of the urgency. To worsen the whole situation, the captain, out of anger, as he passed the route forgot to neither deliver the fuel nor drop refreshment for the lighthouse man. The next time the lighthouse man got to the office to deliver his report he was given query and sack letter. After carefully reading it, he handed the secretary his own report and wrote as well a short note for the captain, he wrote "Sir, I think I rather prefer to purchase your life and family with my gratuity and forever happy for a successful time in serving you. On receiving the report and the note, the captain felt ashamed of his own selfishness after having the full understanding of what happened—being blinded to the farewell of a loyal heart by his own legal heart.

It has been popularly said that customers first and are always right. In other word, it is acceptable for CEOs to rate their customers above their personnel to maintain their sales record. For example, if you have the course to lose either your best personnel or your best customer, which one will you pick as a leader? I know customers are important but not first, in all cases. This is typical order or system in organization that will outlive others.

Personnel ➡ Process ➡ Product ➡ Patronages

To lead a stable and viable organization, a well-informed leader will as well follow this path as order of priority in welfare and necessity. Meaning, he will prefer to have a fall in patronage than to have his product quality reduced. He will rather accept a fall in quantity produced than to short circuit is production process; and above all, he will not mount unnecessary pressure on his men to secure customers pleasure. Learn to be patient in understanding people's weakness, it could the strength you need all along. This is also another interesting illustrative story about leadership emotional skill.

There was a hunter who had a dog that hunts with him. Every time they go for gaming and he cites an animal he will let loose the dog for a hot chase; the dog will catch the animal and drag it to its master or it will weaken it and begin to bark until the master locate it and the prey. He had done this in many occasions, which made the man to like it. One day the dog chased a rabbit to the extreme of the forest, when it caught the rabbit, it weaken it with is fangs and was about dragging it to his master when the roaring of a lion was heard. The dog being frightened dropped the rabbit and ran away; the lion showed up and began to limp to the prey.

It had fallen in to a trap, got injured, and was left behind by its pride. The injury grew worse and it became unable to run after prey anymore relying on luck to survive. When it saw the dog with a captured prey, he chose to be smart by scaring the dog away. Afterward, the lion slowly reached the half-dead rabbit and fed on it. It retrieved in to the little den it struggled to make for itself. When the dog reached its owner, the man was surprised why it could not bring the prey for he was sure of the catch since it had blood on its mouth.

This hunter got angry having concluded that the dog had tried to play smarter by eating the rabbit. He beat the dog with a rod and starved it for the day. The second day the same thing happened with a doe and the third day. Every time the man would maltreat the dog and starve it. Meanwhile the lion was getting better as it was getting well fed as the dog continued to chase the animals to the extreme of thick forest which entraps them preventing them from escaping. This enabled the dog to always catch them near to the lion's abode.

The lion as well had become so familiar to the dog; he saw it as a savior and a friend. Like a tamer of a lion. He so much appreciates the dog's effort to sustain its life. Weeks after weeks the dog began to get use to the experience, anytime he chases animal to the spot and sight the lion afar, it will just leave the animal not allowing the lion to roar. However, the lion began to see it as an understanding friend. Afterward, the lion got well and prepared to go and look for its pride.

Just the following day the dog and the man went for hunting and this time around, the man has changed his mind to hunt the animal together with the dog. So when they sighted a squirrel, the man notified the dog with the chain he had tied to its neck and the belt on his loin. He began to chase the animal using the dog smelling ability for bearing. As usual, the animal moved to the extreme of the bush. As they approached the lion's den, the dog stopped when it almost caught the animal.

The man was very angry and dragged the dog to run but it refused. It had never come closer to the den like that for it knew that king of the jungle lives there. The man said, "Now I know you are a funny and selfish dog. Because you know today you won't be able to feed on the game you refused to catch it." He began to hit the pet with the stick in his hand; the dog began to bark in pain and tried to run away but it could not for the man had tied the chain to his lion belt. The lion was fast asleep when the barking of the dog reached its hearing.

It quickly woke up, by then it had come to identify the barking of its friend. As it stood up, it began to walk to the outside of the den, and there he saw his friend with a man. The man stopped the beating immediately he saw the lion and shouted for help. The lion had thought the friend was barking because of the prey as usual, but he saw a man tied to him. He looked around and saw no animal killed. By this time the man had falling to the ground in fear; he could not attempt to run because the closeness was much, so it would be foolish to attempt running hopelessly.

The dog continued to bark but the lion was so excited to see his friend for the last time since it was planning to leave immediately it wakes up. Gradually, it moved closer to the dog wagging its tail; the dog could not run away because of the chain. When it approached the dog, it too was half-dead literally. The lion licked its fur and smelt the man to know if the dog knew him since they were tied together or he was just a stranger wanting to harm its friend.

Luckily, the man smelt like the dog because they have always been living together. Then the lion turned away, still wagging its tail left the man on the ground breathing heavily; it went in search of its pride. If you have read the account of the prophet in the scripture with his donkey you will understand fully the wisdom behind being patient; that is, considering the past, the present and the future before taking judgmental step upon your team members.

Every member of your team is equally important if you want to raise a flying team—from the head to the tail; from manager to messenger; from director to janitor; from supervisor to lay man. The wing gives the lift; the tail gives the direction while the head leads on. When a cat walks the ground it leaves a footprint; when fish dives the ocean, it leaves surf behind; when the earthworm move on the ground it lives a hole behind but when the eagle flies it leaves no visible path in the sky. Beware and be careful when you are up in the sky of your dream, flying from helipad to airport, living at higher altitude far from the hearts you lead; for often a great temptation will arise to be accessible by fewer minds that are privileged with direct contact, and make lesser impact on the rest.

A skilled leader knows when and how to delegate minor in order to dedicate himself to the major. Leadership is one-man title but not one-man battle.

Paint your dream with brush of time, using a ladder of men resting on the wall of trust, with a can of potential you hold along, the picture is noticed with your self-persistence, intra-patience and conscience. Give your light to all men you can, so when your sun is finally hidden at night the moon of men you have lighted will illuminate the path you led during your days. You will need men to climb up, but remember that as you climb very high, your supporter is not the last rung you rest your leg on, but also all the rest from the ground. From the cleaner as the ground rung, followed by the messenger, the janitor, the gateman, secretary and so on, till the vice president that forms the last rung on which you place your leg, or that you are in direct contact.

There was group of youngsters each with a piece of wood. Suddenly, they came across a fruitful tree that was too tall to be climbed by anyone of them. They concluded that it is impossible to neither climb the tree nor get the fruits. As they were about leaving the tree, one of them said, "I have an idea, can all of you please lend me your piece of wood?" They replied why not, and gladly they donated all. This smart guy used the pieces of wood to make a long ladder and made sure its own was the highest rung.

He placed the ladder on the tree stem and climbed up. On reaching the top he plucked fruits and began to eat. The others below waited for a while expecting him to remember them. When he was satisfied, he began to throw down for them the unripe and defected ones. When they could bear it no more they called out to him. "We want to leave." He said, "You can go—after all I am standing on my own piece of wood." Then each one began to remove his piece of wood from the bottom rung.

When they were almost reaching the top, the young entrepreneurship minded guy realized that ladder was almost gone; he got hold of a branch of the tree and felt secure as he watched the ladder disappeared. He was still boasting of his smartness when he realized no way for him to get to the ground. Quickly, he swallowed his pride, shouted and called out for them asking they contribute their pieces of wood to make the ladder again. He promised to pluck for them the good and ripe fruits as well.

This is the mind orientation of some business minded and blinded entrepreneur. They often fail to realize that they are not building on their idea but men that embrace the idea. Appreciate every one you ever meet in life. The higher a leader goes the more conspicuous he is from afar and the smaller his men appear below; to keep in touch with the lowest from the highest point is the greatest task of outstanding leaders. They see you the more but you see them the less but the gap must not be open because your men are your primary method, the king of 'tools' to achieve anything. Without men money because a burden, machines becomes idle and material rotten away; the master is frustrated.

~They often fail to realize that
they are not building on their idea but men
that embrace the idea~

UNFILTERED LOVE

An old man living in a neighborhood to a young man who use to get angry with everyone once had a course to have a chat with him when they entered the same bus. He asked, young man why is it that you fight with almost everyone? He replied, "No old man, rather everyone fights with me." He said, "Why do you get angry so easily?" "He replied, "No sir, they beget anger in me. I never intend to fight anyone of them but I have to contend for my right." "Old man, do not you also get reactive to people opposing you? He asked. He replied, "No, I respond." He said tell me what is the difference between the two? "When you react you act equal and in opposite reaction. But when you respond it doesn't need to be equal nor opposite, you determine the composite, direction and projection of your reciprocation. When they shout at you and you shout back like an echoe you only react, when they shout at you and you smile that is response." The old man said. "Haven't you read King Solomon's counsel that answer not a fool according to his folly lets you look like a fool like him." He added.

"That is the third law of motion but the first law of emotion. You do not hear everything people say, you only listen; you do not see everything everybody does you only look. So you can choose what you hear and see and the action that follows per time. The second law of emotion is just like the first law, your nerves excitation is principally the product of external force. Your mood will remain stable or in constant direction until the world affects it. But you can choose whether it will set it in correct motion or commotion; your emotion is invisible and untouchable unlike the physical object so no one can really impact it to change its course without you serving as a middle man," explained the wise baldhead.

"You are the gateman for your emotional flood gate. Think of it, " he said further, "When you beam a blue light on an opaque object what will be the color of the shadow?" He said black; likewise, when you beam a red light what will be the shadow color? He said black; what of white light? He replied the same thing; "And the rest of the colors?" the old man asked. He said the shadows of all the colors will remain black. He then faced the young man eyeball to eyeball and told him, "What determines the color of the shadow is not the color of the light but the opaque subject in question, the rays can only determine the sharpness of the shadow." No matter the color of light; the shadow is always black, the same should be of your reciprocation to what people think and talk about your dream and belief. No matter what their comments are, you can choose to be positive. So when men shine on you the red light of disgust and hurt, choose your shadow; when they shine on you the blue light of love choose your shadow; when they shine on you the green light of acceptance choose you shadow; when they beam on you the yellow light of betrayal and hypocrisy you choose your shadow, you have got the power to determine the output color. No matter the action, you can choose your response and not cheat on potential reaction.

The law of friendship

~Sometimes if you can't change the
people that surround you, change
your surroundings~

To change people's temperament sometimes is as difficult as trying to change their sex. To change their attitude is like trying to change their names. Relationships are ladders, you ascend with them or you descend. A friend is a good heart mirror and an act mirror. He or she helps you to review yourself by his reaction or retraction. A friend is the one who loves you before he really knows you and when he knows you, he still loves you just the same only just really. If you want to go down a pit, you will need a ladder, if you want to rise to the peak, you need a ladder and that is the law of friendship. You need to meet some folks to raise your dream; you need to meet some folks to erase your dreams.

Our color is just a variety of packaging and not a variation of worth. Water cycle looks like love cycle; more than 70% of earth surface is covered with water, the human body is about 60% water by weight. This gives us a glimpse of the extent of how love is to occupy in our hearts. Just as the oceans throw up water and get it redistributed as rain to thirsty souls, so is love; as you are rejecting it and throwing in the towels, remember God is filling some souls afresh with love. The scripture says the love of God has been pour abroad on our soul by the Holy Spirit. From him who seems not to have even what he has will be given to some else who already has. Do not hoard love. When you fail to show love to your neighbors, God knows how to use someone else. The rocks can as well sing when men lock their lips. Just as the saying goes, practice makes perfect. Know that you have the capacity to love because you carrythe nature of God—the nature of love.

The same when you start the journey of love in a small way you will witness it waxing strong. Have you imagined how marital love starts between a man and a woman? It begins just casual, until it becomes conjugally mutual. When faith is lost only hope can find it and when hope lost only love can find it. Hope is the anchor of the soul but if the rope is cut in hopelessness love will freeze the ocean to a rock and again ground the storming boat. Love never fails. If the wind is not blowing, you dash against the still air and you will feel the wind—you can generate wind by reaching out so is love, take the first move of love if you are surrounded by only haters and enemies. Start the love path if nobody will make the move, stir the atmosphere to generate the wind. Relationship is like walking over a bridge of love all you have to do is to communicate on the street above and only peep at the sea of weaknesses that passes under the bridge. However, many rather use a canoe of ignorance or worse still, act funnily by jumping in to the sea trying to swim across to relate. This is typically stressful and damaging. Just let the strength of you two, be what is found on the bridge of your relationship. Every relationship, save conjugal, should have two doors the front and the back, so when it is time to unavoidably depart for good; we won't need to create a scene in trying to open the front door again.

Depart in peace and progress, like Joseph planned to put his fiancée away secretly though out of ignorance.

> ~There are some friendships you
> plan to break, there are some you
> plan to make~

Love begins as a solid form, when we only feel it and apply it to ourselves. This is the love for yourself for who you are—accepted or rejected, celebrated or relegated, approved or reproved; then love move on to the second stage as a liquid form, when we extend it like a flowing river of love to any who come to our lives path. We do not only touch those who contact us but like a river we bless also those we contact on the life path. Then love should grow to gaseous form when it spreads to beyond our deliberate path and randomly touch humanity. When we can no longer contain ourselves, when we become self-less that we just want to reach out, not on a narrow river path but a generalized platform like a living sea. We become desperate to help and rescue both friends and enemies. Like the sower, we scatter our seed of love without direction or focus allowing it to fall both on good ground and rocky and thorny soil. When we become like our heavenly father that rains His rain and shines His sun upon all—good and evil.

We go out of our way to make a way for a stranger. We prefer others to ourselves when in turn or queue. We graduate to the new commandment the master gave that supersedes the second great commandment. The old one says, love your neighbor as yourself, the new love command says love one another as I have loved you. How did Jesus love us? He left everything, humbled Himself and sacrificed himself. This is more than loving your neighbor as yourself.

INTELLIGENT EMOTION

> ~In every heart there is a
> hole and there is a hope~

Humanity is like the piano, we compose of black and white keys; if we refuse to let the Creator play us together in harmony, we will miss the tuned symphony of mother earth destiny. On the instrument, both white and black keys are equally important and purposefully placed. Likewise the races, either you are white or black, we must be played together by the great Master who orchestrates all things according opt His purpose. You forgive people not because the pain has gone but that the pains may be gone. If the last time you forgive is father than yesterday, you are having a lot hanging on you for forgiveness. Why? It is impossible to live a day without offences. People will offend you for doing what is right but keep doing what is right by forgiving them.

Every time you drink a cup of, know that billions of people have drunk the same water before you. And as you drink it as well you will release it as urine, sweat, faces or tears. Then the water will find its way to the oceans and ultimately to the atmosphere as vapor, pouring again for other billions of people to drink. Water unifies us together and that is how love was destined to keep us together. God confused the verbal language of the people of Babel and not their love language, because they can't survive without the love language either together in one place or scattered abroad.

~You forgive people not because
the pain has gone but that the
pains may be gone~

Emotional tank

You do not appear for Olympics 100 meters wearing an open parachute. You need to evacuate some thoughts, excessive goals and people from your path to gather strength and time for your flight. Like the space shuttle consists of three major components: a winged orbiter that carries both crew and cargo; an external tank containing liquid hydrogen (fuel) and liquid oxygen (oxidizer) for the Orbiter's three main rocket engines; and a pair of large, solid-propellant, strap-on booster rockets. At lift off the entire system weighs 2 million kilograms (4.4 million pounds) and stands 56 meters (184 feet) high. During launch the boosters and the Orbiter's main engines fire together, producing about 31,000 Kilonewtons (7 million pounds) of thrust.

The boosters are jettisoned about two minutes after lift-off and are returned to earth by parachute for reuse. After attaining 99 Percent of its orbital velocity, the Orbiter has exhausted the propellants in the external tank; it releases the tank, which disintegrates on re-entering the atmosphere. Let us relate this with our discourse; if you want to go higher in life you have to let go of old weight that has used up their time with you. Paul said when he was a child he talked and did everything as a child but when he grew up he put off childish attitudes.

You cannot change your level without changing your in built emotional quotient. You need to discern which relationship and fellowship to embrace or to disengage. The rocket cannot reach its highest orbit with the entire tanks of fuel it takes off with. Let the past weakness not reoccur in your path. Part with them and drop them like an empty jettisoned rocket fuel tank. They are already burnt fuel like ashes. You need to know the emotional character you need to relieve of their services in your relationship and life. Paul said everything is lawful for me but not everything is expedient. You must let go of fellows that are like lead weight in your ship. They will sink your floating ideas in to the depth of fear and you must let go of those who have everything to say but nothing to do. You may be justified to get angry but your anger hardly justifies your intelligence.

One wise leader said in response to New Year planning question; he answered, "I set myself up for a great year by ruthlessly eliminating the bottom 30 percent of activities, projects, and commitments from the previous year, by removing those from my calendar; I get space to focus on the activities with the biggest payoff." Another one echoed the point; "By killing the underperforming tasks and projects," he said; "It opens up all kinds of room for me to be more creative and innovative without running out of margin." The same with you, ten years away from now you will look back and observe those emotional features you have had to shed in the course of the decade. The more you consciously discard them the better the movement achievement.

You must strive to watch the fuel you supply our emotion. It must be a positive emotional fuel. That reminds me of An American aviator, Charles Augustus Lindbergh, one of the best-known figures in aeronautical history, remembered for the first nonstop solo flight across the Atlantic, from New York to Paris, on May 20–21, 1927. Lindbergh's early years were spent chiefly in Little Falls, Minnesota, and in Washington, D.C., where for 10 years his father represented the 6th district of Minnesota in Congress. His formal education ended during his second year at the University of Wisconsin in Madison, when his growing interest in aviation led to enrolment in a flying school in

Lincoln, Nebraska, and the purchase of a World War I Curtiss Jenny, with which he made stunt-flying tours through Southern and Midwestern states.

After a year at the army flying schools in Texas (1924–25), he became an airmail pilot (1926), flying the route from St. Louis, Missouri, to Chicago. During this period he obtained financial backing from a group of St. Louis businessmen to compete for the $25,000 prize offered for the first nonstop flight between New York and Paris. In the monoplane Spirit of St. Louis he made the flight in 33.5 hours on May 20–21, 1927. The plane was a Ryan NYP developed from the Ryan M2, a single-engine, high-wing monoplane, modified to Lindbergh's specifications. In standard conformation the airplane would have seated five people but extra fuel tanks in the "Spirit of St. Louis" occupied much of what had been cabin space.

The "Spirit of St. Louis" was returned from Europe to the United States aboard ship, and Lindbergh flew it extensively throughout North, Central, and South America to promote interest in aeronautics before donating it to the Smithsonian Institution. Overnight Lindbergh became a folk hero on both sides of the Atlantic and a well-known figure in most of the world. There followed a series of goodwill flights in Europe and America. The focus here is that Lindbergh replaced the passenger's seat with fuel for the journey. There are some relationships that you must drop to have a place for enough time, training, treasures, thinking as fuel for your journey in life.

Imagine if he had carried along pessimist as copilot, he had tell him, "Limberge, this is a suicide mission for us but we have a choice to quit it now." If you find it difficult to lose, an association when there is need then at least be loose from the association. Remember, your world rotates on the axis of your relationship. He had to let go of five possible distractive and negativity speculators for increase in fuel capacity for the journey. Impossibility is what happens when we listen too much to those who are advocates of their weaknesses.

If you are confused of what to do, conclude on what to do—leave the crowd of coward, shelve the camp of critics and the action will become clearer. Use your right hand to pursue your need and your left hand your wants, if your right hand needs a helping hand let your left hand lend it, if your left hand need a helping hand, let it end its pursuit—in other word do not keep a company at the expense of your destiny. Look for men with positive motivation that will serve as your additional fuel tank. For the space shuttle to reach the space where the gravitational pull is relaxed it must let go of some components. If you must reach the sky you must be of light content. The sky is for the lights—the stars, the moon, the sun, shooting star, the rainbow, the lightening and the rest.

Patience intelligence

~The beauty of patience is often
revealed in just a little more~

A young curious village boy once heard from his science teacher that what the hen applies to the egg when it tries to incubate them is its body heat. When he got home, he went straight to the family poultry and took five eggs out of ten eggs in the nest of his grandmother hen. He went back to the kitchen and put them on the fire like his mummy used to do. After couple of minutes, he removed them from the cooker and peeled them. To his surprise, he got the same result as his mom use to get, a solid whitish oval shape food. He went back to the poultry and saw the hen already brooding over the remaining five. After some days, he went back and saw five beautiful chicks emerging from the eggs; a new life and product. He became confused and finally went to his grandma to explain things.

The old woman replied, your teacher was right, it is the heat that turns the egg to chicks but the difference is how the heat is applied. The hen is highly patient and takes time to supply the heat gradually giving room for the eggs to refresh anytime it leaves the nest. It shields the hen and does everything in its power to resist intruder. The same with relationship there is none without heat being generated but what determines whether you come out with dead whitish egg or a living testimony of newly born ideas, progress, leverages and testimony is how you, handle the moments in patience or out of it. A little more patience is often the beauty of patience. There is no bad peace; there is no good war in the scope of love.

Water flows up steepest hill, the tallest mountain, neither as turbulent river, nor gentle stream but as gentle and light vapor. If we can take life bit-by-bit and simple as a vapor, we can rise to boundary of heaven. It is not the water that erodes the rock but the rocks that flows in the water. If water cannot move a rock, it just moves round it not to shift it but wear it out. It takes some little rocks along to do the job.

If you cannot solve a problem at a go, go on living and the experiences you reap will wear it off with time. They will comfort you until when God finally confront it to answer your prayer and reward your patience in your relationship. God has answer to every situation, when He is slow, he is not trying to study the problem or consult books; He is just taking time for us to learn in the process He undertakes. Not just for us in future but for others He will send to us with the same features of challenges.

The water storm

A Chemistry teacher asked his high school students, how would you know that the water is boiling? One by one, they began to raise their hands: one said once the water begins to steam; another said once the water begins to bubble; still another said once the temperature is reaching 100^0 degree; the teacher asked if there was any other contribution. Then another three pupils raised their hands; the first said, once the water is making noise; the second said when the pressure it mounts against the atmosphere is increased and equal to it; the third said once the kettle begins to vibrate on the fire.

As the teacher was about to ask the class to clap for all of them for such a brilliant and accurate answers, a hand was raised from the corner of the class. The teacher wondered, what else could this curious boy have to say? Then the young heart said, "Once my father begins to boil, the water is boiling already in the kitchen." The dazed chemist said can you explain further how do you know your father is boiling? He said when he does all what my colleagues have just said: when he begins to fume and steam, have a raised temperature, mounting pressure on our living room atmosphere, begins to have is voice bubble with louder volume resulting in noise from the kitchen and his body begins to vibrate. The teacher said what had that got to do with boiling water? The boy answered, "When that happens mum has been wasting Daddy's gas—the water is boiling already and dad gets to know first."

This is what anger does to the man who welcome and house it in his bosom, it comes with a shake, it is a form of heart quake, accompany with body ache and emotional bubbles. After the exhibition of this deadly sport, the host athletic will experience the phenomenon of a container with liquid enclosed. When you have a water in a keg halve filled, and you get it shaken up and left alone, you discover that the water inside will still be oscillating or waving.

Exactly with you, when you give in to anger; after you are done with the subtle drama, though you are physically settle, your inner man will not, your heart will still be resonating from the negative impact it had on it. Your mind will be filled with echoes of those words you never planned nor imagined to be the mouthpiece; while your anatomical status is still crushing under the shock left behind by the tension you generated for them.

Anger may be short in display but the smoke generated by the spark lingers on and travels beyond the scene. Your words are irrevocable, the scene recorded in the film of your spectators. Why should you create such a horror picture of your weakness and indiscipline? You may be right to be angry by your standard, in fact, every anger warrior are self-justified, they fought for their right that is left behind, but you won't be right at the end. To be angry in a right measure, for the right treasure, in the right period, in the right place, with the right person, with the right procedure, with the right mood texture is so difficult if not impossible to attain; that to do away with it is a gracious and easier alternative recommended. When you are angry for what money can buy you are still a babyish man; when you are angry to defend your weakness you are not strong; when you are angry to defend your strength you are weak.

There is nobody that gets angry that really thinks about it before embarking on the adventure. It is simpler to control yourself-ego than to control your anger. It is better to redefine your love principle and standard in mild terms than to resist the temptation of anger. If you do not want explosion you do not take a gas around those who live with fire. You wisely choose what you present to them. Anger is easily transmitted. Like I picture above, if the gas is joined with the fire both will explode.

Scientifically speaking, water does not need to reach 100°C before boiling; it boils once it has equal temperature with the atmospheric. If you take the water to the top of Mount Everest, it will boil far less than 100°C. You do not need to be heated up before you effectively express your feeling—you can bubble up without being heated up. What you need to do is change your altitude of reasoning by your attitude with seasons.

Kill your monstrous master

There was a houseboy who was being maltreated by his mistress, one of the rules she gave him was that no form of liquid must drop or pour on the floor. One day, the boy slipped with a bottle of water in his hand and right before his mistress the water spilled a little on the floor. The woman, as usual, got angry and gave him a serious beating. To cool her hanger, she took the remaining water in the bottle thinking it was potable water.

As she gulped a good volume in her mouth, she perceived the water was too tasty for drinking, though colorless and odorless. She ordinarily could have spewed the water out because of the obnoxious taste, but in other not to look foolish before the boy she had boasted of her great skill and perfectionism of avoiding water on the floor, she decided to pour the water back in to the bottle, but she has to do it gradually, since the mouth of the bottle couldn't allow all at a go.

Meanwhile, her mouth was highly irritating because of the water, but she forced herself to be patient enough to release the water from her mouth in to the bottle gradually. The boy was already crying, not for the beating again, but the next one to come, because of what was about to happen. Suddenly, he cried out the more and that made the woman to look back at him but now with a gentle look.

In the mean time, the woman had been going through a lesson within. She had been a victim of hot temperament for long, which had actually cost her marriage. She had been meditating, that despite the badness of the water, I was able to hold it a while and succeeded in avoiding it from spilling on the floor by choosing to release it gradually. In other word; I could hold my temper, despite the unpalatable things people might do to me, and I could avoid exploding and scattering things, by gradually releasing by emotion and hurts, in slow word, low voice and gentle touch; without selfishly and angrily splitting emotional commotion all over the atmosphere; nor spitting venom of bitterness over people's peace and joy.

Then she turned to the boy and asked, "Why are you still crying?" He said he cried not because of the beating but because of the next one. She asked which next one? He replied, "Because of the water I had made you to drink." "I have taken one of your bottles from the fridge and kept it all this while. Whenever you maltreat me either by starving me or abusing me and I felt like crying, I used the bottle to collect my tears that they might not fall on the ground to avoid punishment. Over the days the water in the bottle got full and I was about to go and empty it when I slipped and it poured on the floor. The remaining was what you just drank that is why I knew another beating was awaiting me."

"Why did you increase the degree of your crying afterward?" she asked. He said because as he was crying a drop of his tear fell to the floor since the bottle was with her, and for this, he knew the third beating is a possibility. The woman, ashamed of herself, calmed the boy, assuring him that she was now a better mistress. "No more beating, no more anger, I can hold my emotion, it is possible I can. I can release my pain gradually and without multiplying it to disrupt others joy or spitting it out in fury over the emotions and happiness of my surrounding."

When the torrent of anger attempts to tempt you, you have the choice to allow it to steam to gas whereby you fume it out in a rage or conceive, conceal, incubate and freeze it up to bitterness, that it becomes a stone in your heart which you carry all about or let it settle like a gentle stream that it is dried up by the sun of love and patience, before the sun of the goes down on it, as Paul admonished.

Time and anger

Anger will either reduce your words or multiply your word. It makes you talk extensively in malady or talk conservatively in malice. A fool is not only a man that talks extensively but also a man that talks extremely. Anytime we propel more emotion than intuition we have something to wish reversed. Time management is destiny management and it is sometimes best practised in emotional management. Like suffocating your anger; anger will cost you not the moments but the movement of the rest. A mature mind is like a thermostat it acts not reacts like thermometer. It has the capacity to start and stop encounters.

> *Anger -The monster of emotion*
> I do not need you as a servant
> For you destroy my message
> I do not need you as a master
> For you are selfish and subtle
> When I feel to employ a tool of revenge
> I will deploy like a fool a troop of love
> Patience will be the captain of my army
>
> You come in me uninvited
> You leave me but your job lingers
> You make the young and old think alike
> When you hang the sense—oh anger
> Your wings rejoice in the wind of pride
> Your strength feeds on my weakness
> What a manger of danger you are

THE LETTING GO SPIRIT

~Friends fight so they won't become enemies~

Forgive in time forget with time

A butterfly was captured by a lizard; as the reptile held it tight in its mouth looking to settling down to digest it, a falcon sighted the well composed lizard and suddenly, dived down smartly, pinning it down with its sharp claws and up it lifted it, dangling in the air and flying to a safe place to set and digest it. Just some feet in to the air, a man cashing fun with gaming sighted the falcon which was so bold to descend so low above his head, aimed his gun and shot it down.

As the excited man was celebrating his accurate aiming and reaching out to pick the bird on the ground into his cage. A cop who had been watching him shooting the prohibited bird came near challenging him of his offence and straight away gave him a slap and put a handcuff in his hand. As he was being ushered in to the Black Maria, a human right activist who happened to be a lawyer led a crowd who accosted the policeman for taking law in his hands, seized him and began to mob him but he was finally rescued with force by his colleagues who were returning from the check point.

In the meantime, the lizard out of pain released the butterfly in its mouth setting it free to fly away; the falcon as actually being shot with a tranquilizer, it slept off immediate the bullet hit it, and with that the lizard was released right there in the air. The police men finally discovered that the man had only fired a tranquilizer and not actually killing forbidden bird as he released it from the cage to fly away in freedom. The crowd insisted that the man should be set free while the cops finally went away with his colleagues who had come to fight for his freedom.

Sometimes you find yourself in the position as the captor when we are offended and given the privileged to forgive or react. We can choose to let go easily or until we are pressed by a situation that threatens us with pain like the lizard or hold on unto our offender until we sleep off at old age like the falcon, or not until we discover our foolishness of being wrong in the first place like the cops, or when God forcefully deal with us to let go of our victim just like the crowd dealt with the cop; just like the wicked servant in the parable who won't let go of a small debt owned him by his colleagues until their master also determined to collect his own for which he had already forgiven him thereby putting him in the prison. Which way will you let go—by force or by choice?

~Forgiveness is emotional intelligence~

Your enemies are not those who you hate alone but those who love you for hating your enemies. Letting go spirit is the king of relationship attitude. It pilots every order of action and reaction and greases their delivery. Both the "unforgiver" and the "unforgivened" have something to lose—the former his friendship with a man, the latter his friendship with God which is worse.

When the tree shelters the bird and animals, no special or extraordinary favor is done, for the tree is dead if it is hidden from the sun. Sometimes we think we are doing people favor but the fact is that we are doing our self the greater favor when we forgive and let go. In life, we have choice about everything the only thing we do not have choice about is who we are in the eyes of God. The same way, value others' relationship as God values His with you, which makes Him to keep on forgiving and forgiving. When you share your happiness, it is not divided in to halve, I mean happiness share does not diminish in your heart it is rather multiplied on earth. With man there are no 'unforgivable' acts, there are only unforgiving hearts.

To co-exist without tolerance spirit is a path to a turbulent relationship. Birds do not walk on tree, once they perch they keep the deal, not to hurt a leaf, even as they feed on the fruit, knowing that without the leaves the tree is dead but without the fruit the tree lives on to bear much more seed. To preserve your relationship you should know, what and what to touch, also; what and what not to touch per moment. The leaf to preserve in propagating your staying together in peace is forgiveness attribute; if you disregard it as you desire the fruits in your relationships you will cut the life span of your mutual tree short.

There are two ways to shine a light on a traveler who is walking in the dark, you can point the source directly in to his eye to blind his sight and you can point it on his path to brighten his sight. Show love in a lovely way. How you say sorry can further worry the situation.

> Love is detective but not selective
> Love is submissive not suppressive
> Love is permissive not possessive
> Love is progressive not aggressive
> Love is attentive not preventive
> Love is expressive not expensive
> Love is corrective not reactive
> Love is receptive not repulsive
> Love is attractive not defensive

Somebody once asked this question in the Bible study class about forgiveness. The young adult and new convert asked, "Did Joseph actually forgive his ten step brothers seeing that he locked them up for three days when he got hold of them?" The commandment in Lord's Prayer is to forgive and forgive and forgive… up to 7 x 70 daily, not to forgive and forget. It is not out rightly in the ability of a man to forget but the responsibility of time. Well, I want to believe he forgave them but did not forget. After three days of locking them up he told his brothers, "Do this and live for I fear God."

When God says, remember not the former things, He means do not think back. Joseph forgave his brothers but did not forget their deeds of grave hatred towards him. When they reconciled he acted strangely to them; organizing their three-day jailing was not to revenge actually, but to go about his emotion. Moreover, mind you he only gave them a house arrest not reprimanding them in the dungeon where Potiphar locked him. You can read the account again. At the end he said to them do this and live for I fear God.

Paul must have forgiven Demark but he still told Timothy about his disloyalty. Alexandra the copper smith emitted smoke in the eyes of Paul, Paul though with Christian love overlooked and forgave but he in his epistle to his protégée Timothy he reflected on the coppersmith action. If you cannot forget hold no guilt against thyself, to forgive is the law of love, though choose not to reason behind as time and season works on the memory and the harmony of future. It is not the ability forget the past that is a set of compliance to God's will but how we remember the past, is it in a way that glorifies God and edifies good pursuit, Paul had past that he preached and some that he choose to let go off in is thinking memory. "This one thing I do forgetting the things that are behind me…," that does not mean Paul forgot his past mistakes and life, for often he recount his past as he exhorts brethren but what characterize his reminiscence is tailoring it to a texture of testimony and lessons.

"To forgive is a habit of the
wise to forget is a habit of time"

What God says is not to remember the past and not to forget it. To forget means to erase it from memory, not to remember means not to raise it in memory. When we forgive the offender, it makes it easier to forget the offence.

If you can be hurt, it shows you are a human being, if you can forgive it shows you are being human. Forgiveness is a bridge of relationship; 'unforgiveness' is a breach of it. To every action there is an equal and opposite reaction but not necessarily should this be your behavior; often what we need is equal and opposite retraction.

Forgiveness, you can
It is a weapon of peace
It is found in the quiver of lovers
It is the eraser of past shadow
It is the narrow path few past

I will forgive when I forget
But when will I forget, not when I die?
I am not wrong when I was wronged
But what is right if I lose my left hand

When I move my anger, I remove our bridge
For the iron and bars are love and peace
When I am embittered, we are not bettered
For there lies between us a wall we build not a bridge

Offender does not forgive
He is deprived of peace making grace
Isn't the offended revenging when forgiveness is delayed?
Are not the offences multiplying when forgiveness is denied?

In silence our hearts cry,
For our lovebirds are wet
Yet in our voice there lays the choice
To sing again our love lyrics

At last, I will throw my heart over the fence
I will with my act break the wall,
The debris I will temper to raise a bridge
I'll remember my offender, not offence, to forgive freely

Chapter Seven

THE LANDMARK OF STARTING

~Beginning is the first winning~

The rain just beat the eaglets on the mountain placed nest with the mother eagle. She told her little ones to jump out and fly since the nest is not comfortable, but they were scared, "We are not fingerlings that dive the sea sky with wet fins; dear mother we can't for we will drop from the sky, our feathers are wet our wings are heavy, they chorused in unison." So the mother stopped urging further. Afterward the most fragile said, "Mother, I will—because I trust your discretion."

So, the brave jumped out, dropping down the mountain, flapping tirelessly, struggling with the wind current. The rest astonished and scared, gazed down following the trend of event with trembling, but they discovered their loving mother who cares so much for them was just calm and relaxed watching its trusting and thrusting baby, skiing and smiling at the sight.

Then the rate of adrenalin pumping increased for the concerned eaglets, as their peer approached the ground. However, before the crash the little eaglet was seen to dive forward, then thrust further, flapped onward, and then soared upward and farther toward the sky. The wind had dried the wings in the process, and the flight was balanced up. The mother eagle turned its golden-feathered neck and looked at the rest now excited team; it muttered, "Have you learnt."

~There is power in starting; avoidance
is the first key to limitation~

THE POWER IN NOW

I leant a powerful lesson from a great leader and mentor. In one of his leadership books, he talked about how he went to the airport with a gun gift in baggage. He got arrested, but was later vindicated for his innocence. What really stands out to me is how he slightly missed the possibility of avoiding the whole mess. While preparing for one of his talks, after the gun was given to him, to present to his wife as a gift, the thought of the gun came to his mind to get it out of the brief case but he waded it off. "There was one brief moment while I was working on my lesson when I thought to myself, Oh; I need to remember to get that gun out of my bag. However, I was in the middle of writing, and I didn't want to stop because I was on a roll. So I thought, I'll do it later. Time passed. Life was busy. I kept working. And before I knew it, Thursday morning rolled around and off I went to the airport."

Honestly, I have so much imbibed the lesson I learned and it has been a great help for me to do what is best for now at no other time but now. I have escaped many silly mistakes and grabbed a lot of opportunities by gleaning from this story.

~Seize the good opportunities
before they cease~

When opportunity knocks the doors, some never rise on their beds; some open the door and whisper wrong address; some receive him but address him wrongly, while some are not properly or readily dressed to follow him out in time. Procrastination is progress-crashing notion. When we do not work on our possibility, time works on it and makes it impossibility. The best time is now when it comes to some life matters and success ideas. Sometimes you need to leave your reading table or dining table, to fix quickly something you have the tendency of forgetting to do which may be of great regret if forgotten.

The same with life you will sometimes need to drop every other thing to achieve one thing. If you must use a telescope, use the kind of Galileo's time of which one eye is engaged at a time, so you can dream of tomorrow and yet be conscious of today. Do not sleep today to dream of tomorrow. Freedom to plan it is, when you are in charge of your time before the dawn.

The seed of now

The flood of time erodes idea when left for seasons. One day the king of the jungle called for meeting involving the animals in its kingdom. He told them, "I want the jungle gardens to be free of trees," and at random, he asked the dwellers to pick which garden tree to cut. By fate, full-grown gigantic cedar tree was allotted to the woodpecker, and by luck, the same type of cedar tree was allotted to the elephant, but a tender stem in nursery stage. When the result of the lot was announced, the big animal jumped up in overconfidence and in mockery of the woodpecker's helpless fate.

Then the king announced, this business must be completed in the next 50 years, before my return from a long span journey. Immediately the king departed, the woodpecker began to peel the back to have a bite in to the gigantic tree. In boasting and relaxed attitude, the elephant told itself, "This is a minor task though a great command, I will do it any time with a stroke." Years in, years out, the woodpecker worked tirelessly in its own little way while the elephant slept and dreamt of last minute crash program. Unknown to it, the tree was growing in the garden, which it had locked up. Not only that, the elephant was growing old and diminishing in strength by the order of nature. Behold, it got to 50 years since the king's departure, and a noise was heard in the jungle of the arrival of the king.

Quickly, the elephant rushed to the gate of the garden allotted to him and behold a cedar tree has grown to the size of the mini mountain; this big animal try to draw closer but discovered that it could no longer even jump the little stream that crossed the part. Age has worked on him and worse still; the tree was indomitable to be pulled down with a stroke as it would have been possible 50 years ago. At the sounding of the herald of the king's arrival, the gigantic cedar tree received the last peck to bring it down, making a loud noise that resonated the echoes King's welcome shout.

The big animal asked the woodpecker how it managed to do the magic, replying, it said to the big elephant, "When a weakness is dedicated with a planned focus, it becomes strength of genius." Solomon in his preacher's message, told us that desire as expiration period; he said when they shall be afraid of that which is high, and fears shall be in the way, and the almond tree shall flourish, and the grasshopper shall be a burden, and desire shall fail: because man goes to his long home, and the mourners go about the streets.

~A responsibility delayed today
is a possibility denied tomorrow~

Time is not what you can waste it is the only un-renewable natural resources! Time is a friend yet an enemy; It gives you no second chance for its gift. The cheapest of all success resources is time and costliest of them all is time. Some opportunities are like pawpaw they need not all yellow without before they are ripe for food. If you wait for them to be flamboyant on the tree, they are already rotten and devoured by birds. Action is the saving anchor of decisions not determination. Decision is volatile if delayed to condense in to action. Possibility and impossibility are both imagined. Everybody can imagine but the right axis of trailing separate some as optimists and the left axis as pessimists. In fact impossibilities thinkers are more skilled and expansive in thinking world than the other positive folks. Both impossibility and possibility thinking are attitudes not just conclusion. To a pessimist the only thing that is possible is reality.

~When we do not work out our
possibility time walk out on it
and made it impossibility~

Procrastination can be described as progress crashing notion. It is not a thief of time but a robber of the value of time. The value of time is measured by, if it is being used at the right time for the right thing, in a right way and in a right place. Better to spend your time on a right thing than to invest it in a wrong thing. The minor action you procrastinate today will become a major obstruction tomorrow.

Some items do not need to be on your timetable before you live your table to attend to them. Procrastination drags the future too fast and close to us that we are caught unprepared. One beautiful thing about time is that it is never too fast for those who are weak and it is never too slow for those who are strong.

Make the master move

Young poor scholar who aspired to become an entrepreneur always motivates his elder boy child, "Read books if you want to be great in life. If you want to reach higher heights you need to climb up with books."

Meanwhile, his toddler always listened anytime their father charged his brother. The toddler happened to be very active and playful and the father an addicted bookworm. So when the father wants to get him attentive he will collect his toy and keep them on the shelf where his hand can't reach.

One day, the toddler was disturbing his studious daddy who was trying to research more to fulfill his dream. As usual, he collected the boy's toys, went back in to his library and put it on the book shelf. The man dosed off while reading in his haggard library. When the boy came to check on his father and to plead for his toy he met the father sleeping. Not to disturbed his dad, he thought of how to pick the toys after all it is now the right time to play having done his homework.

However, the shelf was too tall for him to pick the toy car. He thought and thought, then something struck his mind—the slogan of their father to his elder brother, "Books will take you up in life, you will reach greater height with books; with books you can climb to the top well beyond what your hand can naturally reach." Then one by one he began to bring the big books of his scholarly dad from the shelf, placed them on the floor in front of the shelf above where his toy was kept. He put the big books of his dad one upon the other making them into a stool and more around the stool as a steps.

Then he climbed the books like staircase and was about taking the toy when his daddy woke up. He saw his boy as he picked the toy but didn't raise any alarm pretend still sleeping. As he rested his head on the desk he was stunned by the site he saw. The young boy successfully picked the toys and came down; picked up the books one by one and returned them to the shelf. Then the man called out to for him, Tom, how did you think that out? The boy rushed to his father, excited about his accomplishment saying, daddy you are awake. I did not want to disturb you with my toy by waking you up to pick it for me, but then I remembered you always say that books will make you to reach greater heights in life, that you can climb up with them. Therefore, I decided to practice it. I took your books, stood on them, and achieved my dream. The man immediately realized a lesson. "I took the books and decided to practice them." He had been gathering knowledge from books all his life but never practiced or took step on one. This thought him a lesson as it dawned on him why he never achieved his dream of business chain; he had not practiced or taken steps on the books he had been reading so he had remained on the ground.

Be ready to sow your today in to tomorrow and never be timed by others watch. Start small with a big dream, a long patience, a strong determination, and a low gratification and with high hope.

~When idea is determined to be born
resources will come to nurse it~

THE SKILL OF SMALL START

Begin from the bottom

A millionaire father wishing to convince his younger son who was bent in taking over his father's business rather than joining the company based on his qualification and capacity applied this. No matter how much the rich old man tried to convince him he would always prove a point that he could start from the top of the cadre as the CEO.

The older just watched thinking about the advice of their father for them—to complete their studies, grow up with capacity and a dream to maintain the success. The man, a retired biologist, decided to employ an art to explain. He told the two boys to get a bag of cereals, which had been feasted on by the bugs. Some were lifeless already, while some were still ok. Then took them to the pool and asked them to pour the seeds in the water. Some dived to the bottom of the small pool while the rest floated.

Then he asked them to leave them in the shallow pool. After one week, they got back to the garden pool and discovered that those that went to the bottom of the pool have begun to shoot out stem while the floating ones did not—they just swelled up, and being tossed by the wave of the water. Based on the observation, he asked them "Why did some grow and the rest did not?" They said because the ones that went to the bottom of the pool have life, and that was why they sank to the base of the pool. They became seedlings because they have life to carry on in to the future but those that floated at the top have no life capacity.

They are empty and that is why they remain on the pool top. Then he faced them straight and said the same with men; those among them that have the capacity it takes to succeed or sustain success to the future are always willing to start from the bottom and not as CEO. They subject themselves to pressure of life like the seed under the pressure of water. But at the end they take root and begin to grow gradually up with responsibility and stability. But those who start at the top swell up like those seeds; they will end up over eating, over sleeping, over playing, over spending and become too fat to move ahead. The sudden comfort will become a burden forthwith. Many got wounded by success they inherited like the prodigal Son in the scripture and in the nearest future they begin to be tossed here and there by life circumstances: bankruptcy, inflation, economic instability, pride, poor people management etc.

~You do not need more than what you
have to have what you need~

Small is beautiful

Four fingerlings hanged roundabout a pool in a little village. They all wished to swim in the Pacific Ocean. One said, "Oh! How I wish this village turned to an ocean; another said, "Oh! How I wish that someone will take me in an aircraft and drop me at a high altitude in the Pacific Ocean;" another said, "Oh! How I wish that there will be a great out pouring of rain that could lead to an ocean overnight in our small village." The fourth one told them, here is water, can we start here and they all laughed at it and asked in mockery, "What does a pool has in comparison with an ocean?" The forth fingerling replied and said, "Both of them are water and that it is better to cool it off in a pool of hope than to dry out at the ocean beach of wishes." After long and failed persuasion it decided to jump in to the pool. So as one of them wished, the rain fell but did not stay as an ocean since there was no depth in the village to accommodate it, but the flood swept the shallow pool of water in to the stream and the stream into a canyon; the canyon in to the river; and river found its way to the ocean all along with the forth fingerling inside.

It is better to fail earlier at lower altitude than at the high altitude. Starting small is an opportunity to fail small, if it is eventuality. Start with is available and obtainable.

You can dream in a hurry but you must tarry to wake it up to reality. The kangaroo delivers a joey, it places it in the outer pouch, where the young can leap out in time of opportunity and jump in when faced with danger. Do not just deliver your dream and hand it over to committee of men to handle. Nurse it and be ready to shield it from discouragement. Be like the kangaroo that delivers just one young per year so that it can fully measure out its guaranteed safety. "Kangaroos normally give birth to one young kangaroo, or joey, per year. A joey is born naked (hairless) at just 2.6 centimeters (1 inch) long. With the help of its claws, it climbs into its mother's pouch and attaches itself to one of the four teats, or nipples. It remains there, feeding on its mother's milk, for the next four months. At the end of this period, it is able to poke out of the pouch and feed on grass. Gradually, it learns to hop out and look for food. When it is seven to ten months old, the joey is ready to leave the pouch. Do not lay eggs more your wing can brood, do not start more than what you have the capacity to spear head per time. Set achievable goals per time.

~Those who are wise enough,
to start small enough never
complain of recourses or capital~

If you do not have enough to start, two things are happening: it is either you do not think enough or you do not plan to start small enough. Do not be disturbed by your starting point all that matters is the point to start. Start from the pit like Joseph if that is where you have the privilege to start. Nothing starts from the peak but the grave and it uses to end in the pit. God started with just two while aspiring for billions to fill the world, Jesus started with just two disciples though He dreamt to disciple the whole world.

The power of smallness

~Small is the beauty of starting~

When you come across the potential power of an atom through nuclear fusion and fission you will wonder, why that the smallest particle yield the greatest physical power that is in tens of multiple of what a dynamite could procure. But the same is the power in the small beginning—just like forest is in a small seed, the giant tree in a mustard seed, the oceans in drops of rain, the potential addiction in routine habits, the billions of men in Adam seed…

When you are in a car and you look out at distant objects, it appears that the moon and the trees are moving and when you are stationed, everything seems stagnant. When you take steps, your obstacle is likely to be forced to take step forward or sideways. There is a psychological power of unconscious reflection determined by our statutory position. When you choose to step out you will suddenly discover that your view has been wrong about opportunities around you that you have been considering as not enough.

When your leg moves your brain apparently move in to action just like the moon seems to in the night. Our brains perform least when we are sleeping the same they perform most when we are on the move like a cyclist, pilot, sailor or motorist will become alerted behind the control and steering. Every neuron becomes at alert. You will never discover your hidden mental power until you tap in to starting power.

The seed of imperfection

No idea comes perfect or complete. When the Creator started the six day work of the universe things didn't start good. God was not discouraged about His work at the beginning of the first day, scripture says when He looked at what He had created; everything was void and without form, filled with darkness. Everything was not very good when God started but He started and at the end when God would not give up on imperfect start, He had course to look at everything He had created and behold they were all very good. Let's see how He handled the challenge of starting.

There are three major features of every beginning, which God experienced as well;

Emptiness: when you are starting out do not be bothered if you feel empty of detailed idea, future outline, and resources. What matters is linking your empty vessel to God's plans. When Elisha will help the indebted widow he told her to go and look for empty vessels and that with her little oil in the jar, the future was settled. All you need is a little oil in the jar; a little idea in your heart. God will multiply it if you will sow it into His purpose and plans. If there is no emptiness what will God fill with His greatness?

Formlessness: Another word for this is shapelessness. Do not be discouraged because your starting is shapeless; that is the beginning of every raw material even the most expensive gold. The planted seed become rotten in the soil before becoming a forest in future. The fact that your idea is formless does not make it valueless. Not everything that has value has regular or uniform shape. It is the nature of every raw material at the starting point.

Darkness: It is good to have the end in view but the process is not always detailed to you. Often the process and paths ahead will seem hidden and unclear as God is going to lead you precept upon precept. So do not be bothered if the path of the idea appears to be dark to your understanding. All you need to do is to start by faith and see by faith ahead through the mist and fog saturated sky. The dream is the title of the book but the number of pages and chapters may be unclear when starting out. God is in the concept of revealing the details step upon step precept upon precept.

Do you know that even the Lord Jesus did not know the details of His assignment on earth when He came; it was revealed to Him precept upon precept. At a point, two of the Old Testament prophets appeared to Him, telling Him the next things for Him to pass through. At a point again, He asked the father, why He forsook him. Meaning He never knew a time would come that it will be as if God has forgotten him.

The beauty of the beginning is not having all you need, to overload your initial ability. Everyone at the finishing line once had the feelings to get more time and more resources to start out, but they took the land mark decision of first leap and at the touch of the ribbon they thank God they started crude. You won't always have all you want to start but you have all you need to start out. The beauty and safety of the starting point is in the smallness. Feelings never fill anything but your emotion, it cannot bring your smallest decision to past. Opportunities throng around us as much excuses, choices are at our custody.

~Starters are not always winners
but winners are always starters~

Time is running but you do not need to fly ahead in worry to meet up. You do not even need to run just walk to time. Winners are fighting starters, losers are quitting starters. Beginning use to be formless, shapeless. Remember God's project was formless in the beginning, the psalmist says your eyes saw my substance being yet unformed; in the beginning God created the heaven and earth and the earth was formless void and filled with darkness. The fact that the start is shapeless does not make it meaningless, like amoeba there is life in its shapeless structure. The darkness does not mean hopelessness and the emptiness is not uselessness.

Starting is like this unicellular organism, your launching is like a unit, like a cell, an atom so it seems shapeless, but as you begin to grow more cells you will become an organ with a definite and regular structure of organization and because your part will shine brighter you will live the realm of organ to system—leading a chain of business conglomeration.

~Do not wait until you feel like before
you do it, start doing it until you
like its feelings~

START WITH FUTURE IN MIND

Have a long span starting pad. You are not starting for today but for tomorrow. Learn to deprive yourself of what you want today so as not to be denied of what you need tomorrow. Two young boys whose father was about dying were given two specially treated fruit seeds as part of their inheritance from a poor farmer. He told them to plant them when they get to their place for he was sure they would germinate there, as it is difficult to grow that kind of fruit in his own area. They came back from the funeral of their father and each went back to his farm to plant it in nursery.

The first-born planted his own while the younger also try to plant his own beside a big and deep abandoned family well. In the process, the seed fell in to the well and he had no choice but to go on with life. The older boy's seed began to grow and at a certain height began to bring forth fruits. Their father had already told them that the specie of fruit use to grow in to a very tall tree but as well begin to bring forth fruit from a very small height. The older boy began to pluck fruits from it to eat, also the younger son seed began to grow in the deep well but he could not reach out to the fruits to pluck as the well was deep. Years later, the tree began to grow tall and taller; the older brother had been enjoying the fruits, as he never needed to even climb or use anything to pluck them, they were hand reach but after some time his hand could not reach the fruits so he made use of long stick to pluck them or he would simply climb the tree. Years later the tree became so tall that not even the longest stick can reach and attempt to climb it became more strenuous. Also age was catching up with him.

Meanwhile the tree in the well was also growing tall and at a point it out grew the depth of the well and the fruits surface out. At this point the two sons have become old. The younger sons visited his farm one day and saw the fruits dangling on the tree and as well touching the ground. He was surprised and happy; he simply moved closer, sat beside the well and plucked the fruits to eat.

He did not even need to stand up not to talk of stretching his hand to pluck. He was so excited that at last I am able to eat from the fruits. The older as well got to the tree and discovered that no stick can reach it any more neither can he climb anymore as old age as dawn on him. He looked up and saw the fruits very ripe, some spoilt and the birds beginning to feed on them.

He was sad at this and decided to visit his brother in his farm to see how he was faring with his own. As the old man approached his brother's farm, he saw his old brother sitting down on rocking chair and at the same time plucking fruits from the tree to eat. He was dazed and said how did you do it? My own fruits are out of reach. He smiled and said, "I have waited patiently all this years, I have not been able to eat from the tree until now. I have been picking on whatever my hands can find from the remaining unpalatable fruits in the garden taking advantage of my available strength then, but you have eaten your tomorrow yesterday and now at old age when strength fails you, you are in want."

You cannot eat your cake and have it. I will advise you that you as well begin to pick all around the garden for the available, unpalatable fruits with your youthful strength. But as for me, I will sit on this rocking chair and eat the sweet fruits till my time ends. Whatever you are starting have it in mind to have a lifetime plan, i.e. a plan that has room for enlargement. When God was creating the earth, He must be having you and me in mind not just Adam and Eve considering the magnitude of the earth size. He has a foresight starting strategy. Create room both in your mind and in drawing table. Be ready to delay self-gratification and self-indulgence.

Those who spend their morning singing I could, their afternoon saying I would will spend their night sighing I should. Things won't be OK with time for you to start but starting will make things OK with time. Smallness is the attitude and the aptitude of starting. Start to dream and dream to start. Ideas comes to everybody in multitude in a lifetime but often few is what you need to fertilizer your imagination. It now tailors down on you to be selective and detective. Every dream is pregnant of another idea. The difference between dreamers and wishers is the attitude to starting. Do not be fed up, be filled up again, and fire up. Stop talking and start working.

Not everything that happens in our lives that we start but almost all that will add value to your lives we must start 80% of them. Some lives are full of actions, some reactions and some inaction; one of the evidences of active life is creative starting decision. If you start nothing you will end with something—regret. The world will need to end when it has no new thing to discover and start, for the purpose of time is for man to search out what his creator has hidden before time began and occupy it till He returns.

Nevertheless, wherever you lay the foundation of the start be it in the pit have the peak in mind and view. Make provision for greater dreams and higher height. It is no surprise that the tallest building in its time has a foundation as high as a bungalow. Built to house a variety of commercial, residential, and hospitality ventures, the tower—whose intended height remained a closely guarded secret throughout its construction—reached completion at 162 floors and a height of 2,717 feet (828 meters). The building, modular in plan, is laid out on a three-lobed footprint that is an abstract rendering of the local Hymenocallis flower. The Y-shaped plan plays a central role in the reduction of wind forces on the tower. A hexagonal central core is buttressed by a series of wings, each with its own concrete core and perimeter columns.

As the tower increases in height, the wings step back in a spiral configuration, changing the building's shape at each tier and so reducing the effect of the wind on the building. The central core emerges at the tower's top and is finished with a spire, which reaches more than 700 feet (200 meters). The spire was constructed inside the tower and hoisted to its final position using a hydraulic pump. At the foundational level, the tower is supported by a reinforced concrete mat nearly 13 feet (4 meters) thick, itself supported by concrete piles 5 feet (1.5 meters) in diameter. How far you will arrive is a factor of how firm you arise. You can't go further than you expand your base. Do not start any how that is, do not start on an emotional foundation, start with aptitude, and start with attitude that can project the altitude you have in mind.

There is no greater giant step in the journey of dreams than the first leap. Have you discovered that when you want to walk or run you take the right leg first, the same if you want to make progress and not just movement, start taking a step, it is the right step. As you progress in life, you will be fortifying your base and expanding your capacity to grow faster, taller and stronger but the seed of greatness is in breaking the siege to starting.

~The wind will only carry the kite as
far as the length of the string~

Passion stretched

As the wind separates the wheat from the chaff so time will separate those who pursue a goal for interest and those who pursue a goal with interest. It is not the color of a wing that determines how high it will lift up but the contour of the design. So is life, it is not your privilege that determines ultimately your altitude but the mold of your knowledge and the mode your pursuit. Until you take a step off your comfort zone, what limits others will limit you. The sky is not our limit but our comfort and satisfaction. Often what we enjoy as daily routine makes our tomorrow to daily rotten. Dream your God's size not your size, see through God's word not your world, dream of the rest not your best you have had; and dream your dreams.

There is tendency of illusion in every conclusion. Sometimes all you need to start is not what you have but who you are. It might not be your age but the stage you have. It might not be your purse but your pulse. Sometimes it is with whose you are that you need to start and not whom you have. It is all about what you have in your hand and carve out in your mind that will do the deal. Jacob crossed the river with a stick but returned with two companies.

With a stick in hand and "trick" in mind, he carved out a niche for himself. It is absurd that some people trust their past more than their future, they live for what they have received not what they can believed, so to let go of the shadow is an impossibility for them. The past might have been great but the future is always greater. We are all prone to fall that is why God daily gives us a fresh sheet of daily paper to re-write and advance.

~There is no eraser designed for
the past for the purpose of it is
to be a riser~

The sky is not the limit after all but our dreams; and the limit of our dreams is our imagination and passion—if those Babel people could imagine building heaven scraper above the sky, it explains it. For those who want to trust their wings and rely on wind of men the sky is the limit, but for those who look up to heaven like space rocket and carry their in-built fuel of determination, desperation and boldness, the horizon is just starting a rung in the ladder of exploits. Just like the sailors sound into the distance and patiently wait for the echo to feed them back of the distance ahead in to their destination, the same with the future as you sail in life you launch a dream in to the future to have a feedback of where you are heading and how to prepare ahead and in head.

~He who stands for nothing will fall
for anything and he who stands for
everything will rise for nothing~

> **Do not look**
> Do not look for a convenient way to start
> Look for convincing why
> Do not look for a convenient day to start
> Look for convincing moment
> Do not look for convenient pay to start
> Look for convincing passion
> Do not look for convenient people to start
> Look for convincing partner

Excuse is often a habit that keeps us in our comfortable limit far outside our dream orbit. The greatest goal is to have a mind that won't let go, a formidable desire to finally start. Passion is a thing of nature; it is more of discovered than developed. If it is not natural it will be cultural and will likely fizzle out with the whistling of time and critics. People who are armed with bows and arrows try to kill the body; the second class of murderer are those armed with disappointment, criticism, discouragement, backbiting, hatred, etc. they want to kill your emotion but lay not down your heart at abattoir of opinion.

Others failed attempt should not be a temptation to your starting success. When you start to work it out people will start to talk you out. There is no beginning without boldness. The giant of all steps in any journey is the first step. There is no greatness that escapes passing through critic's traffic. Two Wright flyers started with bicycles workshop. Honda started by making bicycle as well. Until you start with what you have, you can't end with what you can have.

> ~There is history of starting behind every greatness and there is no greatness behind every historic starting~

There is a starting point before every sterling point. To be different is a crime! Be ready to receive wars of advice why you are wrong to start foolishly and stylishly. When you choose to do the unpopular expect the attack from the cultural. Idea must be strong to stand alone and sit lonely as occasion demands. It is not abnormal for people to attack changes; it is an evidence of beings being alive.

> I asked for a wing, I was given feathers,
> I asked for a sky, I was given clouds,
> I ask for an ocean, I was given drops,
> I asked for a forest, I was given a seed,
> I asked for freedom, I was given a key
> Yet said I have no right to complain
> What do you think?

ACTION POWER

~Execute your dream before time kills it~

Great opportunity approaches us with the tip of their tentacles—a seedling opportunity and often we despise it because we spend the time in making and baking decision. It is good to take time in making decision but do not let decision take your time because life opportunity is on a sail not just on sale. Words are not tools in the workshop of acts, decisions are raw materials, so they are limited without a skillful hand to carry out the operation. What makes idea a landmark is the game of balancing the possibility thinking with reality trading of it—the wisdom of decisiveness. If you cannot walk on the water swim in the water, by all means take a step out the beach of fear. When you take a step of faith you step on fear.

~Action is the talk of winners;
talk is the action of losers~

> With each decision here comes a feather
> With each dream here comes the color
> With each passion here comes the wind
> With each action here comes the soaring
> This is the acronyms of flying attitudes

Think with your hand

In the camp of boys scout, the leader led them to the taps constructed for their use in the camp. There were two taps there; one was very big at mouth while the other was very tiny like a nail's size. When they got to the small tap, they saw the water tricking out of it and he asked them to place a bucket there. They moved to the second one with a very big mouth, he asked them if we place bucket here as well which of the two bucket will be filled up first? All of them wondered at the silly question, nevertheless, they chorused the one at the big tap of course, even if we place a drum there.

Then he asked them to put a big drum there as well. They left and went for gaming. In the evening, he asked them, "Let us go to the taps and see what has happened." By then all of them were very thirsty. He said, "I know many of you are really thirsty and will want to go to the big tap for water in the drum for by now the water supply company must have closed and stopped supplying." All of them said we would go to the big tap and drink from the big drum there. He asked them to follow him. When they got to the small tap the bucket was about to fill up; he said since I am the only one who chose the small tap let me drink. So they moved in to the big tap with the big drum at the mouth. On getting there, the drum was empty.

Then it dawned on them that the tap was locked when they first went there. They were disappointed having thought that by now the water will be over flowing all over the camp. What really happened? They were so fascinated by the bigness of the tap that it took control of their senses in opening it. They all exclaimed how big the tap is and kept on imagining how water will turbulently gush out from it. These were all they argued and debated, and were occupied with, during the tour to the big pipe.

No matter the size of your dream or goal until you start it will end you nowhere. You can imagine and dream of books that fill the universe, but without the skill of starting you will live and leave without writing a unit verse. Truly, idea needs money but starts with idea as well. Every idea is found like gold pebble, do not despise or sell or rate it as such. Take it through the furnace of thoughts, subject it to the workshop of meditation, and ultimately labor it to birth; like a star behind the canopy of cloud when you dress it well, it will create an address for itself. When your ideas are beautiful and mature enough it will attract men, money and the means.

~The longest route to success is series
of decisions the shortest route is series
of actions~

Start the beginning

Making decision without taking action is waste of time; why all the invested time in thinking and planning. Decisions grow old when we do not let it give birth to action, at a point it reaches menopause. The strength of decision is the evidence of action and not emergence of a bigger decision.

You are not a misfit because of your color or race, your background or past, what count is the will to win, the decision to pick your pieces and place it in the hand of your maker not your mockers. Life is a flowing river with the course of luck, chances and fate, those who refuse to swim and wade the waves but rather wait for free flow will be the victims of the voyage. Decisive actions are your fins to swim and paddle the boat of your destiny to the expected destination. You are not creature of eventual ending. God says His plan is to bring you to an expected end not eventual. There are neither small decisions nor micro beliefs, for so they look like drops of thoughts yesterday, today; they link to form streams of choices. The streams tomorrow, join to form canyon of determination and next tomorrow the canyons join to form rivers of desperations. In future, the rivers lead to the seas of action, either dead seas or blue seas.

> **There are ten birds**
> On a snow covered roof;
> Two chose not to fly away
> Two wished to fly away
> Two discussed to fly away
> Two considered flying away
> Two decided to fly away
> How many remain on the roof
> Simple mathematics…ten shivering birds

JUMP START

~Oaks are not grown inside greenhouse~

Intention is lame without a contention for the start; what you dream to become you must wake up to welcome. If you do not know where to start I doubt whether you know where you are, because where you are is the place. Start from where is nearest to you, start with what is dearest to you, start with what is closest to you, start with what is best known to you. Everybody wants to knock at the door, nobody wants to knock at the wall, but both have the potential to fling open. There are some doors with no key hole but there some walls with crack. But everybody focus on the door till further notice.

When there is no keyhole on a door, overlook it and look over a wall that has a window or cracks rather. I mean opportunities that many won't dare nor regard because they are not flamboyant. When there is a crack on a wall, it becomes a potential door, not to stare and peep all they long in futile hope but to expand the hole by persistence and determination until your head can slot through and then your whole body. That man who was sick with palsy in the scripture had friends with unusual orientation. When the door was not approachable, they turned up, instead of turning back. There is no law that says access is only through the door or common rules or route. Anywhere can give you a chance depending on how smart you are—you've got to think anyhow and many hows.

~The greatest and smartest starts
are among the smallest starts~

Sometimes opportunity will often come like a tall wall with no ladder nor scaffold, but you can choose to exclaim, hit your fist against your palm and turn around or you can turn round it to look for a hole to peep and call out through—because sometimes you will always need someone there to get you there. Often our problem is not knowing how to start but rather not knowing what to start, if you know what to start so much like your name, like the breaking of the day, I think you will see the way to start and where to start.

We all dream of the great end but we do not dream of a great start. Today marks the end of yesterday but also the beginning of tomorrow. Not everyone that could do it started with a thought of I can, some like you thought I could not until they did it by deliberate mistake. If you do not feature today, you have no future tomorrow, get up and get back on the time track. Whether you are rolling, crawling, walking, running, flying what matters most is to do it forward. It is better to fall and roll forward than to rise and fly backward.

~It sounds and looks impossible
until you take a screened risk and find it
is possible~

Start to dream and dream to start

Dreams have a natural way of expanding with time in hardworking mind. You only know the commissioning strength of your dream you can't really say the final dimension. Joseph only saw his family bowing to him but the entire world finally came bowing to him. Do not sleep today to dream about tomorrow. Many people sleep in meditation to dream, but continue to sleep in procrastination and the dream slips of their hands while they sleep off.

Some dreams are only big enough to have windows for opportunity to peep in while some are big enough with doors for opportunities to walk in. Let your dream be so big that your heart can't contain, that it just has to overflow in to your acts. Dream what can intimidate your adversities and give room for great mind to slot in their resources. You may not have enough to stand out but you sure have enough to start out. Little things, in little way, in little time, by a brittle man for an ample time are the secret and strength of many folks in the hall of fame.

Our brain is not the source of wisdom it is only a resources for it. Link up with God and you had sharpened up your mind. You may not have everything you want to be a star but you need everything you are to build a start. From a man who lives on excuses do not take an offer of one, rather give another excuse why you must not. Remember, it takes equal time to prepare to fail as to succeed—just 24hrs per day. It is always from nest to next. The first thing the bird learns in the nest is to stand and not to fly, if you can't stand you can't jump and if you can't jump you can't fly—start from the formless, train your heart to celebrate little.

Jump start your plan

In life, you won't always have a wall as back ground to lean your ladder for a climb. Sometimes you will need to plant a fresh ladder and let it grow root to stand. You are born with wings but you are not air borne. Everybody has wings of choices only that some use theirs to cover for comfort, some use theirs for shield to hide their weakness, some use theirs for attention spreading it like peacock, while some use theirs as a glider to fly.

~Not every flapping leads to flying,
some just make noise like penguins~

Your wing always exists but you need to exit the vacuum of mind. Now you may not be able to fly, you may not be able to run, you may not be able to walk, but you can sit down. Jesus said who among you intending to build a tower who won't first sit down and count the cost. Sit down and plan not just what to do but above all plan how to start and plunge in it with an ant step. You do not need to be an elephant before you become relevant in school of starting. He who finally starts so little, in a little place, with a little penny, with a little people is ahead of him who lives to dream, in a big way, of a big ending, in a big place and with great people.

Excuses never make anything possible good or bad, once you are able to find a foot for excuse you are disabled from finding an escape route. Remove excuse from your options, even if you will have to tick none of the above. Better to queue for it again in temporary pain, than to quit it in vain with perpetual pain. Look before you leap but do not always wait to see; many just look, look, and never leap because they couldn't see the details, when the floor was actually not a still water but a solid glass. They look over until they overlook the real thing.

~Starting is the greatest change~

To start is sometimes so scarce among dreamers while to end is so common among real losers. Every start needs training anyway. Of all birds, only eagle is known to give its young ones flight training; little surprise eagles fly like no other bird. If you want to reign in high altitude, you need a training attitude with special aptitude for patience. There is no throne without steps up there, and the tactics to get to the sit and sit long enough is training. Your greatest audience is you—songbirds do not wait for audience before they sing, they sing to themselves from birth and when they are finally noticed, they had become expert.

~The length of failure reveals the
strength of will to succeed~

Conquer the fear to start. There is no infinite failure, there is no finite success. Fear does not leave its spot it only casts its shadow and we give up at the dark reflection. Fear is a shadow when you finally step on it you discover the bump is ground level. No matter how great the fall or rise is, know that your best is not behind you. Some opportunities must be attempted as if they are yours already.

Wet plates and dry plates

~Idea is best molded when wet~

Starting is all about creativity and dexterity. Before the advent of dry plate in 1871 by Eastman photographers then used what is called wet plates. Wet plates were large glass plates on which a photographer spread a photo emulsion (a wet mix of chemicals). When the photographer took a picture, the image was exposed on the wet plate. Before the plate dried out the photographer developed the image by adding more chemicals. The same with innovation—when concept or idea strikes your mind it is a skill to quickly treat your mind as a wet plate by developing the image to a storable stage. Many songs, inspiration, and ideas have surfaced and got submerged, because humankind was not smart to pick them when they sprang up in the mind film for consideration.

~I can't will always be employed by I can~

There is no employer who is not an idea merchant. Entrepreneurs are men who can deviate from the right path to common in other to explore the left path of uncommon. When a jobber sees a forest he only imagines a wilderness, when an entrepreneurial mind gets there he sees a paper mill, he sees parks, he sees furniture's. Every start begins with a change—a change of view; every change begins with a start—a start to review.

The road signs of success

The rule of success is just the same—lies in like trying to get a straight line—either you want to use a red pen or blue or black, all you need is a ruler. The color of success may be different, the pattern may be diverse but the mold is just the same—the path is just the same. When your work becomes your hobby you do not need to lobby to succeed, just live life and you will encroach in to your dream. Success begins with living like yourself, but not for yourself and with a dream per day but not daydreaming.

The challenge we run away from is what some people run to as opportunity, and what we are seeing as opportunity is what some people are running away from as an adversity. The fish will tell the bird, the best world is all water. Life is defined by individual, by the interpretation he gives situation, but the whole picture is that life is neutral we only become our choice, it is a big empty book with our choice of pen to write with the ink of time our autobiography which is called our life style.

The black start

Just start the stupid idea, that is the nature of them all—they always look stupid to start and when started. Disneyland was dedicated at an "International Press Preview" event held on Sunday, July 17, 1955, which was only open to invited guests and the media. Although 28,000 people attended the event, only about half of those were actual invitees, the rest having purchased counterfeit tickets. The following day, it opened to the public, featuring twenty attractions.

The Special Sunday events, including the dedication, were televised nationwide and anchored by three of Walt Disney's friends from Hollywood: Traffic was delayed on the two-lane Harbour Boulevard. Famous figures who were scheduled to show up every two hours showed up all at once. The temperature was an unusually high 101 °F (38 °C), and because of a local plumbers' strike, Disney was given a choice of having working drinking fountains or running toilets. He chose the latter, leaving many drinking fountains dry.

This generated negative publicity since Pepsi sponsored the park's opening; disappointed guests believed the inoperable fountains were a cynical way to sell soda, while other vendors ran out of food. The asphalt that had been poured that morning was soft enough to let ladies' high-heeled shoes sink into it. A gas leak in Fantasyland caused Adventureland, Frontierland, and Fantasyland to close for the afternoon. Some parents threw their children over the crowd's shoulders to get them onto rides, such as the King Arthur Carrousel. In later years, Disney and his 1955 executives referred to July 17, 1955 as "Black Sunday". But see these facts afterward: Disneyland has a larger cumulative attendance than any other theme park in the world, with over 650 million guests since it opened. In 2013, the park hosted approximately 16.2 million guests, making it the third most visited park in the world that calendar year. According to a March 2005 Disney Company report, 65,700 jobs are supported by the Disneyland Resort, including about 20,000 direct Disney employees and 3,800 third-party employees (independent contractors or their employees).

~A black start is not a blank future~

You may have a black start but you will end up a bright star. Starting is a strong power of wining. The shot you never make is intentionally missed. Making mistake is bad but not milking it is worse and masking it is worst.

TIME IS A KILLER

~Time gives birth to ideas; as well bury
them when allowed to nurse them alone~

The time smartness

It is a two edged sword in the hand of decision; I can give you any amount without asking for change but if I give you my time I take back my change. Do not spend time with him who has no watch. If when you invest your time all you harvest is money, you are a waster. In allocating your time for human beings start with you, when you are always available you will soon stop being valuable, if you do not learn how to retreat you will soon retard. We are all served with time, though many a time we seem ought not to have deserved it, for it had often waited for us to use it till it wasted away.

Time waiters are time waster. Time is slow enough to be used fully, and it is fast enough to disappear when abuse making one look like a fool. 24 hours is too long to have nothing well planned undone at the closure, in it you have 86400 sec. Anytime we procrastinate, time laughs for he knows we do not know him. Time is the cheapest of all resources and yet the most expensive. We misuse time because it cost us nothing to buy, but then it cost us what we can't pay for soon. There is always enough time to do enough things. If you want your time to be enough let at least 15 hours make your day and 9 hours your night—I mean it is very likely you need to think more and not just work more. If your 24 hours' time is not enough you do not need more time but rather you need to be more timed and tamed to it.

Learn to respect the power of time. The first application of numerals I think should be to read clock, second to read our age, third to count money, forth for mathematics. Children are known for their experimentation of life, the youth for their exploration of life and the old for their experience of life; because each act on time in custody. A child wishes he were old, the old wishes he were a child, a youth is too busy to reflect. Our lives are only a sandwich between two eternities. You are timed just like everybody. No matter the make, design, size, materials and cost of a clock, it can't have more or less than 24 hours to run a day; the same with life, no matter your make, design, purpose and nature all you need to have to succeed is the same time as everybody. You do not need more than twenty four hours in a day. Do not misinterpret movement as an achievement and do not mistake achievement as a movement.

~Time is your best friend and enemy,
    always available but not always reachable~

Glean your every second

~To be busy means to be occupied,
    to be in business means to occupy~

Andrew Johnson's 39th president of the United States who served as the nation's chief executive during a time of serious problems at home and abroad teaches about time art with its life acts. In 1826, when he had just turned 17, having broken his indenture, he and his family moved to Greeneville, Tennessee. Johnson opened his own tailor shop, which bore the simple sign "A. Johnson, tailor." (When Johnson was president, he remarked that he still knew how to sew a coat). He hired a man to read to him while he worked with needle and thread. From a book containing some of the world's great orations, he began to learn history. Another subject he studied was the Constitution of the United States, which he was soon able to recite from memory in large part.

Harry Truman said that Johnson knew the Constitution better than any other president, and many of his later political battles were framed in terms of the constitutionality of proposed legislation. His copy of the Constitution was buried with him. Johnson never went to school and taught himself how to read and spell. In 1827, now 18 years old, he married 16-year-old Eliza Mc Cardle (Eliza Johnson), whose father was a shoemaker. She taught her husband to read and write more fluently and to do arithmetic. She, too, often read to him as he worked.

~As he tailored with his hand, he tailored
his mind at the same time~

FEED YOUR FUTURE WITH TIME

It is not a magic that you may end where you face. It is so much easy to roll backward, it is easy to crawl backward, it is a little bit difficult to walk back ward, it is more difficult to run back ward but it is impossible to fly backward. Those who carry flying mentality do not patronize the past. Often what will relieve you will cause you pain. Tomorrow will generate answers to today's question and today can only generate anxiety to tomorrow's question. Every dawning bring us a brand new day, if the used yesterday must flow in to it filter it and above all let it not alter today's joy package.

If you do not see the changes you desire in your life, do not change your mind, change happens when we are busy chasing it. If you have opportunity to travel to your past what will you return with? If it is not the future you dreamt any other thing is wrong. If you have opportunity to travel to the future what will you take along? I think your today for a glimpse and not yesterday. The purpose of the day is not to seek the past but to see tomorrow.

~Work out your plans or time
will walk out on them~

Failure is success under construction; do not down the tools nor desert the site; it is easier to create the future you needed than the past you wanted. One day, a partially deaf four year old kid came home with a note in his pocket from his teacher, "Your Tommy is too stupid to learn, get him out of the school." His mother read the note and answered, "My Tommy is not stupid to learn, I will teach him myself." And that Tommy grew up to be the great Thomas Edison. Thomas Edison had only three months of formal schooling and he was partially deaf. When you take a right decision you will be left with who are right. If anybody walks away on you, keep on walking on your way, you are not sent to everybody.

Nobody can give you wing, they can only donate feathers for you, you are not armless, so knit the feathers of counsels and motivations together to create your wing of originality! First give what you have to people, then who you are, do not cast your pearls before the swine. Do not live trying to make your opinion count, just leave this world as a champion and your every word said will become a quote, your biography a philosophy, your failure will become a tutor and your memory will become museum. Sometimes what we are running after is running after us. The shadow of others opinion about us we put at the front and that of our deepest reflection we neglect behind, but shadows have no colour apart from black no matter the colour of the light that makes it—it can't make you a rainbow.

Your own opinion that you leave behind could be all to make you greater. If you want to live like a rainbow and not a dark image learn to invest your time in discovering and deploying yourself. Tough time separates those who have ability to succeed from those who take up responsibility to succeed. Strive to be corrected by your mistake and not to correct it. Life is not symbolically about correcting our mistakes but making the best of the residue.

May you make your entire mistakes as a follower
May you fall all your fallings at the small strides
May you get all your scars behind the scene
May you be pruned in mirror light and not before the lime light
May your flame go mild before your fame go wild
May you grow legs before you launch wings
May you rather fall seven times and then rise than other wise
May you maximize the beauty of beginning

Chapter Eight

TAKE STEPS IN POSSIBILITY

~A dreamed believed is half achieved~

    A young man went in to the garden of an old gardener, who watches over an unusual orchard. The young man approached him and said, "Old man, I want a special fruits about life affairs." The wise gardener responded, "I have all sorts of fruits in my garden, kindly go in and look for the one you desire." The young man went in and spent half of the day in the big orchard. When the sun was about setting he emerged from the gate of the orchard empty handed. He met the gardener there and said, "Sir I have not found what I wanted in your garden; thanks all the same for the privilege." The man replied, "What kind of fruits do you want?" "I want the fruits of success, leadership, progress, greatness and much more," he said. He replied "And what, how come you couldn't find them?"

    The young man said, "I have searched all through your garden and the only tree I saw was the tree of courage, no other tree in the whole expanse of land. I felt a bit disappointed and discouraged." "Go back and climb any of the trees." The old man instructed. He reluctantly went back and on sighting the first tree of courage he met, he reluctantly and hopelessly climbed it up and to his amazement hanging and dangling on the tree are fruits of good success, greatness, leadership, progress and much more than he wished. As he got down with much of these fruits he met the old man on his way out and was very thankful. The old man said my name is Joshua.

Your life Success = (Your Mentor + Your Best friend + Your Favorite books) k

Where k=Courage. When k=0, Life is void!

A good example of the illustration above is Joshua. Looking at the heavenly inauguration speech God delivered on his commissioning ceremony. God told him, if you want to have a good success then study yourself approved of the book of the law; he has Caleb as his best friend and Moses as his mentor. To crown it all God said again and again and again be very strong and be very courageous as the conclusion of His strategy for him.

The real strength of dreamers is revealed when their dreams are rejected, when their words fail to echo beyond the nearest audience. Big dreams requires big planning, big planning requires big courage and big mind geography. When that foremost engineer was demonstrating his new engine, Rudolf Diesel was almost killed by his engine, when it exploded. This brain behind the internal combustion engine, which is the heart of all automobiles and nearly all prime movers, could have given up. He could have let go at the incidence, rather, Diesel forged ahead and in the late 18th century, he demonstrated another model with the theoretical efficiency of 75 per cent, in contrast to the ten per cent efficiency of the steam engine after the years of experimentation.

In 1898, Rudolf Diesel was granted patent #608,845 for an "internal combustion engine." The diesel engines of today are refined and improved versions of Rudolf Diesel's original concept. Think of technology today without the courage of the Diesel heart—the earthmovers, submarines, heavy-duty electrical generators and all sorts of machines that run with diesel engine.

~Failure is an emotional pain,
quitting is a physical scar~

Great minds are not born like they rather choose to burn out excess emotional weight of fear and scariness oozing from the commentary of their blind spectators. Marvin Kitman, I think humorous and humbly asked a natural question, he quoted it questionably, "If God wanted us to be brave, why did He give us legs?" David will be a good lad to answer it the way I imagined. From distance I can reflects the echo of his answer "To run towards our Goliath." Fear always tries to tailor our faith in to a costume of doubt, but the key to the wardrobe is in our choice pocket. We choose what we wear whether a dress of anxiety that wears out our passion and pursuit or outfit of faith that befits our future and dream. The great Nobel Laureate who invented the dynamite explosive once had his factory exploded killing some of his staff including his relative but instead of giving up the game, Mr. Nobel persisted and ended with an idea that rules the world wars, leaving behind such a name that offers the highest awards in world of inventions and discoveries.

~Courage is not simply one of the
virtues but the form of every virtue at
the testing point ~C.S. Lewis

SUBTLE FIELD OF THE MIND

The power of multiplication is strongest in the mind field. Watch the things that touch your mind, they leave footprints there. In 1850 three pairs of European rabbits were turned loose in Australia. Within a few years the rabbits were everywhere. Millions of dollars were spent there on research for devices to kill rabbits and protect crops. New Zealand had a similar experience a few years later. In the western United States jackrabbits increase enormously in numbers every five to ten years and cause great damage to crops. At such times, thousands are killed by poisoning and by organized hunts.

In the same vein, everything in the geography of mind has the capacity to multiply; the belief we entertain as attitude will multiply like virus in to every system of our endeavor. If your line of word is I can't always, it will soon become a paragraph of I can't do this, I can't do that…and before you know it, spreads to a page of impossibilities list and ultimately a life book of stagnation. Do not hang around limitations advocates. When the twelve spies came back from spying the Canaan, they brought a bad report to the people—"We are not able to go up and possess the land," like an epidemic, millions of souls were corrupted same hour. Just like faith comes by hearing fear comes by hearing the word of cowards.

Mind Shift

~People who cry a thing is impossible
mostly never try enough~

In spite of the opinion expressed by some distinguished mathematicians that the curvature of the Earth would limit practical communication by means of electric waves to a distance of 161–322 km (100–200 miles), Marconi succeeded in December 1901 in receiving at St. John's, Newfoundland, signals transmitted across the Atlantic Ocean from Poldhu in Cornwall, England. This achievement created an immense sensation in every part of the civilized world, and, though much remained to be learned about the laws of propagation of radio waves around the Earth and through the atmosphere, it was the starting point of the vast development of radio communications, broadcasting, and navigation services that took place in the next 50 years, in much of which Marconi himself continued to play an important part.

Somebody must believe in possibility, somebody not necessarily with the ability but with responsibility to be different and determined. He who complies with history of beliefs, who never applies any positive doubts, will buoyantly multiply ignorance. In spite of the rapid and widespread developments, then taking place in radio and its applications to maritime use, Marconi's intuition and urge to experiment were by no means exhausted. In 1916, during World War I, he saw the possible advantages of shorter wavelengths that would permit the use of reflectors around the aerial, thus minimizing the interception of transmitted signals by the enemy and also effecting an increase in signal strength.

~Tough time separates those who want and
 wish success from those who hunt and need it~

Tough time will either leave you tough or rough. This is life humor what we seek is not always what we see and what we see is not always what we seek, but whatever life presents to you in it is a present wrapped. It is easier to rise with an elevator, than a ladder but you can't move the elevator to another spot of need. This means if you want to be a success coach, you need to build your own strategy from the scratch not trying to feed on others ideology. When you successfully handle and conquer challenge by faith power, you have got hold of the formula which will likely be applicable to many other life gladiators. One humorous thing about idea is that they are hardly caught when hunted for but they choose to visit every soul with a mask on, leaving the task of identification for the opportunist. Do not look for opportunity, look for what need is never met, look for what resources we call waste, listen to what your neighbors complain about, look for what everyone listen to but never hear then you have the opportunity without measure.

One thing that is possible is the reversal of culture and belief, but we have made it so important that we allow them to make us impotent. A great political icon and father, about his country once said, "There is a great physical difference between the white and black races which I believe will forever forbid the two races living together on terms of social and political equality." But over time, this has been proved as a possibility and it's been ultimately practiced in white house.

Leadership and life is for both white and black skin—and anyone with wise and not blank mind is welcome to the high throne. To be black is not synonymous to being blank and to be white is not a ticket to being wise, each race is equally and intellectually equipped for the race. But some are just more smartly diligent that others and it shows. Mental difference I think contributes immensely to the physical. One thing giants do not know is the height of their shoulder, which they had made available for followers to climb. They could often be proved wrong by their trainee who stands taller on their shoulder to see farther than their fathers. Like Isaac Newton said his case was.

~A loser is not the one who loses the
interest of his business deal but the one who loses
interest in his business because of the loss~

KILL YOUR EXCUSES

Idea may come by chance, but never become a plus by luck but work. Idea needs finance but first your faith. Do not think money first but more ideas to replace unavailable money. No matter your height you can reach higher if you will apply the heat of un-satisfaction and new goal settings. Nothing is absolutely free especially freedom for it comes with responsibility. Failure is an achievement we did not plan for; it is not part of our goal, it is outside the scope of our dream. Nevertheless, the lesson is that it is not the end of our dreams, it has not come to stray us, nor stay with us, nor to slay us within, it is just comment on our endeavors.

Excuses are the bricks for raising the tower of failure; we bind them with the mortar of complaints and paint them with emulsion of wishes while we wait for luck to inhabit the house. Excuses will save you from today's laxity but won't abase tomorrow's reality. When you face challenges do not give way for it to pass you by, because you can leave the road of success in the meantime only to look back and see that dreadful tractor of challenge has the implement of opportunity attached behind; which implies you could have confronted it and laid hold of its gift; but it could be too late to catch up.

Rather face the oncoming adversity, pass through it and come out at the back to meet the moment you have been waiting for. God says we should pass through it all not jump over. You can only make story when you live to make excuses, you cannot make history by manufacturing excuses. Excuses will make you a self-story teller and pitiful auto-biographer, but if you want people to write of you a biography worthy of history then milk your excuses, squeeze out the opportunities in them.

Dodge your good excuse and judge the bad ones, by all means excuse yourself from this common monster of its master. Excuse is a gentle man; he looks for no one rather everybody looks for it. People make excuses but excuses cannot make anyone. Thank God, you are passing through not failing through. Those who develop interest in their past forfeit the interest the future can yield. Bad planning makes man a failure; good excuses keep him a failure. What you have done is limited, what you can do is unlimited. Mistakes are the broken rung of the success ladder; you need it after all to step higher, so mend your strategy and do not end it. If you let go of a rung you will find it difficult to climb up. You may need to bend but do not end it

~ There are no obstacles around you
until there is within you~

If you want to be noticed, draw and paint your dream, and with zero tolerance for excuse and paste it on the notice board of time. Little mind stare up at global sky counting the stars, average mind discuss their brightness, bright mind reflect their light. The songbird sings for no one in the nest, it rehearses its lines and scales to unseen audience yet we hear it enough to give it name. Start now do not wait for spectators; when you finally catch fire all legs and wheels including wings will stop by to watch your flames as it rises up the sky to perch among the stars. Know that God trains like mother eagle for He will let you down from the hills, then watch you as you learn to unfold your wings to learn the flight of destiny and if the wind is supersonic or your wing is wetted by the rain, or they are still babyish to soar, then He will dive down like the mother eagle in the sky to bear you on the eagles wing. One thing is common to all those who fly, those who walk, those who crawl—all have shadows, i.e. everyone at one stage or the other has past failure.

And this is the truth that we all have past to be tempted to let accompany us, the shadow cast when light of old wishes is shone on our past time. The great at the top have failures to count, the small one crawling has the horror of small starting to recall; average result could frown at the need to repeat the same ordeal of past contoured exercises but whatever your lot keep your shadow of failures below, keep it behind keep it like a non-existing thing under and leap with your future for in it your hope lies.

Those who fly do not have any structured shape of their shadow for anything anyone can intercept it below them and paint a disfigured shape of their image on the ground. So is your turn will be when you rise above all your battles, crawl all your tunnels and finally emerge at the lime light. Then tongues will wag in rhythm—the melody of critics; the painters of rumor will engage their brush cropping your reputation, editing your work, exchanging your good deed intension for your omissions. But when your root foundation is firm and buttressed, the wind will only blow off leaves from your tree, and if it succeeds to blow off fruits it will soon turn in to forest, for what has just happened is your seed dispersal.

~We can see the stars in the dark
because the stars are burning not
just because they are up~

Back your obstacles

In 1968 Olympics a medical student and athletics jolted the world when he used an unconventional way to take the gold in the high jump segment. He chose to approach the obstacle to jump with his back contrary to what was prevalent at the time—diving over or hurdling while the jumper faces the bar and looking down. The same theory can be applied to life terrain when you are faced with life challenges; turn your back to your obstacle not in fear or coward attitudes but not to allow it to magnify itself above its size. Rather, you face up and focus on the One Who lives behind the cloud for cheers and strength. Learn from Peter, as long as he pretends as if the storm was not exiting and focused on the Master he threaded on the stormy water.

~ Tough time will shake you
but not to shackle your faith~

Carve out room of faith

A seven old boy told his aged uncle that he was looking for faith—he found it hard to believe in anything or himself and God's ability in him. After he told his old uncle his problem, he decided to help him. He took the young boy to a farm and told him, this farm is a special farm, in the midst of it is buried a container inside which is a virtue of faith. But the soil of this farm is made of fear, anxiety and worry; while the air is made of faith. He took him to the exact spot where to find the container. As he began to dig, he got to a point that he could not dig anymore. His tool was banging a rock. He stood up and went to his uncle, "Sir I can't continue the digging, I am stuck, yet I am yet to get the container of faith. So he followed him there.

When they got there, he said the vessel of faith is the hole you have dug. "He asked the boy, what is inside the hole?" He replied, "Air;" and that is what? The boy said, "Faith, since the air of this place is made of faith." His uncle analyzed further, "Like I told you that the soil of this farm is called fear, worry, and anxiety. Once you get them out the space is occupied by faith." Again, he said, "Do you notice I did not give you any tool?" "Yes I do," he replied. The uncle asked, how did you come about the tool you used? He said choice. The uncle replied, the same about life adventure, you choose to reach out to faith and evacuate fear and its entourage by the tools of choices and decisions.

Your passion - your failure = your success

So when your passion only equals your failure success is void

Your passion to override excuses and limits must be greater than the failure you encounter; the extra is what acts as material for your success.

THE HERO'S MIND

Roadless and the road less journey

There are two paths to greatness in life: a Road Less Journeyed and a Roadless Journey. The Road less journeyed is the path many dreaded to partner with and the Roadless Journey is the pathless wilderness waiting for adventures. Your imagination will determine your mentality and note that anything that gives you comforts has the power to conform you.

~No mistake is useless;
it is just a painful discovery~

Let your dream be so big that you can't but just hit your target. Small dreams are liable to slip off. Great people fail elegantly and gallantly until they fail in to success. Prepare enough that even your failure will justify you if it is eventuality. You have a duty to spread those feathers. The wing is useless in the cocoon nor is it useful in the nest; when will you escape your comfort zone? Do not be tempted by a failed attempt to quit. Death is not the worst thing but to die for nothing. When the storm has passed, tough trees stands upright again; bend if you will but do not break. Winners bend losers blend or finally end it. Nobody is too busy to breathe so anything you want as your breath you will have time for it; you will live for it.

If you are not told your age how aged will you look like today and how urgent will you treat life. Forest is different from a bush, in the forest the top is clouded but the base is scanty; trying to start small while hiding under the comfort of giants all the while will make you live scanty, just as the trees shade the sun from reaching the floor of the forest hence depriving the young seedlings from reaching out to the sky. Comfort will cloud your growth. In the bush, every plant grows all over the land but not without struggling for survival in the thicket—but they grow!

A wise farmer knows when to transplant a seedling from the comfort of nursery. There is a time to leave the green house of comfort to the open field, direct to the scorching and wind of life. This will help you grow strong root to stand the test of time and above all to bear fruits according to your own kind. You are not to maintain success you are to update it—yesterday success must be turned to a seed for today's process or it becomes a siege for tomorrow's progress. If you do not structure your mind today you have no future tomorrow—get up and get back on the course.

The captain of defeat

Only those who go below the ground level are not needful to rise again and run for they have finished the race. But as for you as long as your falling is on the ground and not below the ground you are commanded to rise and run. Failure is like a seed when it stays long on a spot it begins to germinate, being watered by the whispers of critics and shout of mockers and with time it gets rooted. When allowed for seasons to pass over it, it bears the fruits of frustration and termination with a fizzled out self-esteem. Then hope becomes a thing of question. When life throws you at the wall of failure do not slips through the window of hopelessness, rather bounce back with reactive momentum and spring through the door again. Do not we say for every action there is an equal and opposite reaction.

In your life make faith matters or you make fear master. Faith comes by hearing and hearing by the word of God likewise fear comes by hearing and hearing by the words of speculation. Fear will make what is before you to finally befall you; it has the power to make things happen. Fear does not knock before it enters, so lock your mind with all diligence and intelligence. Our life ship challenge is not the tip of Ice Berge of retardation visible on the sea but much more the remaining 90% built of fear is submerged deep in the sea of heart.

When you fail in an attempt, before you erase the past memory, trace back the path and this for two things: to gather experience and momentum. We are not fools to have made mistake, but we are when we make the mistake of learning not from it or let the accompanied loss build limiting fear. Your past may follow you wherever you go today but can't follow ahead to your future without your conscious leadership. Successful people are not failure proof but have been failure proved overtime, they thought of victory, they fought for victory and they caught up with victory. They dream of palace in the pit, they make stepping stones out their stopping stones. Everything about fearful men anatomy is bilateral, including their minds, double minded.

Fear could be spelt out thus;
Future Expectations At Risk

Failure brings us close to success but we must open up to our mistake, acknowledge it and get in it knowledge to proceed more accurately. You may fall on your path but do not fall apart.

Heart on the rock

~Making a decision is 1% courage,
taking a decision is 99% courage~

The route of the journey of failure often ends at the root of success, for from there, the stem of wisdom watered with experience springs up; the seeds of great achievements have best been planted in the middle of challenges and in the season of oppositions. The winners mentality never fails, for even when they fall they see it as a form of movement, they roll forward! It is not every genius that is extremely gifted, educated or privileged; it is not every leader that is born with the skills, nor into the system; it is not every hero that is error free or without limitation, but all have one thing in common they are valiant and radiant in decision education.

All that finally succeeded once failed but not all that ever failed finally succeeded because they succeeded to quit while the former failed to quit. Great men failed as much as they succeeded, they had seasons of fear but as much they had reasons for hard faith to carry on. They have many excuses to quit at every season but quit the feeling for their initial findings. What ultimately stops men in life exploration is not those mountain or valleys, they are not horrible past or terrific future—what limited men in the past is still what does it today—poor heart management.

~Take your time in taking decision
but and do not let taking decision take
your time~

Solomon put it proverbially, that a man ought to guide his heart with all diligence, where the life issues spring out. Life is matter of the heart, the acts are only the product. Life is like the race of huddles you do not slow down because of the obstruction, it is part of the race, do not stand and stare at the Jordan, step in it in faith; you do not just start to dream all the while, dream as well to start. Something must leave you for you to outlive your existence. A seed does not become a tree in the shell nor in the fruit on the branch.

Every exemplary success was once a temporary failure. It is just natural to be criticised whether you are right or wrong, passive or active, quite or loud, rich or poor, male or female, black or white, bold or cold— breath alone is what qualifies us all for criticism but you have the choice to harden your heart against the blow of men. Though, sometimes you may need to listen to your critics especially if they are in harmony, not to dance to their symphony, but to review your script or if possible that your instrument is not tuned.

Think before you give it up. What if the last time is the last step to the result; if Thomas Edison had stopped 9999 times then he could not have seen the light at the end of the tunnel. He said, "Many of life's failures are people who did not realize how close they were to success when they gave up." Sometime all you need is a better approach, sometimes a greater passion, sometime a stronger patience. Winners are quitters who postpone it to the end.

Develop fearless faith

~Fight your fear before you
fight your enemy~

If you do not have faith, fate will have you. Fear is a force to make things happen; faith has the potency to make things happen; yours is playing the host for either. When the pressure of fear is equal to the treasure of faith in us doubt sets in and when the pressure of fear is finally greater, unbelief settles. Giving all diligence add to your faith. Heroes are not men of zero fear but as well not of zero faith. What operates in a leader that separates him from followers is not age but courage; it is not the height he stands but the depth he understands, it is not his title phase but battle faced. A focussed mind knows when to resign from credential cage to act on the potential stage assigned for him—when to take destiny risk like Jacob for his financial freedom.

Dreams are brave leader they will guide you not only in the path to thread but much on the magnitude to think and altitude to talk. Talent are wings to fly, charisma adorn it with colour but character of decision is the wind. To attain success outside being boldly decisive is like trying to fly in a vacuum. The strength of failure is the failure of strength to dream again. Fear pulls you to your past faith pushes you to your future. Do not fear what is to happen fear Who makes things to happen. You are not fit for success when you see every opinion to befit you.

When you want to fix into every mould you will have to live shapeless and homeless. Fear can't take you beyond your past; it can't lift you beyond your height. When a man thinks fear he will hear fear in every news; he will see fear in every good; he will feel fear in every touch; he will smell fear in every flower; and he will think sting in every honey drop.

FAILING SMART

~Failure is like dirty soap what
it takes to clean up is in it~

Both failure and success are time of test not a time of rest. Stars learn to shine in the dark night and shine brighter in the darker and brightest in the darkest. If failure could discourage you then success has never motivated you enough at the onset. Nobody succeeds once and for all and nobody fails once and for all. Either success or failure none is once and for all. Nobody's falling makes a lifetime failure. Failure does not remove your strength it only reveals your weakness. Failure is to remould you not to be a mould for destructive emotional element—the likes of depression, bitterness etc.

Successful people are not failure exempted but rather failure examined. Turn your gain to pain. The storm is not a reason to adjourn your sail but to adjust it. Failure is a temptation to stop likewise success. Do not give it up rather take it up. In his defeat Washington displayed the combination of coolness and determination, the alliance of unconquerable energy with complete poise that was the secret of so many of his successes. It is better to fail 50% and succeed 50% than never to try and fail 100%. It is better to try and make a mistake than to make a mistake of not trying.

~What lies behind us and what lies before
us are tiny matters compared to what
lies within us~ Oliver Wendell Holmes

Failure is relaxing

Success is like a high rise edifice; to reach the summit you must not climb all the stair cases at once. Every story you get to you must pause, go in and master the level in other to gather experience and resilience to climb the next but to us it looks like a failing time rather a trying and training moments. Those who try to climb the peak at a time hardly live to tell the story of success as they seem frustrated by imaginary, unrealistic, smooth, failure free journey.

You can ask the first conqueror of the highest point on earth, Sir Edmund will tell you 'Mount Everest means ever rest as you mount'. Attempt to succeed and be tempted to proceed when you fail, it is the simple science of becoming valiant and heroic. The peak of success is when a successor picks it and thoughtfully makes it an input for a successive accomplishment. Be your own successor a while, pick it up. Failure can be described as a time of compulsory rest and a test of determination, passion and decision.

~If at all you will draw the circle
of your limit use the radius of time~

A tree grows old and fresh and tall because it has learnt to shed old leaves for the new. If a dream must remain beautiful and taller, each old goal must be replaced by the new. The more the tree grows taller and emerging new branches the more it grows deeper and spreading its new root, both for strength and nutrient. The higher goals you conceive the higher relationship you build and the more of knowledge you hunt for.

Dreams should be broken down to daily fragments of goals; check out your pursuit if it is burdensome, probably you are taking too heavy a bite per time. Failure may reduce yours but not you, what you have not whom you are, who you have but not whose you are. Failure that reduces your fame is not it but which do your flame. Either you fail or succeed keep trying, it is the secret to endless winning. When we fail we demonstrate our ignorance and estimate out knowledge. Many fail not because they are too weak to succeed but because they are too weakened by fear of failure. Do not quit trying and do not try to quit for when you give it up some else take it up. Either you fail or succeed everything is a beginning not the end. Life is to be lived in a cycle and not in a circle.

~Either you fail or succeed keep trying,
it is the secret to endless winning~

Interview your self

If need be come out of yourself to become yourself—I mean you may need to win yourself before any other battle. Fight off false self-representation and intimidated self-value and ask yourself question like the prodigal son and you will be surprised the answer you will get. Establish basic life knowledge that can guide against your weakness and excesses.

Do not begin again without accessing your falling point and be ready to sit and learn. Anyone you see at the top chooses to stop there through faith they had those reasons to quit earlier. Success and failure are like the two wheels of a bicycle the former like the rare to activate motion the latter like the front to activate direction.

~If you do not first learn
to sit you stand to fall~

Wet not soak

A king whose son was to ascend the throne after his death refused to show up in the palace for preparation. When his father contacted him, my son why are you running away from your inheritance? He said, "Father I have lived my life to witness how your administration was unendingly criticized. I am not ready for such a time." The king told him, "My son let me explain life to you." "I want you to help me do something tomorrow morning before the sun rises. You know the tree at the back of my palace, you will help me to paint it thoroughly with black paint, when you are through come and tell me," he requested. The boy went out to do just as his father said the following day. After painting, he came back to the father and said he had done as he wished.

The king said, "Are you sure? Go back and check it out; make sure you paint the tree black. He went back and checked. Finally, the father went with him to see for himself. On getting there, he saw that the boy had done a good job, painting the trunk and the branches but left the fruits and leaves and the roots. "Do you see that you have not succeeded to do just as I wished," the king queried. He said what? The king replied; you did not paint the fruits, the leaves and the roots or are they not part of the tree? He said, "Oh father I am sorry I never thought they should be painted."

The king responded, "The same with you; people may paint you with different colors of criticism but your fruits which are the product of your integrity can't be covered. Your leaves of sincerity that give shade to people you rule can't be covered and those you are shadowed by it will praise you. Above all, your entire root which is your passion, truthfulness and principle can't be painted as well, which of course are your driving forces. With that, you will stand the storm of critics."

The Master when confronting the adversaries of His dream said to them, John came neither eating nor drinking and you people said he had demon, and now, the Son of man came eating and drinking and you said He is gluttonous. When Paul had a poisonous snake wrapped around his hand on the Malta Island during the stormy voyage the dwellers said he must be a wicked man though he escaped the sea storm yet justice won't let him be go free. However, after he shook the beast in to the fire, they changed their mind and said he was a supernatural man. Men's opinions are sensitively climatic they change with emotional tides and seasons.

Chapter Nine

TAP THE POWER OF NEW IDEAS

~You are too loaded to
be a load to humanity~

Young mountain climbers stumbled at a spot on the mountain heights where he saw an eagle's thorny nest. Carefully, he picked one eaglet successfully while the rest flew away. As he climbed down, he took it along and placed it in a cage on getting home. The eaglet grew gradually in the light wooden frame cage to an adult. One day the young man decided to view the eagle outside the cage. So he tied a rope to its leg and tied it to the cage. Then he opened the cage and let out the bird. As the eagle reached outside it spread its wing and stretched. The young man watched, suddenly the young creature saw other birds flying and remembered who it was and where it came from. It too decided to fly to the extent to which the rope will permit. But to its surprised as it took off and reached the longest length of the rope the cage took off it the air with along and up to the mountain it flew, where it rested and took time to chop off the rope.

The cage it later turned in to a nesting material to breed. Its freedom had always been in the reach of its capacity but positioned tagged. What had been hindering the bird from flying was not the cage all the while, but the position. When you dwell inside your problem, you can hardly escape from it; but when you think outside its influence, you are set to handle it faster. You do not solve a problem by thinking about it, you think on it. In the same way, ideas are pioneer of freedom from the cobwebs of culture and miniature mindsets. You will amaze yourself from the potential you can unleash, when you set out of the organization policy to have a glimpse of what your contemporary offers. The cage is the tradition, protocol, policy, culture, rules, laws, theory, belief, notion, norms and much more that we consciously or unconsciously design and appoint to be our master and bottle neck. When you think outside all these you can effect change as you dream appropriate. Jesus told the blind leaders of His time, that the Sabbath was made for man and not man for the Sabbath. Every litigation, in whatever form it is painted should be subject to probation. When the bird was given a chance to come out of the box, its potential was maximally revealed. When you think outside the box, you will discover a new world of freedom and possibilities.

Ideas never end, as long as time never ends. Idea is what you see when you close your eyes to what you can see; it is what you hear when you close you hear to what the world fears; it is where you go when you miss the foot path of culture. When you are inside the box of culture you are as limited as the history until you choose to be upset and finally think offset.

~What stops organisations from going
ahead is often what the head stop from
letting go from his head~

The story that was told of J.P. Guilford, an acknowledged figure in new age creativity is very capturing. As an employed psychologist during the World War II to select viable fighter pilots for the success of the battle he came to a great insight to the power of idea dexterity. He discovered that a counterpart old retired pilot was also engaged for the same assignment. Feeling funny about the rivalry and assumed incompetence, he forged ahead with the selection. During the war, he came to realise that most fighters that were downed by the German army were from his selection.

This made him feel depressed to suicide contemplation for being accountable for such a loss of lives due to his weak and stereotype expertise. On the other side the pilots approved by the old pilot fared well at the battle front. He summoned courage, swallowed his pride and asked the old man for his secret though he had felt a bit offended for the Ministry having to bring on board another expert. He replied, he engaged just one question to separate those with potentials from those with credentials. I had asked "What would you do if your plane was shot at by German anti-aircraft when you were flying over Germany?" Every trainee that responded "I had fly higher" were nullified. Those who answered, "I do not know—maybe I'd dive" or "I'd zigzag" or "I'd roll and try to avoid the gunfire by turning" he considered. The retired pilot considered those who gave the intelligent and credential answer as unqualified.

They proposed to apply the well know tactics to fight the expert in the field. These are those chosen by the psychologist as capable. They depended on their credential and educational manual. The logic is that the enemy was able to predict their move when under fire and was already laying ambush for them at the upper cloud to be downed easily. Tree lives to the maximum potential because they are not living under the roof of men; men sometimes fail to achieve all possibilities because they live under the roof of their mind.

Think creatively

~Always think about what's missing
it's amazing what you will find~
William H. Swanson

The skill of mind is the ability to think differently, unpredictably, suddenly, unexpectedly and creatively. A man and his team went on a journey along the narrow path walled by mountains on each side. He told them I had walked this path before which I want you to walk ahead of me as I planned to meet you on the other side latter in the day. Along the path, was a pit dug to obstruct the movement of passers-by with no space to turn on either side to bypass it, since the mountains were standing as wall.

The hole was 20m deep and 9m wide in both sides. Close to it, the man had placed two ladders constructed for the purpose of crossing the pit. The ladders were 10m long each. So they set out for the journey. When they were about getting to the pit, they met the two ladders on the road which they left behind. When they came across the pit, they halted and stop the journey. They tried to see if they could jump but it looked too dangerous. As they were about giving up on the journey they suddenly remembered they had seen two ladders on their path as they were coming, so they sent two of them to go and get one.

When they brought the ladder, they read the calibration on the wall of the pit and saw it to be 20m deep and 9m wide on both sides.

They were disappointed when they discovered the ladder was just 10m long, the length being shorter than the pit's depth, and admitted it will be dangerous to throw the ladder of 10m long in to the 20m deep hole to climb down on one side to walk through the bottom of the hole and climb up on the other side. So they resolved to fate and one by one slept off as they waited for their boss.

When the man got to the place where he propped the ladders, he discovered one had been taken. He picked the other one and continued with the journey. He met his team camping around the pit, grounded and sleeping. Quickly, he perceived what halted them. When he got to the hole, instead of dropping the ladder in the hole to impossibly climb down and up, he stretched it rather on the pit with 1m excess, used it as a bridge to cross. When he got to the other side he removed it and called out for them.

They all jumped up from deep sleep and marveled seeing their boss on the other side with the other 10m long ladder. They were curious and amazed. Finally, they were able to gather much courage enough to ask him how he did it. Without much ado he repeated the process to cross over to meet them for the unnecessary explanation. What kept that team back is the same that is keeping you back. Status quo! They had been conditioned, that ladders should only be used to climb up and down.

~Where all think alike, no one thinks
very much~ Walter Lippmann

THE IDEAS LAW OF OPPORTUNITY

Man desires are dynamic and to meet up mind design must be creative. Thinkers complement a situation they do not complain. They see better in the moonlight than in the sunlight, for the rays of silence illuminate the floor of their heart ocean to pick the lost axe's head. Thinking is our homework; we should go home with it at the end of each day in the class of life and ruminate on the lecture life delivers during the day's work. When you are thinking you sweat more than when you are working for in the former you labor to work out the latter. To turn the world upside down you must be ready to turn inside out. The earth movement teaches us not to only try to revolute round the subject to change but also to rotate on our own axis as object of change. Idea is the heart of creativity, when idea is recycled and the mind is allowed to metamorphose it in the cocoon of time, there is always an emergence of a better fly. People who could think ahead and travel a bit of miles upfront in the world of imaginations always wait for others to only come and be ultimately led. Our heart is the greatest soil for cultivation of dreams. Many people leave it uncultivated they just want to live as buyers and servants. This is why innovators will keep up with excess job choices because man's needs and desires are ever changing. When a product meets their specifications, it is just for a season, they will soon trade it off in quest for the new trend. Dreams are ideas in large scale.

Opportunity accompanies problems

In every disadvantage, there is advantage and vice versa you see base on how you look. There was a stormy rain sometimes in a small village, almost all the houses had one or two sheets removed from the roof. When they tried to repair them there were holes left in all. Being an agrarian community, with poor economy, most of them were unable to repair their roofs. Following this, a long session of rain began and they had to stay in door to evacuate the water from the leaking roof. In the process, their cloths and other cloth material always become dirty. One day a farmer who seemed to be the poorest among them thought of something, "What if I begin to collect the stained and rain messed up cloths and put up a laundry service?" I can easily use the water that leaks down in my roof for the washing instead of just spending time to evacuate it. Moreover, since everybody complains of dirty cloths piling up in the bedrooms, there will be a ready market. The farmers had tried to maximize the little sunny time they had to be spent on their farms. So he started the business; when everybody was in door during the long session of rain complaining and busy mopping up their house he was busy gathering the water and to wash. When the rain stops he would come out spread the clothes and went to join other on the farm. Gradually, his income began to increase while other kept on complaining about having little time to spend on the farm and their leaking roofs.

By the end of the raining season, his colleagues had almost nothing to boast of financially. Realizing his sudden wealth at the end of the season, they asked him how he did it. We all had become wretched because of the inability to work on the farm. How come? The wise farmer replied when you were all complaining of the weather and the leaking roof, coupled with having to spend most of the day in door I was not, I was taking the advantage of the situation.

The birth of Linux Operating System was a result of a man who will leverage on the difficulties he encountered in operating the system he just bought. In trying to fix the bug that won't allow him to enjoy his property to maximum, he ended up configuring a differently new programming idea. Problems often come coupled with solution but we are stuck because we have a presumed readymade way out, the last one that worked for us. We let history be our mirror and manage our mind.

> ~One should never impose one's views
> on a problem; one should rather study it,
> and in time a solution will reveal itself. ~
> Albert Einstein

Some abilities in you will only answer to your responsibility to embrace challenges in the light of squeezing out ideas from them. Do not lurk for opportunity all around, rather look around all. Just hold your string and let the wind fly your kite; that is a whole lot of how millionaires think, they get cart of idea and attach it to labour of men as horse. Little minds look at opportunity and overlook it because of its present state, great mind saw the opportunity and looked over it to its present state.

> ~Coloring outside the lines
> is a fine art ~Kim Nance

I love the story of the great America farmer and inventor of the first successful steel plow. John Deere ended up contributing immensely to the field of agriculture, taking his country to prominence in the field. As a young man in his early twenty, he mastered the trade of blacksmith after which he began making tools in the like of shovels, pitchforks and similar tools; his customers were farmers. In a bid for better operation and market, he relocated to another state where starting out farmers there were facing serious problem with the soil type and tool they used. The soil being a hard rich prairie soil, though good for crops but being visited with difficulty of the soil getting stuck to the iron plow available from the East blacksmiths. The indigenous famers had to have a frequent and frustrating stop over as they scrape off the blades of the plow. This was a major challenge for the community but John was seeing a great opportunity to further his skill.

In 1837 Deere conceived that if the plow were made of smooth surface the force of adhesion between the metal and soil could be reduced and that was it. He turned a broken steel saw to plow and gave it a high polish work. This turned out to work very well. John established a company and became a leading figure in farm implements manufacturing. He began to import steel form neighbouring country and produced in large scale for farmers to order. By the end of 1857, his production rate scaled up to 10,000 plows annually.

This is the law of opportunity, leveraging on what people complain as problem. When life throws at you challenge it is not for you complain but to explain, it is not for you to back out but to start out a new order in the field. There is no great idea but rather small thoughts that were allowed to stay a season longer in the soil of imagination until they grow out of hand in to an institution. You are here for the change. You are here not to be counted but to count and amount. You are the change.

THE IDEAS LAW OF FLEXIBILITY

~Whatever age: stone, iron,
bronze, silicone…, every state of
humanity is crude, with time~

Good ideas one day becomes old idea, if not replaced won't really die but kill minds around; it takes a bold and new idea to finally bury it alive. Old ideas do not die they must be buried alive and this is the logic leaders need to master. The goal of every goal should partly be not to just make it bigger and longer but better and easier for humanity. You do not expect everything to change 360^0 at the onset. This is practically impossible but at the same time do not wait till people imbibe your idea rather introduces it and with time it will have the good old idea buried with the soil of time. You ask a critic how to cover a bottle that contains your idea for it not to slip away; he will tell you to turn it upside down on the floor and the mouth is covered. But how do you take it up and not have the water of ideas wasted or splashed over insignificantly. So do not let critics or the world determines the implication and implementation of your idea.

Largest national heart

It is just normal to see leading leaders with a different leadership aptitude when it comes to being creative in welcoming ideas especially in its crude state when it is so formless to be recognised by other team leaders. It is not an overstatement to assume that the 20th century has indeed been a turning point for United States in technological capacity and leadership as it rose to be a super state. It has been a rise based upon tremendous natural resources exploited to secure increased productivity through widespread industrialization, and the success of the United States in achieving this objective has been tested and demonstrated in the two world wars.

Technological leadership passed from Britain and the European nations to the United States in the course of these wars. This is not to say that the springs of innovation went dry in Europe: many important inventions of the 20th century originated there. But it has been the United States that has had the capacity to assimilate innovations and to take full advantage from them at times when other nations have been deficient in one or other of the vital social resources without which a brilliant invention can't be converted into a commercial success.

As with Britain in the Industrial Revolution, the technological vitality of the United States in the 20th century has been demonstrated less by any particular innovations than by its ability to adopt new ideas from whatever source they come. America as a nation has been very skilful in incorporating minds which have something to offer because of their national orientation about giving room for self-expression and solid support to those who have something say or contribute regardless of geographical differences. Being willing to change and move on with trends not as they come but even hunting of targets.

~The gift of leadership is the gift
of friendship with people and ideas~

Break the chain thought

~Daily addition births addiction~

For years humanity had engrossed itself with the childish fact that the only way to fly metal or man in the air is to follow the manner of birds in developing a model that will engage the flapping technique to generate a lift until in the 19th century when a British scientist Sir George Cayley, known as the father of aeronautics came to the scene with a flexible mind deviation. He used modified arch-type kites to make "flying machines," which in 1853 led to the first recorded manned flight in a glider ending the long-time held belief.

His comprehensive and illuminated understanding of both thrust and lift was the key in invention that would ultimately overthrow the ancient and faulty ideology with flapping wings a clue to manned flight. Imagine if we still tailor toward a flapping winged airplane. Anyone who can make you think is a leader; a manager will only make you talk his mind and walk his path to norms. To be free you need to awake your ability to think, to remain free, you need to awake to responsibility live it. People may forget what you said; they may age out how you make them feel, but how you make them think they won't live out in a hurry; the power of hearty influence has lifetime trait potency. To be free means to be able to think without the background of the past.

~To be free from ignorance
is the king of liberty~

Think outside the box; think from the balcony of the world, treating the mass conclusion as mushroom to create much room for your unconventional mind. Either things are working or not our mind must be working for a better way. There is no limit to improvement except of short-sightedness.

The bridge of idea

A young girl close to three entered her dad's office in the morning excited and running toward him shouting, dad see, see as she pointed to the necklace graced around the neck by her mom. She was just all out to get a word of affirmation and admiration from her father. On reaching her dad he cuddled her and looking to her face he said, "My baby what do you do first in the morning when you see your daddy?" She replied, "Good morning." "Have you done that?" He demanded. She replied no, the father said do it. The girl calmly and soberly said good morning my daddy. The father said "Let me see your neck lace, it's such a beauty! I love it, who gave you?" The little girl coldly replied my mummy with faded excitement and tailored enthusiasm. Immediately, the father realized what he had done wrong, doing right thing at the wrong time to the neutral soul.

On a good day, she would have been pumped up with excitement at the complementary of her father with joy radiating and laughter beaming on her face. This had been her response every time following her father's acknowledgement and admiration, but that morning he was protocol driven and legality blinded. He discovered he had played killjoy to an innocent child who was just identifying what the rules of life are all about by polarizing her excitement with the rules of social behavior. Any way I was that man. I placed protocol above love.

When they brought the exited kids to Jesus to touch and bless them the protocol oriented Philip and the security conscious Peter flared at the parents for coming to disrupt and disturb the busy no nonsense master. But Jesus was displeased while He quickly reached out to them. Many times, the bridge to link idea to realization must be constructed by the materials gotten from the broken wall of protocol; consciously watching principles encroached and eroded. The idea processing will definitely subtract from you but it will infinitely add to you. It will change order but will birth a system. It will reverse your principle but will make things possible.

~Someday, somewhere, somehow,
someone will believe in your idea,
but you first~

Give room for needful mistakes

There is a time to defend your mistake and there is a time to let it be subject to critics refine but setting the boundary is very important. A newly wedded man desired to bring flower for his new wife every day so he asked a horticulturist to help him plant a flowering plant at his courtyard. The man being a perfectionist took care of the plant from the seedling. As the plant began to grow, the branches began to go in different direction, this young man as a perfectionist dislike the disarray and started a good pruning work on the plant. Anytime a branch tried to shoot out than the other he had pruned it off. Months after months the plant couldn't produce any flower, the man becoming frustrated called for the horticulturist, he lamented; but sir I told you I wanted a flowering plant that is so unique and not common at all, like something I have never seen in my life or around.

The man said for the past twenty years I have been in the profession I have not had such a complaint from my customers. He said, "Sir, something is wrong somewhere;" he asked, have you been watering it daily? He said yes. He asked, is it exposed to sunlight? He said yes. Then he asked him to come down to his horticultural garden. On getting there the young man saw the same type of plant blossoming with flowers. He was thrilled at the same time bewildered. He asked, "Sir, what went wrong?" The man looked for a while and from experience asked the man a question.

He said how often do you prune the flower? Every time a branch tries to shoot out disorderly above others. He responded. "I have never allowed the plant to make such a mistake of missing the beautiful rhyme. I am an addicted perfectionist; I always want things to be perfectly carried out." Then the horticulturist laughed and said sir, you are responsible for the flowerless state of your plant. You must allow the plant to shoot out some branches that will grow enough to produce tender stem that will give birth to the flower you want.

When you are so careful to take a risk, give room for the unknown or make necessary mistake, you will be at risk of a great and common mistake. If a baby would desire not to fall at all, it will never walk. You can't be more than your thinking, so think more than this. You can't expand more than your faith so dare more than this. Do not just try to perfect your mistakes; rather let your mistake makes you perfect.

~Anything that is successful is a
series of mistakes~ Billie Armstrong

Bend your thinking

Bend your thinking and ideas will never end. One of the ways God blesses us is through creativity. Think of Jacob. But how people respect the awe of history, in a way that chains humanity, in such a way that it never changes our story. Capsize your thought and you will be surprised that you have been sailing against opportunity for long. A young agile farmer went to a piece of land he just bought for farming. When he started to till the ground, he discovered that it was full of little rocks. The first three days of work ended up destroying his farm tools.

Frustrated and disgusted, he thought of how he would explain his new financial struggle to his wife so he decided to carry a piece of the little rocks home to show his wife and children the reason for his inability to provide for their needs, what had been standing as obstacle to him.

On his way home, he felt he needed to drink water and branched to a gently flowing stream. As he tried to drop the stone he carried on his head down, it rolled in to the middle of the stream. As his eyes traced the little rock to the middle of the stream, he discovered something; the stream on colliding with the little rock could not climb it, but gradually it began to hit the little rock and afterward spilt in to different paths. As the water flow past the rock, the different path began to join again a few steps after the little rock. He began to reason though the stream could not drag the stone along not overflow it but had managed to maneuver its way through.

Then he began to see what he could do to the same stone that had stood as obstacle in his farmland. He reasoned, "Instead of farming, I could rare animals, I could start poultry farming and at the end I will still get money which I could not get through tilling the soil."

The world could remain in darkness if not that a man chose to bend its thinking from the common beliefs. For about 1400 years, until the AD 1500s, scholars accepted the ideas of the ancient astronomer Ptolemy. His theory stated that Earth was the center of the universe and that the sun, stars and planets revolved around it. The first person to question these ideas was Copernicus, who claimed that Earth rotates on its axis and that all the planets revolve around the sun. This breakthrough opened the way to a truly scientific approach to astronomy. He put the idea in a book but it was not published for years. However, because it opposed the standard beliefs of the time. According to one story, Copernicus did not see a published copy of his book until the day he died – 24 May 1543. Copernicus' theory influenced two other great astronomers, Johannes Kepler and Galileo Galilei.

As long as white light travels in a straight line, the beauty it contains won't be revealed; but when it is subjected to density of the cloud rainbow emerges as the rays are bent at different speed to give birth to spectrums. Let your thinking pass through the prism of obstacles for new colors of idea lights to emerge.

~Adventures looks opportunist sees~

> **The soil of soul**
> On which all thoughts grow
> The tree of attitude, there spring out
> The fruits of character drop off
> With spreading stems of reputation
> A man inside out is formed on the film of time
> His nature trails him as his shadow
> And his life rolls out the picture

THE IDEA LAW OF OBSERVATION

Galileo made one of his earliest scientific discoveries in the cathedral of Pisa. As he watched a chandelier swinging back and forth, he realized that it took the same time for each swing, whether the swings were large or small. This discovery became known as the law of the pendulum. It led to the use of the pendulum to measure time. Idea comes not with a title or existing terms; they often are uninvited mistakes, accidents, errors, distraction, digression, natural implications etc. All these can be caught with the net of inquisitive observation. There is a need to free your mind and be ready to dignify necessary stupid insight that may seem your lot as you choose to think offset from the natural laws and conclusions. Just like how the real knowledge is gotten by students before they start preparing for exams, when their minds are free and only panting to process and to possess knowledge—when they are triggered to examine why and what and not being eager to be examined under pressure. Much scientific ideas came from simple and everyday life occurrences. They are just smartness of inversion of normal thought and senses.

Nature is an embodiment of teachings and source of inspiration. God gave us our geography not just to appreciate the landscape, the trees and the animals but to as well be tutored by them. See how a curious man maximized the blessing of shadow. In 240 B.C., the Greek astronomer Eratosthenes made the first good measurement of the size of Earth. By noting the angles of shadows in two cities on the Summer Solstice, and by performing the right calculations using his knowledge of geometry and the distance between the cities, Eratosthenes was able to make a remarkably accurate calculation of the circumference of Earth. Eratosthenes lived in the city of Alexandria, near the mouth of the Nile River by the Mediterranean coast, in northern Egypt.

He knew that on a certain day each year, the Summer Solstice, in the town of Syene in southern Egypt, there was no shadow at the bottom of a well. He realized that this meant the Sun was directly overhead in Syene at noon on that day each year. Eratosthenes knew that the Sun was never directly overhead on the Summer Solstice, in his home city of Alexandria, which is further north than Syene. He realized that he could determine how far away from directly overhead the Sun was in Alexandria by measuring the angle formed by a shadow from a vertical object. Eratosthenes had someone measure the distance between Alexandria and Syene.

He used that distance, what he knew about the Sun's angles, and a bit of geometry to figure out the size of the Earth. He ended up with a crude but respectable measurement of the earth dimension. Solomon said as he was passing through the field of a lazy man he observed and receive instruction that a little sleep and slumber is what needed to acquire a life time of penury in the fourth chapter of his proverbs. Do not just live to look and take picture, go a mind mile to capture what lesson nature and the happenings are delivering. The world is a big lecture theatre for the souls that go around with the student attitude.

There is no citadel or terrain of inspiration it is free fall availability for all who can think walk and think live. The man who made telephone mouth piece was involved in installation of transmission cable across the Atlantic when he discovered that the amount of current flowing varies with the depth of the cable. In other words he interpreted that the cable current carrying capacity varies with the pressure mounted on it. This was developed to the telephone mouthpiece that worked on compressed and decompressed carbon particles. Whatever degree you obtain in school, it is a preparation to begin learning. When you prepare and fail, learn, when you learn and succeed, prepare. Learning stops when living stops. The only two things you do not learn in life to do is how be born and how to die. There is a chunk of ideas to capture by the tool of intentional observation.

~Invention sometimes is nothing,
but just ability to know that if x=y and
y=z, then x=z~

Look long enough to see

We often neglect gold dust because they do not glitter. Considering a marble sculpture executed from 1501 to 1504 by the Italian Renaissance artist Michelangelo. The statue was commissioned for one of the buttresses of the cathedral of Florence and was carved from a block of marble that had been partially blocked out by other sculptors and left outdoors. After Michelangelo completed the sculpture, the Florentine government decided instead to place it in front of the Palazzo Vecchio.

The original is now in the Accademia, and copies have been installed in the Piazza dellaSignoria and the Piazzale Michelangelo, which overlooks Florence. To be smart means to be timely and environmentally wise—to look over when others overlook. When others are sleeping, smart heart is dreaming, when they are dreaming he is awake already and when they are awake they open their eyes only to behold and be dumbfounded by his product of foresight.

~Those who focus on their credentials
run after opportunity, those who focus
on their potential have opportunities
looking for them~

When Saul was depressed they recommended David for him as a talented musician so he went looking for him. When pharaoh was having foreseen economic problem they recommended Joseph for him and he went looking for Joseph in the prison. When you choose to live and explore inward you will have many opportunities outward looking for you. There are physical five senses and there is one analytical sense: perception, this draws the thin line of separation between genius and indigenous brain. Some things appear nonsense to some people because they have no sense lens to magnify the seedling opportunity in it. The beginning of limitation is not fear to act but the art of hearing and seeing of the heart. Be careful how you are trained, it forms habit that training may not succeed to reverse.

~To unlearn is often more difficult to learn~

Our limit is not our challenges but what we fail to challenge—a form of notion, belief, philosophy and tradition. Often we neglect what seems has no value because we do not have the value to explain it in us yet. The more knowledge we grow the more opportunity seems to exist: to a toddler money is a paper like his diaper; when he grows to six, money is all about using it to purchase; when he grows to teenage money becomes an object to save sometimes, but to a man money means much more including investment. Everybody looks at adversity somebody sees the opportunity. You need time to purchase knowledge, the market place not being the library alone nor the seller being a scholar alone but everywhere in the room and on the street, with every fool and wise you meet, by every sense, eyes and the ear, at every time night and day. Great lives are 80% of action and 20% reaction, for they often wait for themselves alone to dare and bear.

~If the escalator is slow start walking
on its stairs~

We wait for opportunity endlessly at home why it waits for us at bus stop to make the journey faster. We allow history to determine our sight and pace. We exchange experience for experiment. When you go to the house of opportunity, go with a touch of smartness for many have turned back after he opens to their knock because his room was dark and they couldn't see him.

Possibility harvests ideas

After some leading financiers established the Edison Electric Light Company and advanced him $30,000 for research and development, Edison proposed to connect his lights in a parallel circuit by subdividing the current, so that, unlike arc lights, which were connected in a series circuit, the failure of one light bulb would not cause a whole circuit to fail. Some eminent scientists predicted that such a circuit could never be feasible, but their findings were based on systems of lamps with low resistance—the only successful type of electric light at the time.

Edison, however, determined that a bulb with high resistance would serve his purpose, and he began searching for a suitable one. He had the assistance of 26-year-old Francis Upton, a graduate of Princeton University with an M.A. in science. Upton, who joined the laboratory force in December 1878, provided the mathematical and theoretical expertise that Edison himself lacked. Aristotle's put it thus, whenever there is a conflict between theory and observation, one must trust observation, he insisted, and Theories are to be trusted only if their results conform to the observed.

~The laws are to guide us to master
life not to master or guard us from living~

Edison later revealed, "At the time I experimented on the incandescent lamp I did not understand Ohm's law." On another occasion he said, "I do not depend on figures at all. I try an experiment and reason out the result, somehow, by methods which I could not explain."

Gift of serendipity

Interruptions are cloners of ideas, when things go wrong it could be to become strong. When unplanned happened it does not mean it is bunch of disadvantages or disappointment. On Sept. 3, 1928, shortly after his appointment as professor of bacteriology, Fleming noticed that a culture plate of Staphylococcus Aureushe had been working on had become contaminated by a fungus.

A mould, later identified as PenicilliumNotatum, had inhibited the growth of the bacteria. He at first called the substance "mould juice" and then "penicillin," after the mold that produced it. Fleming decided to investigate further, because he thought that he had found an enzyme more potent than lysozyme. In fact, it was not an enzyme but an antibiotic—one of the first to be discovered. By the time Fleming had established this, he was interested in penicillin for itself. Very much the lone researcher with an eye for the unusual, Fleming had the freedom to pursue anything that interested him.

While this approach was ideal for taking advantage of a chance observation, the therapeutic development of penicillin required multidisciplinary teamwork. Fleming, working with two young researchers, failed to stabilize and purify penicillin. However, he did point out that penicillin had clinical potential, both as a topical antiseptic and as an injectable antibiotic, if it could be isolated and purified.

Do not be too busy to be distracted by an unplanned insight. Edison invented many items, including the carbon transmitter, in response to specific demands for new products or improvements. But he also had the gift of serendipity: When some unexpected phenomenon was observed, he did not hesitate to halt work in progress and turn off course in a new direction. This was how, in 1877, he achieved his most original discovery, the phonograph. Some earlier researchers, notably the French inventor Léon Scott, had theorized that each sound, if it could be graphically recorded, would produce a distinct shape resembling shorthand, or phonograph ("sound writing"), as it was then known. Edison hoped to reify this concept by employing a stylus-tipped carbon transmitter to make impressions on a strip of paraffinic paper.

To his astonishment, the scarcely visible indentations generated a vague reproduction of sound when the paper was pulled back beneath the stylus. Edison unveiled the tinfoil phonograph, which replaced the strip of paper with a cylinder wrapped in tinfoil, in December 1877. It was greeted with incredulity. Indeed, a leading French scientist declared it to be the trick device of a clever ventriloquist.The public's amazement was quickly followed by universal acclaim.

Edison was projected into worldwide prominence and was dubbed the Wizard of Menlo Park, although a decade passed before the phonograph was transformed from a laboratory curiosity into a commercial product.

If your principle is not working then observe your mind background for our ideology can't be smarter than our thinking anatomy. Many ideas have died on the drawing table as they were not laboured into actuality. Think something new and try something new you will be surprised about other unplanned ideas that will ambush you on the way. There are discoveries and opportunities that only answer to the law of starting. You will never come across them until you decide to start out.

~Ideas are nothing but positive
mistakes caught by inquisitive senses~

The diligence of silence

~A midnight candle gives light to your
eyes and to your mind~

Often Jesus will go to the seaside alone with nothing really stated out as His mission but I perceive, to reflect and receive inspiration from God. At a time, the oppositions came to Him with a question of what punishment to be for a trespassing woman caught in the very act. He stooped down as they talked, in silence and after a while He gave them a knock out answer, then he stooped down again writing on the ground with his finger. People go to beaches to have fun but isn't it funny to make of beaches such conclusion. Such serene is the library of nature. Though void of books but can lead to the birth of history by the breeze of inspirations that the still sea and lonely waves hydrosphere reflects to ventilate the minds for idea infusion and cultural diffusion, budding a well-groomed land marking meditated product. Darkness did not come in the night it has been there on the earth waiting for the sun to set; discovery won't come it's been there in your heart waiting for your mind to rest. If you must remain valuable you must not always be available. You are like what you think like. The power of silence is the secret tool of known wise. The art of selfless-discipline is the pad-lock for mouth door. God has done much anatomically and physiologically to help us guard our tongue, by "imprisoning" it in a house barred with Iron Gate made of white iron—the teeth and muzzling double door made of —the lips.

~A wise man has much to say
and have much unsaid~

Meditation and observation are soul twin engines of idea. Be stingy with your time when you are with critics. Generals do not live general life. Your determination must produce more thrust for you to rise above discouragement of failure. Nobody can hold you responsible for listening but you will for your speaking. Everything that has to do with mouth should be done slowly, in measure and softly for whatever comes out from the mouth or goes in to the mouth can hardly be recovered. If you do not have something better than silence then keep silent.

~Self-control begins with mouth control~

MANAGING IDEA SECRETS

~The wise produce in pain,
 the smart reproduces in gain~

John Augustus Sutter, German-born Swiss pioneer settler and colonizer in California; the discovery of gold on his land in 1848 precipitated the California Gold Rush. Sutter spent much of his early life in Switzerland; he was a Swiss citizen and served in the Swiss army. Fleeing from bankruptcy and financial failures and leaving his wife and children in Switzerland, he reached California in 1839 and persuaded the Mexican governor to grant him lands on the Sacramento River.

There, at its junction with the American River, he established the colony of Nueva Helvetia (New Switzerland), later to become Sacramento. He built "Sutter's Fort" (1841), set up frontier industries, and, in spite of his enormous debts, provided lavish hospitality, and often employment, to traders, trappers, immigrants, and Native Americans who came to his fort.

Discovery of gold on his land brought disaster to Sutter. In the process of building a water-powered sawmill, a carpenter named James W. Marshall found flakes of gold in a streambed (January 24, 1848). The two men tried to keep the findings a secret, but the news leaked out. Workers deserted the colony; gold seekers and squatters overran Sutter's land, stealing and destroying his goods and livestock. When the U.S. courts denied title to his Mexican grants, his ruin was complete. By 1852 he was bankrupt. When Elisha was instructing the widow on how to get out of debt, he told her to go in, get empty vessels, and lock the door behind her.

Why was he concerned about the secrecy of the idea? You need to be wise in handling the seed of change from subtle crowd. You must not only be busy with your idea you must learn the skill to do progressive business with it. Solomon gave the account of a city that was besieged by another greater king to make war with it. In the little city was a wise man that through his wisdom delivered the city but afterward was forgotten and remained poor. He could have learnt from David. When he was about to go and fight Goliath he asked what will be given to the man who conquers the gigantic enemy. He did the business part very well. Men could be dubious and inconsiderate that is why you need to be business skilled with your idea.

The Wright brothers are young men with bright order. Their claim to have flown was widely doubted during the years 1906–07. During that period a handful of European and American pioneers struggled into the air in machines designed on the basis of an incomplete understanding of Wright technology. Meanwhile the brothers, confident that they retained a commanding lead over their rivals, continued to negotiate with financiers and government purchasing agents on two continents. Determined to move from the marginal success of 1903 to a practical airplane. The Wrights in 1904 and 1905 built and flew two more aircraft from Huffman Prairie, a pasture near Dayton.

They continued to improve the design of their machine during these years, gaining skill and confidence in the air. By October 1905 the brothers could remain aloft for up to 39 minutes at a time, performing circles and other maneuvers. Then, no longer able to hide the extent of their success from the press, and concerned that the essential features of their machine would be understood and copied by knowledgeable observers, the Wrights decided to cease flying and remain on the ground until their invention was protected by patents and they had negotiated a contract for its sale. Their ideas of manned flight could have been hijacked and flopped financially.

The skill of foresight

An old traveler use to pass through a village where a cunning famer lived who had an oak tree behind his courtyard. One day, the traveler being wearied in the scorching sun, branched close to the oak tree to relax. When the farmer saw him, he challenged him of his mission. After the man explained he was there to relax the farmer said you have to pay: Either for the shadow of the tree, the shade, the tree or the ground they cost the same each. "I will pay for the shadow that's all I need;" the traveler said.

The next day he was passing by and he decided to branch under the tree as it was raining. Then the farmer came out and challenged him, what are you are doing there? He said he was using what he paid for. The farmer said the sun is not out and there is no shadow you have no right to stay under the tree unless you want to pay for a shade. So the traveler agreed to pay. Another time the man was travelling and decided to lodge on the tree. When he got there, he climbed the tree for a shade, to have glance of the landscape and to avoid crawling animals as he was planning to sleep on it overnight. The farmer came out and said what are you doing on my tree? He said, to be safe from crawling creatures; the farmer replied, we did not agree that you would touch my tree.

So he paid to climb the tree. Another day the traveler was on top of the tree and became hungry, so he decided to pluck the fruits that surrounded him. Then the famer came out and said; old man who gave you permission to eat of the fruit? You will have to pay. Therefore, he paid for the tree. The next time the old man was on the tree eating the fruits with his family having picnic under it. Then the famer rushed out what are you people doing here? The traveler replied, we are enjoying the shade and the tree I paid for. The farmer answered you have no right of such you did not pay for the ground. I want to use my courtyard for something else come and remove your tree.

The traveler had the choice of buying the tree, the shadow, the shade and the land but went for the shadow to meet his immediate need when he could have gone for the land and got the tree, the fruit, the shadow and the shade almost free. Foresight could be described as four eyes: two for today and two for tomorrow. You will need to have a plan for your idea. You can hardly know the size an idea could grow up to so do not cheap it out. Have a forest in mind not just the seed at hand.

No idea is peanuts

Peanuts may be pearl worth, before you sell an idea do the cost not based on what it worth's today but what it will tomorrow. Ideas is a forest in a seed, do not cost a seedling, price tag a plantation. In 1947 Schulz began drawing a comic strip called "Li'l Folks." "Li'l Folks" ran in a newspaper and a magazine. In 1950 Schulz sold "Li'l Folks" to a company that sells comic strips to newspapers. The company renamed the strip "Peanuts," even though Schulz did not like the name. Peanuts" appeared in seven U.S. newspapers in 1950. By 1958 "Peanuts" appeared in 355 U.S. newspapers and 40 newspapers in other countries. "Peanuts" eventually ran in about 2,600 newspapers in 75 countries.

Those who walk away on impossibility create room for those behind to walk on possibility. In February 2008, Microsoft Corporation made an unsolicited bid to acquire Yahoo for US$44.6 billion. Yahoo formally rejected the bid, claiming that it "substantially undervalues" the company and was not in the interest of its shareholders. Three years later, Yahoo had a market capitalization of US$22.24 billion. Guess what yahoo will capitalize market wise in three more years.

~The size of the seed is not what determines
the space of its planting but the future.
Nobody plants the smallest mustard seed
in biggest flower pot~

THE CYCLE OF REVOLUTION

Idea changes the world. Ideas are always good risks. Ideas lead, the world follows. You do not need a committee for a good idea; all you need is commitment to go beyond that very point of discouragement. There are no ideas born by the crowd only those they will burn with word of criticisms.

~Why and how makes producers;
what and when makes consumers~

Ideas can be viewed in the light of the following progressive terminologies:

Intuition- This is the first state. God endows every one with it even the animals. They think of how to make nest from the available, how to burrow and keep their young ones.

*Imagination-*This is the free gift of the mind. It is the core anatomy of the mind. It is as powerful as the mouth. It is the action within and carries the same power and consequence as those performed by the limbs. Imagination is a tool for surfing the unavailable to generate inspiration for possibility. This is where the superiority of human beings over the animals is beginning to emphasise. So a soul without active and productive imagination could appear to have lower value.

*Inspiration-*This is streamlined to men and this separate men from the animals. This the power of humanism. Which means a life time without inspiration exposes itself in competition with that of animals capacity in creativity wise.

*Initiative-*This is first, simple, unconscious, common application of inspiration. Any time you engage your initiative it is a form of deployed inspiration. We often only engage it for daily activities but not for intentional goal and this is what separates the genius from the rest. They task there initiative for the task: normal challenges and as well for acquired challenges

*Intelligence-*When you live every second on initiative you are seen as intelligent.

*Idea-*This is the outcome of intelligence garnished with diligence. It is the official title for intelligence.

Innovation- When idea is planted and cultured innovation is the tree that springs up.

Industrialisation- These are the fruits that fall from the tree of innovation.

Association of ideas

A further influential section of Book II is Locke's treatment of the association of ideas. Ideas, Locke observes, can become linked in the mind in such a way that having one idea immediately leads one to form another idea, even though the two ideas are not necessarily connected with each other. Instead, they are linked through their having been experienced together on numerous occasions in the past. This can be applicable as an individual or as a group. Like earlier said every idea is pregnant with the seed of another idea, either involving grafting or cloning of fresh ones.

Association of ideas is observed in a team work when a chain of inspiration is developed among the group. This happens when the leader is open enough to allow every head to contribute. In the beginning of astrology when the knowledge is being used as a compass for travellers on the sea, the sailors are recorded as using the constellation of stars to determine their location per time on the infinite sea. They depend on the position of the group of stars to find their ways when they can go on with their limited sight and telescope.

Just the same is applicable to the leader in the board room; sometimes the simple way out is found on the board floor where heads of ideas are collated, giving chance for collective innovation. One star can't lead the sailor always there is a time for constellation of stars to play the role. When you allow others to light their candle from yours, you only have a time to share and not a dime to lose and illumination to gain for the atmosphere shines brighter and stronger, and more heat is generated for all in the moment. This is the idea of constellation of stars; it is useful for navigation because of the coming together of stars that makes the sky special and eye dazzling giving direction to sailors.

This is the law of discovery, when you share ideas with others of like mind to dig and remix; the team comes out with sharpened tool like the robbing of iron is with iron. Two good heads are burden until they are fused to link and connect ideas.

Idea spelt

If you cannot generate answers, generate question and make it general. The original definition of question I think is quest for solution. Get the beautiful child out of the ark. Moses mother was bold to keep the beautiful gift but hidden out of fear. As the boy was crying on the sea bank the same is your gifted idea. Do not burry it in fear, get it out of the ark of timidity before someone else get hold of it and later employ you to take care of it on salary basis like Pharaoh's daughter did to Moses mother and Laban to Jacob. Idea could be alphabetically spelt does:

I=*Inspiration*

D=*Development*

E= *Experimentation*

A=*Application*

I = Inspiration

A Physics teacher once tested his students during practical session. He brought out a 100 liters container, 75 liters, 50 liters, and 25 liters. He brought out as well, 100 liters of water. He told them how many of the four empty containers could the 100 liters of water fill at a time? They all said two at most. They said it can fill the empty 100 liters alone or 75 and 25 together or 50 and 25 together; so at most it could only fill two containers per time. The instructor admonished, think very well. He asked again, "How many of the containers can the water fill at a go? I think it can fill all the four containers."

They replied him with the same answer. Then he left them asking them to think it out. They began to think and do calculation but finally resolved it is impossible to achieve more with 100 liters of water. They need more to fill all the four vessels (I know if you are asked as well, you may fully support them). Just then, the teacher entered. He said place the empty 25 liters container in the 50 liters and then the 50 liters in the 75 liters and finally place the 75 liters container in the 100 liters container. After that was done, he said take the 100 liters of water and poured everything in the 25 liters.

As they began to pour, the 25 liters got filled then overflowed in to the 50 liters; the 50 liters got filled then overflowed into the 75 liters; the 75 got filled and overflowed in to the 100 liters. As the 100 liters container got filled the water got exhausted. Then he asked which of the container is empty they said none, all were filled.

Some times what you have is quite enough to start out and meet multiple needs if you can think enough in multiplication. If you want to engage the power of excuse, it will always serve you right, but you have the potential to skillfully maximize the available not in normal way but thoughtful way.

D=Development

~I never did anything by accident,
nor did any of my inventions come by
accident; they came by work~ Thomas Edison

A young girl saw his father business rubber stamp and try to read the impression but it was difficult as the letters were cut in lateral inversion as usual. After struggling to no avail, she took it to her father asking him to read it for her. A dreaming man who was lost in thought quickly jacked back to reality and discovered he had been engrossed with the idea he felt so good not to be remembered. He had been thinking on changing his company name and watchword, many great ideas have crossed his mind but it took little cognisance of them.

He was in the act when his little daughter took away the pad from his table without knowing. He wondered how and when she took it away. After listening to her request, the man having the understanding of what was happening and what was impressed there, asked her to bring the ink pad and a sheet of paper. He pulled out the stamp and pressed it on the ink pad to soak the ink after which he pressed it on the paper.

Clearly, the name of her father's company was portrayed on the paper. The girl exclaimed, it is your company's name. I can read it out even off hand. As the man reasoned about what had just happened, he realized that when the impression you have in mind about an idea is written down it becomes clearer and readable by all who are stakeholders especially you and becomes impossible to forget.

He wisely pull out his drawer, took his writing tools before the last inspiration get lost in the ocean of mind activities. Moses was a great leader having the mindset of documentation. We could not tell what the master was writing on the ground when they accosted Him to give a verdict on the case of the adulterous woman brought to Him. Who knows whether He was writing down the idea for the answer, for immediately He gave the unquestionable answer He continued to write on the ground. God said you are to write down the vision and make it plain so you can run with it, in other word so you can develop it.

The first step to developing any idea is documentation. It is like turning the negative photo film in to a picture. Documentation brings about clarity and reality of the process ahead. Researchers say the average lead pencil will write a line about 35 miles long or write approximately 50,000 English words. Engage the power of pen.

Anton Van Leeuwenhoek who invented the first practical microscopes, and used them to become the first person to see and describe bacteria, among other microscopic discoveries said "My work, which I've done for a long time, was not pursued in order to gain the praise I now enjoy, but chiefly from a craving after knowledge, which I notice resides in me more than in most other men. And therewithal, whenever I found out anything remarkable, I have thought it my duty to put down my discovery on paper, so that all ingenious people might be informed thereof"—in his letter of June 12, 1716.

After using your hand to write you still need it to work it. A genius is not a man who is a good thinker, but a man with a twin attitudes— perseverance and possibility. John Maynard Keynes said about Isaac "His peculiar gift was the power of holding continuously in his mind a purely mental problem until he had seen straight through it. I fancy his pre-eminence is due to his muscles of intuition being the strongest and most enduring with which a man has ever been gifted. ... I believe that Newton could hold a problem in his head for hours and days and weeks until it surrendered to him its secret. Then being a supreme mathematical technician he could dress it up, how you will, for the purposes of exposition, but it was his intuition that was pre-eminently extraordinary"

E= Experimentation

The only secret of genius is the reversal of their natural order. They are desirous of their thoughts breakthrough as others desire food, sleep and chatting. They make their laboratory a general merchant of bedroom and dining room annex. Edison revealed, "At the time I experimented on the incandescent lamp I did not understand Ohm's law." Like he was quoted above "I do not depend on figures at all. I try an experiment and reason out the result, somehow, by methods which I could not explain." Experience is good, but it is limited to what it had achieved, but experimentation frees the heart and hand to pursue fresh and greater discoveries. Edward Jenner, English surgeon and discoverer of vaccination for smallpox who was born at a time when the patterns of British medical practice and education were undergoing gradual change was a country youth, the son of a clergyman. On completing his apprenticeship at the age of 21, he went to London and became the house pupil of John Hunter, who was on the staff of St. George's Hospital and was one of the most prominent surgeons in London. The firm friendship that grew between the two men lasted until Hunter's death in 1793. From no one else could Jenner have received the stimuli that so confirmed his natural bent...The young inherited from his mentor "...interest in biological phenomena, disciplined powers of observation, sharpening of critical faculties, and a reliance on experimental investigation. From Hunter, Jenner received the characteristic advice, "Why think [i.e., speculate]—why not try the experiment?"

~At the time I experimented on
the incandescent lamp I did not
understand Ohm's law~ Thomas Edison

A=Application

Almost all ideas can be traced to being a need created idea on the platform of decision to be practical in resource adaptation and application. So it is of no use to stop the idea walk on paper work. Sometimes you can't really determine the extent to wish idea will soar or sail. The engine that bears his name set off a new chapter in the industrial revolution, but Rudolf Diesel initially thought his invention would help small businesses and artisans, not industrialists. His true love lay in engine design, however, and over the next few years he began exploring a number of ideas. One concerned is finding a way to help small businesses compete with big industries, which had the money to harness the power of steam engines. Another was how to use the laws of thermodynamics to create a more efficient engine.

In his mind, building a better engine would help the little guy. Rudolf Diesel's inventions have three points in common they were initially motivated by the inventor's concept of sociological needs—by finding a way to enable independent craftsmen and artisans to compete with large industry. That last goal did not exactly pan out as Diesel expected. His invention could be used by small businesses, but it was embraced eagerly by the industrialists, as well. His engines were used to power pipelines, electric and water plants, automobiles and trucks, and marine craft, and soon after were used in mines, oil fields, factories, and transoceanic shipping. Diesel became a millionaire by the end of the 20th century. So whatever the idea you have, apply it to meet a need and you will be surprised by the masses that really need it.

~Until you apply it, it won't multiply~

DRESS UP YOUR IDEA

~Everything begins with an idea~ Earl Nightengale

Every idea comes like a seed, very small insignificant, unnoticed and despicable. But if you can invest time and curiosity in them, exposing them to dexterity of mind power and piercing it through the box of normality you will often come out with something of difference with consequential influence. When your idea is well dressed and tender to maturity like a groom it will find the bride of opportunity.

A group of boys went on camping in a mild jungle. Along the line, one of them got missing from the team. The rest did not realize it until late in the evening. The missing boy began to look for his friends. At a point, he thought within himself, "They too must be looking for me and if I can't find them they can find me." So he stood up from under the tree and looked for the highest mountain around, took time to climb to the peak waving his cloth which he removed. As the friends were about giving up the search, they moved in the direction of the mountain and faintly saw a red shirt of the group dangling in the air. Easily, they found out their missing friend.

The young boy is an idea while his friends are the opportunities. Sometime we hawk aimlessly and fruitlessly around the life we live looking for opportunities for our undeveloped idea when we could develop the idea and let opportunities begin to look for it. Nobody will help you to develop and deliver your idea; they will only come to collaborate with its growth. When your idea is ripe in composition and in right position, opportunities will find it. It is like a pregnant woman, nobody can help in developing the child; as she will have to eat well and sleep well to nourish the seed to fruition, which no one else could do. She can only be helped a little to deliver the child. People will only come to help nursing the child after the delivery. Take pain to nurture your brainchild instead of looking for opportunity to nurture it. Ideas look for opportunity not money. Your pocket is not the midwives for your ideas but your power of passion. See this young shepherd boy "…when the words were heard which David spoke, they rehearsed [them] before Saul: and he sent for him." When your idea stage is commendable, you will be recommended.

~If you burn enough your
flame will catch attention~

I once read about a young inventor and entrepreneur who developed a device that can enable you see the visitor at your door on your mobile phone wherever you are at a time. As a proactive entrepreneur, he took the idea to the sharks, a group of investors known as financier for emerging companies. At the interview, he was rejected out rightly by some, and as well offered a seemingly underrated ball game by some. He left the panel to develop his idea on his own. One day, a billionaire came across the device when he accompanied a colleague to a house on which the device was installed. Quite impressed, he called the young man and offered to buy a substantial and favorable share in the company. It was like a dream come through for the young heart. Before you decide to sell your idea, remove the drowse from the gold. Ideas are like matches you have to get it out of the box and rob it with your time, treasure, and talent for it to generate spark. David was just in the wilderness enjoying the dexterity he had achieved in playing the harp when they came all the way from the palace to come and buy in to his idea. Dress up your idea for a proper address by its suitor. If the world had made use of all the ideas that have come across the heart of all who had lived there, it would have been a paradise of wonders. But out of ten ideas that cross the mind of an average man less than 20% were utilized. Think of songs that have come and gone over a soul.

Think of inventions that came knocking as a flash thought but was taken ugly because it came with a bone alone and no flesh. The sky is wider in space than the ground below; I mean if the whole earth surface is finally inhabited with every dust carrying a sole of man we can still have enough space to fly in the sky without choking our liberty to soar. Everybody can be great, God did not design success to resemble a pointing mountaintop where only few can inhabit but like a plateau, an altitude where a city can be built.

His Son said we are a city set on the hill that can't be hidden not a mansion but a city. There is no mind without an idea, because every mind is an idea from God individually fashioned. Success is not race bound, is not tribe trimmed, nor tongue glued, it is not a native of any language success answer to its master call, the principles and laws.

~When your idea is polished enough,
it will be published~

Tailor your excuse to your outfit

Friction hinders our speed when we walk, run and fly, but we all need friction to walk and run even to fly we need friction to take off, so are those mistakes, you need them to learn the true success. We talk through wire today because a man yesterday will work through the day and think through the night. "It takes 24-hour to plan to succeed; it takes 24-hours to plan to fail; you need just 24-hours to fail or succeed. If your time is not enough it is either your intelligence of planning or diligence of handling is not enough or both.

When your idea is ripe enough, birds of men will come to taste the nectar and propagate the pollens of its seed. Young Bell recorded achievements on behalf of the deaf and his invention of the telephone before his 30th birthday are evidences of his persistence and diligence coupled with thoroughness of his training. Never adept with his hands, Bell had the good fortune to discover and inspire Thomas Watson, a young repair mechanic and model maker, who assisted him enthusiastically in devising an apparatus for transmitting sound by electricity. Ironically, the telephone—until then all too often regarded as a joke and its creator-prophet as, at best, an eccentric—was the subject of the most involved patent litigation in history.

Their long nightly sessions began to produce tangible results. The fathers of George Sanders and Mabel Hubbard, two deaf students whom he helped, were sufficiently impressed with the young teacher to assist him financially in his scientific pursuits.

~Your pocket is the cart; your passion
is the horse; you only need the latter
to take off, and the former latter~

Nevertheless, during normal working hours Bell and Watson were still obliged to fulfill a busy schedule of professional demands. It is scarcely surprising that Bell's health again suffered. On April 6, 1875, he was granted the patent for his multiple telegraphs;

Ideas take time to grow, it takes time to glow, it takes time to show, it takes time to flow. Every seed is despised while on the ground, some step on it, some sweep it away, some overlook it, a potential prey for birds, but in it is an ark as big as Noah's, in it is a forest as stretched as game reserve, in it is paper mill.

After another exhausting six months of long nightly sessions in the workshop, while maintaining his daily professional schedule, Bell had to return to his parents' home in Canada to recuperate. In September 1875 he began to write the specifications for the telephone. On March 7, 1876, the United States Patent Office granted to Bell Patent Number 174,465 covering "The method of, and apparatus for, transmitting vocal or other sounds telegraphically…by causing electrical undulations, similar in form to the vibrations of the air accompanying the said vocal or other sounds. Alexander Graham Bell, who patented the telephone in 1876, inaugurated the 1,520-km (944-mile).

The most noteworthy contemporaries of Bell were Antonio Meucci, who filed a caveat (rather than a full patent) in 1871 and let it lapse through lack of funds, and Elisha Gray, who filed a caveat on February 14, 1876, just a few hours after Bell submitted a patent claim. The Bell story does not end with the invention of the telephone; indeed, in many ways it was a beginning.

Do not sleep over an idea for behold others are dreaming. What you invest your life on, will be harvested in your memory, live to empty yourself and so die to fill lives. When Bell died, the whole America telephone line was stopped for 60 seconds to honor Bell. How great the bell of an idea can ring and echo in the tunnel of time when a voice of diligence is given to it! There is no gift or idea that God has given you that is a waste or to be buried. Some ideas are to project you, some are to perpetuate your once existence here on earth. Some are to be shared and some are to be chaired by you.

There is no natural resources that is a waste except those that humanity is yet to discover its use, the same with you there is no gift in you or idea that is a waste except the ones you are yet discover existing or what it's reasons for existence, or how to explore.

~Nobody will buy into your idea
until you are sold out in it~

The seed success

On a sunny day, little boy riding a bike got to a point beside a big tree when suddenly the rain began. He quickly rode under the tree and propped the bike for a shelter. The rain did not pour much but much enough to have him wet up. When the rain stopped, the boy thought why not stay longer to rest before entering the rising sun again. As he sat there, water began to drop from the tree. Surprised and disappointed, that it had started raining again and the tree fail to cover him this time. He angrily stormed out only to discover that it was not raining outside the tree shade. He was surprised.

When he got home he explained his ordeal to his mother, who gave him explanation that when it rains the tree shield by transferring the rain drop from one leaf to another with a speed that ensure it get to the extreme leave when it pours to the ground therefore shielding from the rain. But as soon as the rain stopped the remaining water on the leaves, because of low speed and volume began to drop to the ground right under the host tree. When you try to stay longer in a comfort zone it gradually becomes a combat zone and when you decide to stay long enough in your combat zone it turns out to be comfort zone with time. You need to step out of every success to keep it from collapsing on you.

Chapter Ten

THE NEED TO BE CHANGE CREATIVE

~Embrace change but do not marry it~

Two sales men from a manual hair clipper manufacturing company, were sent to a remote village for sales promotion as their last market hope, since electric clipper had suddenly taken over the market in the urban. On getting to the village, they discovered they were all wearing a dread luck—they do not barb nor comb their hair. One of the two sales reps said, "This is a dead luck, how are we even going make them understand the name of the equipment they had never seen? Worse still they have no such custom." The other one replied, "Well, let's see what happens."

Then he proceeded to the palace of their village head. The man was having a dread lock so long and bushy. He said, "Sir, I know you are all great farmers here, and I want to ask you a question." The old men said speak on my son. He asked, "Sir, when you have a piece of land right at the back of your house and weeds grow on it, becoming very tall and bushy what do you think will begin to happen?" He said, "Wild animals will begin to inhabit the parcel of land and it will become dangerous to my family especially the children." The sales rep asked further, "Sir what then will you do? "Of course, I will get a cutlass to cut it and clear with a rake." Sir, the same with your hair, when it becomes so long and bushy wild insects begin to live there and it becomes dangerous to your comfort especially your health as I can see you scratching your head, it is because of wild insect called lice," the sales man said.

The elderly ruler answered, "But my son, we can't use cutlass and rake for our head, what do you say to that?" "That is why we have come," he replied. Here with us is a special cutlass for the hair and special rake for it. Then he brought out the manual clipper and a comb. He asked the man to let him use one of his sons as example and right there in their presence he turned the boy to cutely looking chap. They were so amazed and excited and bought in to his idea of change. All what some people see in life is what could not work but those who see why it must work will finally discover how it will work. When the will is dead the way is a dread and when the mind is blind, every door is a wall.

~Dreams make you to feel your future;
attitude to change makes you to fill it~

Comb your brain for innovation

A teacher of psychology was trying to teach his students how to think outside the bone box. He took a board, placed it on the stand right in front of the class and drew a car on it. After the drawing, he asked them what was missing. They said sir, "You have not drawn the tires." "It was intentional," he replied. "Now, I want somebody to push this car from the middle of the class to the door post."

Some of them were teens; they responded "But sir, how can you push a car without tire?" After some minutes of arguments and bewilderments, some of them woke up to reality and said, "Sir, the issue is not even the tires that were not drawn, assuming the tires were drawn is it possible to push a car drawn on the board?" They all chorused, common Charisa you are talking—the eldest among them who stood to be their mouthpiece. They chanted, "You are talking what fools we have played this long." He asked them again, "Who can push this car for us?" Everybody said no one as it is practically impossible.

Then he called the cleaner who was mopping the corridor, he said, "Sir please we want you to sweep the base of this board and the surrounding floor." The man focusing on what he was asked to do, primarily to sweep the base of the board stand, just went to the board and the stand, pushed it to the door side and swept the base and the surrounding. The teacher asked, was the job done? None could answer him back. Sometimes we are engrossed with what is obtainable that we overlook what is attainable. Like the story told of builders who were contacted by a hotel to solve the problem of in-house traffic. Right at the top floor of the hotel, they were discussing the serious problem to be encountered in the installation of a lift.

As they were thinking and talking about the difficulty and cost implication of having to break through the floor of the building right from the base to the top, a cleaner who worked in the hotel overheard them. This is going to be a lot of work for me having to sweep all the dirt of broken concrete, he thought. At a time, he summoned courage and went straight to the chief engineer, "Sir, why do not you install the lift outside the building and enclose it?" he suggested. Like a man, waking up from dream, it dawned on him a possibility they never imagined. With excitement, he replied the cleaner what a great idea. Immediately, he called his colleagues and shared the idea with them, they were all dazed: this will cost us much lesser than the stipulated cost and with lesser effort.

~Every problem has a solution and
every solution has a problem, you
get your choice of view~

There is a constant need to fine-tune your means. Activity should not be mistaken for productivity neither should effectiveness be replaced with efficiency. An expert in muscle building wrote many fall victims of excessive stress in trying to build their muscle by banking on the number of repetition they make or the heaviness of the weight engaged. This notion is common and wrong, as effort ought to have been channeled to the particular muscle to be built. What are the old good methods you must subject to effective change?

THINK VAST NOT JUST FAST

~Gift without skills is lame,
skill without gift is load~

Two friends were having a time out in a boat, with a reserve fuel for their long journey in the plastic can. In the big cruiser, they chose to have a picnic of roasted stick meat when the gas accidentally cut fire. The exploded fuel splashed fire on their body causing their clothes to catch fire. As their raiment began to burn, the two quickly thought of what to do in a twinkling of an eye. The first man without consideration, jumped in to the river, and the fire was quenched immediately but as well, remembered instantly, he could not swim. He shouted for help while the second one finally endured to remove his burning cloth with some minor degree of burnt. With a brief relief, he finally came to himself and heard the screaming of his friend for help. Rather than jumping in to sea as expected being a professional lifeguard, he let down a bucket with a rope. His friend quickly dragged himself towards the life rope but to utter his amazement his friend lifted it up with water in the bucket.

He did the same the second time and the third time. In pain, he let down the anchor rope and rescued his drowning friend. When they were back in the boat the drowning friend asked his friend "Why didn't you rescue me in time by jumping in the sea since you can swim very well and why didn't you get me up with the rope the three times you let it down?" He replied, if I had immediately jumped I would not have rescued you in time alone but I could have rescued myself in time as well without much burnt I as experienced in struggling to remove my burning cloth since the water would do the job faster and easier. Then he looked to his face and said, "Those three times I had used the bucket to draw water saved the boat from burning in to capsizing. We both could have escaped the fire smartly but could have perished in the sea unadvisedly."

A good leader won't be all out to change things because the business environment is changing. Before you dive in to the decision of change you need to dissect the emotional technicality surrounding it. Impulse should be paused while a room is being given to insight.

In 1985 the Coca-Cola Co. declared that it will change the label of its flagship product in the U.S. from Coca-Cola Classic to simply Coca-Cola; the designation "Classic" was added after a change in the beverage's formula. It was ill received and the original formula revived. The company had good intention of variety but the nature of man is to resist change unless the crusader appeals to his emotional judgments and mental dexterity in such a creative and initiative way. Change should be approached creatively and advisedly.

~ Change is the evidence of life~

THE LONELY CHANGE PATH

In the 17th century devout young man, came up with a new discovery in which truth was revealed and God was preserved. Isaac Newton's three laws of motion and his principle of universal gravitation sufficed to regulate the new cosmos, but only, Newton believed, with the help of God. Gravity, he more than once hinted, was direct divine action, as were all forces for order and vitality. When you try to be different, you will develop inherent critics. To be different you do not need to stretch to the north or the south, for your uniqueness is in you being you and getting used to it.

Galileo became unpopular at the university because of his attacks on long-held scientific beliefs. The story reported that he dropped objects from the famous Leaning Tower of Pisa to prove that objects of different weights fall at the same speed. His new theory of gravity contradicts the ideas of his predecessors, who believed that weightier objects fall faster than light ones. You will be rejected when you choose to see from unusual angle. But to be static is to be a natural self-critic in the school of ideas. When an idea has been observed with scrutiny and has served humanity, men metamorphosis it to law but such laws must be able to bend if not breaks when need be. Every idea must be subject to retirement after serving generations.

For long, the world has been kept in darkness. With the aid of pieces of lens improved upon as telescope by trial and error beyond what was obtainable in his time Galileo sketched the Moon's phases as observed through the telescope, showing that the Moon's surface is not smooth, as had been proposed, but is rough and far from evenly distributed. These discoveries were earth shaking, triumphing over the theory of ignorance. With a telescope as an instrument of change, he ended up re-orientating the world that the moon is not a perfect circle but as rough as the earth with mountains and valleys.

Galileo's conversion to new school of taught and diversion from the world belief would be a key turning point in the scientific revolution that the earth is not the center of the universe as it had long been believed and taught. But how receptive was the world of his time? Of course, he had to spear his new crusade amidst opposition and persecution until the light it beamed could not be ignored.

Another case of the lonely path of change is of the F.M system by Edwin H. Armstrong. A shy lad fascinated from childhood with science and machines. As teenager, he was inspired by the exploits of the leading communication scientist of his time in sending the first wireless message across the Atlantic Ocean. He concluded to join the hall of inventors. Using his family attic as a secretive laboratory, he designed a circuit of wireless apparatus and started the journey solitarily, a secretive work that absorbed his life. Wireless was then in the stage of crude spark-gap transmitters and iron-filing receivers, producing faint Morse-code signals, barely audible through tight earphones. Armstrong joined in the hunt for improved instruments. Armstrong made exhaustive measurements to find out how the tube worked and devised a circuit, called the regenerative, or feedback, circuit that suddenly, in the autumn of 1912, brought in signals with a thousand fold amplification; loud enough to be heard across a room. Moreover, he discovered how to use the same circuit to generate waves at its highest amplification,

~Winners are quitters who
postpone it to the end~

This youthful invention that opened the age of electronics had profound effects on Armstrong's life. Armstrong secured four patents on advanced circuits that were to solve a basic problem in wireless adventure using the Frequency Modulated circuit. They revealed an entirely new radio system, from transmitter to receiver. Instead of varying the amplitude, or power, of radio waves to carry voice or music, as in all radio before then, the new system varied, or modulated, the waves' frequency (number of waves per second) over a wide band of frequencies. This created a carrier wave that natural static—an amplitude phenomenon created by electrical storms—could not break into.

As a result, FM's wide frequency range made possible the first clear, practical method of high-fidelity broadcasting. "Because the new system required a basic change in transmitters and receivers, the established radio industry gave it a cold welcome as it were for every emergence of change waves. Armstrong had to foot the building of the first full-scale FM station himself in 1939 costing hundreds of thousands of dollars to prove its worth. He then had to develop and promote the system, sustain it through Second World War and the after war effects. This is one of the price of change agents you may need to bear the whole burden alone but it is for a while, though you are overlooked and walked over you will soon be a topic of discussion and center of art.

~If you want to choke your idea in the tunnel
of time get committee to sit on it, if you want it
to see the light of the day get committed~

During the crisis of trying to prove his point with strenuous financial demand coupling with ageing and fight over patent right, with most of his resources gone in the battle for his brainchild, he took his own life. As usual, time fought for Armstrong as it does for other change agents. Over time, FM came to be recognized and preferred system in radio and television sound transmission and the dominant medium in mobile radio, microwave relay, and space-satellite communications. As mark of honor Armstrong was elected to the hall of fame to join such figures as André-Marie Ampère, Alexander Graham Bell, Michael Faraday, and Guglielmo Marconi as he dreamt of as a lad. Today we celebrate his achievement not only in words of acceptance but also in application.

Bold thinkers

~Nobody flies who never takes risk~

When you succeed you have earned a new thing, when you fail you have learned a new thing. Be content with what you have today but not tomorrow. Boldness is not in face, it is in pace the heart is ready to take when the ground disappear. If you are not bold you are cold, and if you are cold you are naturally common, water exist anywhere in the north and south pole at such a low degree of temperature but hot water is made to happen. Anyone that tells you, you are not qualified to win could as well have said you are not qualified to live. To the living alone is the hope to win.

If successful people do not surround you, you go around them, the people you are close to determines a lot what you are next to. The fact that you want to give up shows you have something to give to your generation, so do not let it go. Success is not just about becoming somebody in life but what people come to be because you once lived. Men are God's formulae for idea, with us, He wants to generate and thereby recreate. The work of creation in the first seven days of the world were partially works of recreation, for bible says in the beginning God created the heaven and the earth but the earth was without form, so God began to recreate it for the next six days.

Those who move in head move ahead. Those who only move on legs will soon be removed from being head. Not everybody that determined wins but everybody that wins determined. We won't stop thinking and seeing why things won't work when we naturally always see reasoning as work and interruption. Often ideas come as interruption, like an eruption of thoughts from background imagination. Starters are potential winners but the ultimate winners are always members of the finishers who dare and endear their ideas.

~If you want to kill any idea in the
world, get a committee working on it~
Charles Kettering

CHANGE IS UNCHANGEBLE

In the late eighteen century, a motion was raised by patent office director of America, insinuating that the department be scraped on the verdict that new invention is no more feasible hammering his proposal on the basis that all innovations and ideas had been accomplished. This sounds funny in the light of what has formed the heart of technology and science today. But not only this mind sail in the same boat, many leaders and managers are voicing the same by their attitude to giving rooms for uncomfortable change. There is nothing we can do to change than to change with it. It is the only constant thing that can't be changed.

Change is inevitable
Change is irresistible
Change is indispensable
Change is unchangeable
Change is approachable

Change is possibility
Change is responsibility
Change is adaptability
Change is mentality
Change is positivity

Change is every thing
Change is everyday
Change is every time
Change is everywhere
Change is evermore

Change is always fought

~There is no beauty in changing but
there is beauty in change~

When Lee De Forest announced the possibility of transmitting voice signals across the Atlantic, to the crude and limited world it was a case of fraudulence that was leveled against him as an attempt to lure people to buy into his proposal of the triodes tube. Can you imagine where we would be without his invention? Or think of what Armstrong the inventor of FM would have built upon. But see how change has always been fought by generations. The Eiffel Tower was another world turning point that faced rigorous and wide criticism before it came in to existence, simply because of its second to none, as nothing of such has ever been done.

As the French government was organizing a fair to celebrate a century of revolution this monument meant to mark it was attacked with various points among the rest that were submitted, but was executed with small cost with a record breaking period of two years. There are two ways to bend iron, you either heat it up and bend it or beat it up and bend it; in either case heat is involved. You are the one who will be ready to stand the reaction by the world or your organization to the heat evolved and involved, this planet is always aggressive to maintain its culture of ignorance. It takes heat to have change of state like the height of the Eiffel Tower that varies by 15 cm due to temperature—before any change or variation there is bound to heat. From stagnant ice to moving water and from moving water to flying vapors, heat plays major and progressive roles—from stagnation to motion and eventual translation.

When Edward Jenner would discover the vaccine for small pox, it was another story of stigmatization and isolation of change agents as usual. He had been fascinated by the fact that those contracted cowpox get immunized against small pox be it accidentally or intentionally. He took time to ponder on this and concluded that the cowpox could be transmitted to someone else who is not having it to serve as immunization against the small pox since the cowpox is relatively harmless. After carrying out the experiment and ascertained it, he published a book on it but as usual, the public unfavorably reacted to it.

Jenner kept on to being actively involved in promoting it until it spread worldwide across continents.

Ready for the reactions

When relativity was first announced, the public was typically awestruck by its complexity, a justified response to the intricate mathematics of general relativity. But the abstract, non-visceral nature of the theory also generated reactions against its apparent violation of common sense. These reactions included a political undertone; in some quarters, it was considered undemocratic to present or support a theory that could not be immediately understood by the common person. But today, laws have got to bend toward the light theory it carries. Nothing new will escape being treated as a stranger and intruder of common sense. You need lion heart to enthrone your idea. If you can't defend it the world will bend it in your mind and end it in your hand.

~Do not go for what is ripe, rather what is right~

Inside every idea is another idea but the old must dominantly die to birth the new, better to say it thus, you can't have the beautiful flying butterfly and the rough caterpillar at the same time. You must let go to let grow and let glow. Creativity is a gift of opportunity. Courage is a cool rage against the obtainable and certified attainable. Winners are quitters to normal, lovers of positive distraction and god managers of discouragement—i.e. they are used to criticism and are good in using the bricks of obstacle haul at them to construct leverage for their desired miracle. Learn to exchange the good for the better. When the cloud releases the rain it is brighter, it is happier, it is lighter, let go and let glow. Your talent is subject to revolution if you will let loose the absolute latent power in it by giving room for seasonal change despite the weather of cold acceptance.

HABIT OF CURIOSITY

~People will praise you when you
discover and explain a problem but will
pay you only when you solve it~

Success that is not turned into process overtime is a future potential failure in its overtime. Let the ideas you trip on yesterday becomes background you walk over today. Feed on your success only for a while before you turn it into a seed. Question your success and find answer for the future process. If you cannot generate answers, generate question and make it general. The original definition of question I think is quest for solution. No tree grows taller than its root goes deeper. Deep questions exhume deep answers.

Not every opportunity appears open; some are veiled like a bride reserved only for the guy who can pay the dowry and that of the length of the courtship of perseverance. Often, very, few know when opportunity comes but very many know when it leaves. To be creative is not to be independent but to be a good correspondence of exiting clues for your ideas. Ideas often come when we are looking for the ideal and we are too busy to welcome it or deluded by easy way out. Old ideology is the chief enemy of new ideas.

~Let the ideas you trip on yesterday
becomes background you walk over today~

The power of question

Engaging the wisdom of question to solve problems is a great asset to genius and access to idea. Just like white house is open to all, it's only that, it can harbor black man but not of blank mind neither is it reserved for white man but wise mind. The same is the dam of inspiration anyone who gives to curiosity will reach the flood gate of change. You may have a redundant spare tire but do not have a redundant spare time success is not to be maintained but applied. When you chase your goal and finally catch it, shoot another one and begin the race again. Let the end of one success generate a question and questioning that will give a new answer for the next success.

The success that makes you rest will turn your future to a forest, never fully fruitfully cultivated but left to grow weed with time while your seed rests in you crying and drying. It takes wind for fire to burn, it takes wind for fire to quench, so it takes success to come to lime light it takes success to become a lame height—attitude is the factor.

When success is not in progress it is failing, when it is not in reprocess it is fading. Success is always in process. Innovations are ever dynamic. This is the law of true success.

THE POWER OF PONDERING

~When you have nothing to say speak silence~

According to statistic, most homes worth over $250,000 are equipped with a library. In other word, wealth is inclined to those who have value for their mind. That should tell us something that books are experience at hand, each page you open makes you wiser than time since you have others failure and success as a ready-made experiment. Books are potable friends. The cost of a book is not the price tag talk less of the cost of ignorance if not read. You are the books you read or do not read and the association you keep or do not keep. Silence is the language of the great minds only like minds get the information. Thinkers are always welcome either literate or illiterate because schooling only provides us with information and not revelation that is why many great inventors are half schooled. Great minds never die. Think more before you risk more. Tomorrow is too far to stretch your mind in anxiety to reach, and it is to near to shrink your mind to think just for today. Our limitation starts where our imagination stops. Education teaches us what can be done and sometimes also teaches us what can't be done. It teaches us what we can do and also teaches us what we can't do. The only limitations a person has are those that are self-imposed. Do not let education put limitation on your imagination. Do not put your potential at the mercy of your credentials. Try out new thing from new thinking not giving reservation to fear of failure; every success story is also a story of great failure.

~Great mind focus more on less,
little mind focus less on more~

There is a close relationship between the device called mortar and pestle being use to pond things and the process called pondering in the mind. When you ponder with the mortar and pestle the item changes states from the original nature to another, the same, when you ponder on a matter in your mind you change the state of orientation it offers you.

Take time to talk less and think more. Silence is not quotable. Sometimes a million words weigh lesser that minute silence. Speak not when you are chanced but when you are balanced in your thoughts. Silence is the first topic to be learnt in the school of wisdom. When word fails to win a fool in an argument silence will never. Silence is not consent; it is a blind assumption to presume so. To be quite means to leave unnoticed to be silent means to leave a notice. When you do not have what to say, say hi for halve time and stay silent until quarter to time when you say bye as you leave for the rest of time.

Good listeners are good thinkers, good thinkers are good talkers. The wise work more in the morning , talk more in the noon about the work, think more in the night on the work. A fool talk more in the morning, think less in the noon about the talk, and work hard in the evening life. You can learn as much as you can imagine, if you are willing and you are time prudent and information desperate. There is thin line of disparity between an ignoramus and a fool, the former knows nothing and keep silent, the latter knows nothing likewise and keep talking. It is better to think, think, and forget to talk than to talk and talk and forget to think.

~Self control begins and ends with mouth control~

Creativity is distinction

~Change is the hope of hope~

One of the most vigorously contested architectural competitions in many years ended on Feb. 26, 2003, when representatives of the Lower Manhattan Development Corp. (LMDC), the Port Authority of New York and New Jersey, and the governments of New York state and New York City chose Daniel Libeskind (see Biographies) to develop the 6.5-ha (16-ac) site of the World Trade Center, destroyed by the terrorist attacks. Libeskind's design featured a park sunk 9.1 m (30 ft) below street level that would be a memorial to those killed in the attacks, and 70 stories of offices topped by a spire that would rise to a height of 538 m (1,776 ft [the height of the structure was selected to coincide with the year that the Declaration of Independence was signed]) and thereby become the world's tallest building (Freedom Tower).

The shape of the spire was likened to that of the upraised arm of the Statue of Liberty. Other parts of the design included visible "footprints" marking where the Twin Towers once stood, a cultural quarter with a museum at its core, a transportation hub, a performing arts center, and four additional office towers.

In winning the competition, Libeskind triumphed over some of the world's most prominent architects by simply applying reality to dexterity. The six other finalists included Foster and Partners, whose design featured a single tower that appeared to be formed from two entwined buildings; Meier Eisenman Gwathmey Holl, which offered five towers, three of them connected by a walkway and two other buildings connected to each other by a walkway and erected perpendicular to the other three; the THINK Team, an international group whose design featured very tall twin towers composed of exposed steel latticework; United Architects, which submitted a plan that comprised several very high towers fused together to form a helix-shaped structure; Peterson/Littenberg, which offered tall twin towers with a promenade between them; and Skidmore, Owings, and Merrill, which presented a design featuring a cluster of 80-story buildings. Earlier, in 2002, six designs had been submitted for consideration, but all were rejected as prosaic and unimaginative.

Inventors are not extra ordinary minds but unsatisfied souls who dare to question answers in other to have find answers to questions. Ideas truly rule the world but no idea should be allowed on the throne forever without a challenge. No idea is perfect, in both illustration and application; every inspiration is an input for another brain's imagination. Idea is not a culture of any race some only take the advantage of the factual knowledge that there is a thin line distancing guessing from idea, for ideas are bold guessing. There is no idea born by a group of people only those burn by crowd, so guard your brain child. If knowledge is light then ignorance is darkness. There is no difference between a blind man and a man walking in darkness so is man with half information.

~Change leads, ideas follow~

BE RISK CREATIVE

In the early eighteen century a French tailor, inventor and parachuting pioneer, now sometimes referred to as the Flying Tailor, came to be remembered for jumping to his death from the Eiffel Tower while testing a wearable parachute of his own design. There was a great need in the aviator sector for effective parachuting device. After joining the league to proffer solution he designed one that he tested with a dummy which worked but with subsequent failed attempts of others. He attributed this to as a result of short distance he had to test run the flights and the operation of the device. He was finally given permission to make use of the Eiffel tower after series of demand. He hid his intention until the last moment to use himself as specimen and not a dummy as agreed upon.

He ignored all attempts to dissuade him by the witnesses. When he would not listen to them, they pointed his attention to the wind strength to convince him at least to wait for the wind to subside for his own safety but he refused despite his past failed attempts with his dummies. When he was further pressurized as to whether he will engage additional precaution like safety rope he replied that he would not, since he intended to trust his life entirely to his parachute: "I want to try the experiment myself and without trickery, as I intend to prove the worth of my invention." Even a renowned and experienced expert pointed to him the lapses in his technicalities indicating that the device will need a longer time to disengage. Not even the security who had witnessed his past failed attempts could stop him.

Despite further attempts by his friends and spectators to dissuade him, he jumped from the first platform of the tower wearing his invention. The parachute failed to deploy and he crashed into the icy ground at the foot of the tower.

~Never invest in any idea you can't
illustrate with a crayon ~Peter Lynch

Change your approach

~Change is the purpose of time~
What you need sometimes is not more time, more talent, more treasure, more team but more training on type of approach. When there is no strategy change looks like a tragedy. The southern route via the Khumbu Icefall and the South Col is the one most commonly taken by climbers attempting to summit Everest. It is the route used by the 1953

British expedition when New Zealander Edmund (later Sir Edmund) Hillary and Sherpa Tenzing Norgay became the first men known to have reached Everest's summit. The first recorded efforts to reach Everest's summit were made by British mountaineers. With Nepal not allowing foreigners into the country at the time, the British made several attempts on the north ridge route from the Tibetan side.

After the first reconnaissance expedition by the British in 1921 reached 7,000 m (22,970 ft) on the North Col, the 1922 expedition pushed the North ridge route up to 8,320 m (27,300 ft) marking the first time a human had climbed above 8,000 m (26,247 ft). Tragedy struck on the descent from the North col when seven porters were killed in an avalanche. The 1924 expedition resulted in the greatest mystery on Everest to this day: George Mallory and Andrew Irvine made a final summit attempt on 8 June but never returned, sparking debate as to whether they were the first to reach the top.

They had been spotted high on the mountain that day but disappeared in the clouds, never to be seen again, until Mallory's body was found in 1999 at 8,155 m (26,755 ft) on the North face. Tenzing Norgay and Edmund Hillary made the first official ascent of Everest in 1953 using the southeast ridge route.

Their success could be traced to their change of approach of direction. Sometimes you can't change your obstacle but you can change your spectacle—the way you see it and your strategy the way you approach it.

ACTIVATING DECISION

~Change is the true evidence of decision~

Decision gives wings to imagination. This is the danger of sitting on the fence for so long deciding on which side to jump, the fence may collapse leaving you to fate of either side you least wish. When we take too much time to decide time decide for us. This is the danger of a life time of decision making, like a smouldering wood it reduces to ashes but never gives a light to illuminate its world nor to ignite others. Decision could be informational or situational oriented. The quality of your decision is directly affected by the accuracy of information you are exposed to and the quantity is determined by the amount of transformation you want to explore. In situational decision, it is like how Samuel told Saul to do as the occasion demands. Situational decision is one of the skilled assets of real leaders—ability to make decision on the spot without spots. You will often find yourself on the fence that will look safe to relax on, but the truth is that sitting on the fence is an undecided decision. Hence, rather do wisdom thing and head on the right side now.

> Winners are not failure proof
> They are only failure proved
> Winners are not failure immune
> They are only success consumed
> Winners are not genius folks
> They are only sincerely genuine
> Winners are not of principal might
> They are only of principled mind
> Winners are not unchangeable leaders
> They are only incurable dreamers

Successful people do not do great things; they only do small things in a great way though encounter failures or hindrances in a great way. Henry Ford did not or forgot to put the reverse gear in the first car he built. They succeeded in spite of problems, not in the absence of them. But to the outside world, it appears as though they just got lucky. All success stories are stories of great failures as preludes. The only difference is that every time they failed, they bounced back. This is called failing forward, rather than re-thinking backward. You learn and move forward, this the critical decision period when many losers establish their lots. Learn from your failure and that is what you can earn for your input. Problems do not come with any apparel, rather we wear on them different costumes of: fear, impossibility, difficulties and the rest; nor do they come with altitude like we rate them with our attitude.

Do not try to erase your past attempt to pioneer change, time writes with ink and you can use the wind of present season to flip a new page for fresh history. To the fish the ocean is a sky, the wave is the wind, the river is the storm, the iceberg is a rock, and floras carry the aura of roses, so you can as well define an atmosphere for yourself; appreciate where are today, celebrate where you are planted. Man's need is ever changing so your idea, they will one day welcome. Just decide to be determined.

Too far

~What you attack you can't attract~

Do not go near those who always say you are going too far. A man without dreams will always have a better yesterday. It is in dream that our thoughts find expression; dream is the breathe of soul, it keeps it less in touch with the reality of the past, more with the responsibility of today and the possibility of tomorrow. Every new day comes with a wing, ready to fly but has nothing to carry but your hopes and dreams. To be dreamless is to be hopeless and to be hopeless is to be dreamless. Have a dream so big that life is worth living and the beginning is worth starting. Out of all the fruits only the coconuts have flowing juice within. But it is not a surprise that it has the hardest back as well. Those who will keep rare treasure will have capacity to keep under check rear pressure. To live is courage, to die is courage. If courage is a gift it had come rapped, rammed and roped. Fear will either keep you going for left over or stop you over from the right. In either way it can't keep your going or stopping safely.

> You are entitled to:
> As much as your eyes can sight
> As much as your mouth can confess
> As much as your faith can fight
> As much as your hand can work
> As much as your mind can conceive
> As much as your feelings can conquer
> As much as your thoughts can blossom
> As much as your dreams can soar
> As much is yours.

MANAGING CHANGE ATMOSPHERE

~There is an attitude required for every altitude~

Make room for idea driven change

There were four fish in a little pool at the river course of a village. Information got to the community of fishes that a great flood of change is coming and it will likely sweep all away. But that they had been given opportunity to turn in to anything they think will save them from the flood. The four fish friends were happy when they heard this clause attached. They began to think of what they could change to so as to resist the flood that was coming. One said it would turn in to a tree with a deep and widespread root to resist the flood. Another said it would turn into a rock to resist the flood. The third said, "I will turn in to whale with big fins and great swimming ability," while the forth one said, "I will turn in to a pit." Then they all laughed at the forth fish's plan saying what a foolish idea—to turn in to a big hole to resist the flood.

Then the flood came and one by one, they were exposed to the challenges. The flood hit the tree and unsuccessfully, but with time it began to remove the soil surrounding the root, and one day the tree lost stability and fell off, immediately it was washed away by the flood. As well, the rock resisted the flood but due to wear and tear of abrasion and attrition, it wore out to a little piece of rock which was sooner carried away by the flood. The third fish truly vigorously swim against the tide of the river, going in the opposite direction to avoid being washed away but a time came when its energy failed, it became tired and surrendered to the torrent and current of the water waves.

The fourth fish now a pit at the base of the river was soonest filled with water and remained under the base of the sea until the flood was over. When the community returned to the village, they saw the same fish in the regular pool and were curious of how it made it why others were washed away. He replied, while they chose to turn in to a proud tree, overconfidence rock and arrogant swimmer, I simply and humbly turned in to a smart pit there by creating room for the oncoming flood of change. Change is great strategy for globalization process but resistance to it could be a tragedy to an organizations' progress. Now where do you stand as a leader: a proud CEO, overconfidence chairman or arrogant president that will resist every transitional and revolution advancement at arm's length; or a change oriented leader. No leadership or establishment or institution can last more than changeability intuition.

~You can proceed without changing
  but can't succeed without it~

Flexibility nurses sustainability

Creativity births leadership without boundary. Iwata led Nintendo's development into a global company, with its hit Wii home console and DS handheld, and also through its recent troubles caused by the popularity of smartphones. Iwata had been poised to lead Nintendo through another stage after it recently did an about-face and said it will start making games for smartphones, meaning that Super Mario the plumber would soon start arriving on cellphones and tablets. The falloff in appetite for game machines in the past few years was partly because people are increasingly playing games or doing social media and other activities on smartphones. Nintendo has repeatedly had to lower prices on gadgets to woo buyers. The company returned to profit in the fiscal year ended March 2015 after several years of losses. Until the recent shift in strategy, company officials including Iwata had repeatedly rejected the idea of developing games for mobile devices, a market that they brushed off for years as irrelevant. In March, Nintendo announced an alliance with Japanese mobile game company DeNA Co. to develop games for mobile devices.

Nintendo pioneered game machines since the 1980s, developing one of the first machines and the hit Game Boy hand-held device. Its main rivals in the business are Sony Corp. with its PlayStation machines and Microsoft Corp. with the Xbox One. Both companies have done better in adapting to the era of online and mobile games. Iwata succeeded Hiroshi Yamauchi, who ruled over the Kyoto-based company for half a century, transforming it from a traditional playing-card company to a technological powerhouse. When change is delayed it could cost more to effect it and what it affects. Choice making is by force in life for they come either as an action, reaction or inaction. Often what we know to count is what limits us from what we can count to achieve.

This informs me about the story of two puppies that strayed from their mother while hunting. The owner had used same rope to belt the duo together to keep them from going apart or wondering away. At a spot, as they surfed the jungle, they came across an old wounded lion, too weak to run but hungry. On sighting the old jungle king, they barked and took to their heels with their little pace, while the old lion hopelessly dragged itself in a chase if at all luck will drop on his empty tummy. In front of the puppies, was a tree but they could not see it ahead in fear, hence ran in to it.

One to the right and the other to the left, of course the tree stopped them as the rope got wrapped around the stem. So halting side by side each other, they barked louder in fear as the lion approached. The old jungle king approached the one at the right, weakened it with its claw and ready to feed on it. The rope now loose because the weakened had ceased pulling the other puppy. When the other frightened puppy saw the potential death as well, it came back to reality, grew unusual courage and a sense of progress to pull the more. Taking the advantage of the loose rope, it fled; but now having to drag the other weak puppy.

After a while, the weakened puppy gained its consciousness and again it ran along. Before the relaxed old lion could get up from rest, the preys were on again. Being already tired, it stood up stressed, and with the same weak and slow pace it watched them as they dashed away.

The old lion is time and season while the two puppies are organizations interest (profit) and interest (emotional attachment), and the tree is the market force.

~Idea and change come and go, time remains~

The latter means what they have feelings for or their emotional interest, organization belief and protocol, while the former means their profit or turnover. Many firms allow their interest, culture and sense of value to dogmatically stagnate their profit margin from being progressive by opposing market force until the season of time weakens and feeds on them. They want un-changeability and profitability to march together. The tree is all about the market force. It stops both the old strategy and turnover making them potential prey for time and tide. Many individuals and institutions have had to pay for this with their progress and before they finally woke up from the sleep damages had been done. Like the other puppy, wise organization had to pick the injured market rate by letting free long time held down change proposal, like Nintendo did in the game world, wake up to reality, develop sense of progress and new courage to fight and recover. It is a thinker's world, it is a changing world; you are here because your mind was there.

~I can't understand why people are frightened
of new ideas. I'm frightened of the old ones~
John Cage

The Philosophy of change can be likened to the cycle of butterfly metamorphosis. The life begins like an egg, the place where the change concept is conceived. It is the moment of thought revolution when we take a break from what is normal and common, to mentally explore the world of untold possibility. Then we set out like the hatched egg of the butterfly, we migrate like the caterpillar from our orientation and mental habitation to next available bus stop of transition. Then here comes opposition and the urge to change our mind not to change the man again but it is a time like the pupa stage to reflect back on the need for the voyage and hibernate in cocoon to gather more courage and determination to drive through the mist of comments.

It is a stage where conviction is fortified and submission is consolidated. At this point people may think we have complied with the norm and shouts of critics but the silence here is not so but a licence in process. Then the wings emerge from the pupa's shell, the bright elegant butterfly force itself out the shell. In the process it struggles and seems to be in need of help. Rather it never bothers for in its struggling and forging through the challenges of traditions and culture the beauty is being compiled and edified. It is left alone in the struggle for change.

~Change seems to make things fall
apart but in the right path~

At the end of the process, it emerges with a rainbow wing, laden with spectrum of natural artistic. Not only filled with glamour of change, the product is equipped with wings to fly and scale what limits its caterpillar and other common culture—leaping the bounds and boundary of blind humanity custom to demonstrate the transformation.

One of the rules of a professional mountain climbing coach who focuses on the youth is the altitude building capacity by making sure the team spend quality time at each stage at the base camp, not only to learn climbing skills but also to become adapted to environmental changes such as the atmospheric pressure exertion on their skulls.

The higher you go the pressure changes and this why some people lose bearing to the change environment. They are inflated by the pressing forces around them in a negative way such that they become victims of emotional instability giving room to competitive challenges and unexpected or unplanned events to take over. But there is a need to adapt and utilise the change elements either temperature or pressure. Learn to get accustomed to an altitude before you move ahead. The peak of every success is the platform for another process to start up; in other word success in never final, it is in progression. If the roof top is your limit you need a tall ladder, if it is Mount Everest is it, you need a tight rope; if the sky is your limit you need a wing of dream in the wind of change. The beauty of idea is when it changes to bring the next change. To be dogmatic is to be a dramatic fool in the science of concept. Nobody succeeds once and for all; nobody fails once and for all. Winners are change trainees.

~The success in failure is learning
from it and the failure in success is
leaning on it~

Climb high, sleep low

One of the ways to increase your income is to reduce your expenses. One of the ways to manage a progressive change is to feed less on the result. Do not let your achievement equals your entitlement. Learn to separate your need from your want. Learn to delay gratification. Have you discovered that if you want to jump higher you need to bend lower? Every lasting peak begins from the pit. Perhaps, because most of the early climbers on Everest had military backgrounds, the traditional method of ascending it has been called "siege" climbing. With this technique, a large team of climbers establishes a series of tented camps farther and farther up the mountain's side.

For instance, on the most frequently climbed southern route, the Base Camp on the Khumbu Glacier is at an elevation of about 17,600 feet (5,400 metres). The theory is that the climbers ascend higher and higher to establish camps farther up the route, then come down to sleep at night at the camp below the one being established. (Mountain climbers express this in the phrase, "Climb high, sleep low.") This practice allows climbers to acclimatize to the high altitude. Camps are established along the route about every 1,500 feet (450 metres) of vertical elevation and are given designations of Camp I, Camp II, and so on.

Finally, a last camp is set up close enough to the summit (usually about 3,000 feet [900 metres] below) to allow a small group (called the "assault" team) to reach the peak. This was the way the British organized their expeditions; most of the large commercial expeditions continue to use it—except that all paying clients are now given a chance at the summit. One of the main skills or change creativity is discipline, to live and lead sacrificially. This climbers' style also teaches those who aim for the top that patience to master each stage of change before proceeding to build on it.

~Spend less, have more~

MENTAL FLEX

~One idea can't hold the world to ransom~

Heroes are not extraordinary species but men of like passion; men of unsatisfied soul who dare to question answers in other to find answers to question. When an idea has been observed, with scrutiny, and has served humanity, men metamorphosis it to law but such laws must be able to bend if not breaks, when need be. Nothing should defy the law of constancy like phenomenon of change. America is not the most gifted country, nor the most populated race, nor the most resourced geography, nor the oldest independent nation, nor with the best naturally resourced, but the best in idea, talent and people management and it shows.

Headship or leadership

There is no team that can ride above the skill and integrity of its leadership. When you want to increase the growth of a company change its workers, but if you want to increase its development change the leader. Bringing in more qualified workers will only improve the gross output of the organization—I mean efficiency wise, they will jack up—more quantity per hour that may lose acceptability and market with time; but when you want the company to develop new product and be effective that is, having maximized output and desired quality with innovative product, that meets the current needs of consumers, then consider changing the leadership.

This is why no matter the size of a container it can't deliver per time more than the throttling neck and that which the cork permits. So if you want to witness increased output then start to change the leadership in you—your mindset. Time changes things but what changes first is the thinking, otherwise the direction and the dimension may be disappointing. There is nothing that does not change except change itself; it is the law of time. If nothing should change then let everything excuse time. Many people try to avoid change because they cannot afford it, but time will work with tides to give the alternative they ask for—wishes change to fate with the time. Some people are held down not by a strong rope but a wrong hope; they hope in wishes and wish their hope would one day come to pass.

Ideas overthrown

~Change is the author of idea~

In the 19th century, there were two pillars of physics: Newton's laws of motion and Maxwell's theory of light. Einstein was alone in realizing that they were in contradiction and that one of them must fall. After the war, two expeditions were sent to test Einstein's prediction of deflected starlight near the Sun. One set sail for the island of Principe, off the coast of West Africa, and the other to Sobral in northern Brazil in order to observe the solar eclipse of May 29, 1919. On Nov. 6, 1919, the results were announced in London at a joint meeting of the Royal Society and the Royal Astronomical Society. Nobel laureate J.J. Thomson, president of the Royal Society, stated: This result is not an isolated one, it is a whole continent of scientific ideas.

This is the most important result obtained in connection with the theory of gravitation since Newton's day, and it is fitting that it should be announced at a meeting of the Society so closely connected with him. The headline of *The Times* of London read, "Revolution in Science—New Theory of the Universe—Newton's Ideas Overthrown—Momentous Pronouncement—Space 'Warped.'" Almost immediately, Einstein became a world-renowned physicist, the successor to Isaac Newton. How was it able to achieve this by leveraging with the terrain around it. When idea gives birth to another it is usually on a greater scale. Every existing idea must be leverage for another and not to be used to level up future revolution.

~Ideas truly rules the globe but no idea
of renown should be allowed on the throne
of change forever~

www.ingramcontent.com/pod-product-compliance
Lightning Source LLC
Chambersburg PA
CBHW070048080526
44586CB00013B/962